I0083726

Institutional Harassment

Institutional Harassment

Divorce, Abuse, and the Legal System

Miguel Clemente
Translated by Daniel Migueláñez Munilla

LEXINGTON BOOKS
Lanham • Boulder • New York • London

Published by Lexington Books
An imprint of The Rowman & Littlefield Publishing Group, Inc.
4501 Forbes Boulevard, Suite 200, Lanham, Maryland 20706
www.rowman.com

86-90 Paul Street, London EC2A 4NE

Copyright © 2022 by The Rowman & Littlefield Publishing Group, Inc.

All rights reserved. No part of this book may be reproduced in any form or by any electronic or mechanical means, including information storage and retrieval systems, without written permission from the publisher, except by a reviewer who may quote passages in a review.

British Library Cataloguing in Publication Information Available

Library of Congress Cataloging-in-Publication Data

Names: Clemente Díaz, Miguel, author. | Munilla, Daniel Migueláñez, translator.
  Title: Institutional harassment : divorce, abuse, and the legal system / Miguel Clemente-Díaz ; translated by Daniel Migueláñez Munilla.
  Description: Lanham : Lexington Books, [2022] | Includes bibliographical references and index. | Summary: "This book offers a psychological approach to several forms of harassment often experienced in divorce cases in the justice system, including intimate partner aggression, sexual abuse of children, the unscientific parental alienation syndrome, and the weaponization of the legal system from aggressors seeking revenge"-- Provided by publisher.
  Identifiers: LCCN 2022021657 (print) | LCCN 2022021658 (ebook) | ISBN 9781666902532 (cloth) | ISBN 9781666902556 (pbk) | ISBN 9781666902549 (epub)
  Subjects: LCSH: Divorce--Psychological aspects. | Divorced people--Psychology. | Harassment. | Revenge.
  Classification: LCC HQ814 .C56 2022 (print) | LCC HQ814 (ebook) | DDC 306.89--dc23/eng/20220518
  LC record available at https://lccn.loc.gov/2022021657
  LC ebook record available at https://lccn.loc.gov/2022021658

Contents

Acknowledgments

To all the people that I have been able to evaluate for years in order to make psychological-forensic reports. Almost all women, all victims, and most of them legally harassed.

To Jo-Anne Cardinal, for her detailed review of Daniel Miguelañez's translation. Her work has been essential to faithfully communicate the style and content of the original text.

Introduction

The Beginning of the Judicial Process: Child Sexual Abuse

The validity of psychological profiling is relative; in some cases, some individuals who have a behavioral disorder may not be identified as such (what is called type I error in statistics, or false negative), and those who do not have a disorder may be linked to the collective of those who have it (type II error, or false positive). And yet, when the technique is properly carried out, the resulting psychological pictures of offenders are highly reliable. Perhaps for that reason, after several years of analyzing cases—and of researching—as an expert in the field of forensic psychology, I think there are certain elements that can help us understand what happens to several women—and to some men—when dealing with a completely new problem that they never thought they would have to face.

What follows is the summary of a story that has been used as part of an experiment to verify how individuals react when they see themselves reflected in it (Clemente and Padilla-Racero, 2021); the story is divided into steps that serve as the index and the body of this book.

Let us suppose that you are the divorced mother of a 6-year-old girl. You have been granted the custody, and according to the visiting arrangements, the girl's father has the right to spend a weekend with her, from Friday afternoon until Monday morning every other week, as well as two afternoons during the week. For some time now, when your daughter arrives home on Mondays (after it was the father's turn and having spent the weekend with him), you notice that she is just a little sadder each time. She starts wetting her bed, having nightmares, and behaving poorly; she insults you and tries to hit you. The same happens when it is getting closer to Friday and she must return with her father; the nightmares begin, the cries, the enuresis and encopresis—and she tells you that she does not want to go with him. After the next weekend with the father, you verify that her genital labia are increasingly swollen. Upon your suspicions, the pediatrician states that it cannot be determined whether there has been touching by the father or not, and that the hymen is intact. After much crying, the girl begins to speak and says that her father touches her genitals; he insists on bathing her, touches her, and introduces objects into her vagina and her anus. One Monday, your daughter arrives with bloody panties; however, at the emergency ward of a hospital, they again verify that the hymen is intact and say that they do not know for certain if she has been abused. The girl says that her father put an object in her genitals again and that he hurt her very much. Upon the preventative complaint filed by the hospital on suspicion of sexual abuse, a judge suspends the father's visitation rights, but on the impossibility to demonstrate that the father abused the girl (except by her testimony), the visitation arrangements are resumed, and she must spend the weekends with her father. The father also files a complaint against you, the mother, claiming that you were the one who provoked the wounds in the girl, stating that you gave instructions to the girl to touch her genitals and anus and later say that it was him; and that, therefore, it is the mother who is manipulating the daughter to be able to file a complaint pleading sexual abuse, and take away the contact with his daughter. In essence, mutual complaints are being filed.

Your daughter tells you that she refuses to go back with her father; that, if she has to go back, she will commit suicide; she says that she trusts you and that, as her mother, you should defend her. You consult a lawyer, and you are told that you have no options but to obey the judge. The following Monday, after the new visit with her father, the girl returns, one more time, with bloody panties, and she cannot go to school because she cannot sustain herself standing up; she is unable to close her legs; the labia of her vagina are completely red, and she says that her father tied her up and put something in her vagina that made a lot of noise and hurt a lot. Once again, in the emergency ward of the hospital they say that the hymen is intact, that they cannot determine if there has been rape, and neither do they know if there has been a sexual aggression.

It is worth noting that this case is based on several real-life accounts. Our research team presented it to a large sample of mothers, along with the following questions—the results are also included.

1. What decisions would you take on that Monday, when your daughter returns home with her panties full of blood, barely able to walk, and saying that her father had introduced an object into her vagina provoking pain? The results indicated that practically 100 percent of the mothers chose the option "file a complaint, because a crime has been committed, and to protect the child." Thus, the mothers primarily trust the justice system, taking for granted that it will protect their son or daughter by avoiding contact with the father, as everything indicates that he is the alleged aggressor.

2. The story continues. Fifteen days have gone by, and the moment arrives when your daughter must return with her father for the weekend. She is terrified and both of you fear that the same thing will happen again. What would you do? In this case, answers were grouped into two large blocks: those who opted to look for an excuse for the visit not to take place (42 percent) and those who chose not to comply with the law and avoid the contact of the girl with her father (58 percent); that is, none of the mothers would comply with the judicial decision; in addition, those who use ruses to not comply and those who would directly not comply with the judicial decision would end up being equally distributed. This demonstrates that mothers still trust in the justice system, thinking that it would react and defend their children. Let us continue with the story.

3. Let us suppose that you have avoided the contact of the girl with her father. Your daughter's self-esteem has gradually increased; she no longer has nightmares, but the father has filed a complaint against you for not complying with the visits. First you have been fined; but now, as you still refuse to comply with the visitation arrangements, the judge has ordered the police to go to your house and take your daughter to a juvenile center, where she is to receive psychological treatment until she accepts going with her father. What would you do? In this case, the answers were grouped into obeying (handing your daughter over to her father, as that is what justice demands) or disobeying (refusing to open the door to the police and evade them or run off with your daughter). Most of the mothers (81 percent) chose to disobey, and the remaining 19 percent of them chose to hand the girl over to the police. The data allows for a double interpretation; first, that the vast majority of mothers would act defending their daughter; second, that knowing that their daughter would be sexually abused by the father, 20 percent of them would obey justice and put the minor at risk.

4. The police have obtained access to your daughter and have handed her over to her father. You are completely forbidden to have any type of communication with her, and he is the one who holds the custody now. You cannot even see her, call her on the phone, or communicate in any way. What would you do? The decisions in this case can be grouped into two large blocks: obey justice (wait until it is judicially determined that the girl can have contact again with her mother) or find a way to be in contact with her, even if that means kidnapping her. Results: 12.94 percent of the mothers opted for obedience, against an 87.06 percent who would try to be in contact with the child, even if that meant kidnapping. We should point out that each participant took a personality test, and that, in the case of those mothers who opted for disobedience, there

was a higher level of paranoid ideation, that is, of thinking that the others—and above all, the institutions—were against them.

5. After two years in which you have not been able to see your daughter again, there is going to be a court hearing to determine if you may resume visitation with her. How do you think you will react upon being interrogated by the judge, the district attorney, and the lawyer of the girl's father? Answers could be classified in two large groups: the mothers who opted to remain calm, in control of themselves, and accept the situation (45.88 percent), and those who showed sadness and lack of control, and confronted the judge and district attorney (54.12 percent). There were notable differences from the psychological point of view between the two groups: The mothers who stated that they would show sadness and lack of control scored higher in somatization, obsession-compulsion, interpersonal sensitivity, and phobic anxiety. The story continues in the following way:

6. In the court hearing in which you are right now, the judge orders your daughter to go to the visitor room and make a statement before him about whether she wants to go back to you or continue living with her father. Your daughter does not look at you in the eye upon entering, and states that she wants to continue living with her father. Why do you think she did that? The answers can be grouped in two blocks: She did it due to coercion or fear and because she accepted the situation (66 percent) or due to the feeling of hatred toward you as her mother for having made her feel abandoned (34 percent). There were no major psychological differences between those who think one way or the other.

7. Suppose that, in fact, your daughter has expressed that she wants to continue living with her father. How would you feel? This question concerns the emotional reaction that the mother would have when the child expresses that she wants to remain with her abuser. The answers may be grouped into two blocks: Some said they would feel very bad (73 percent), whereas others stated that it would not affect them (27 percent). Furthermore, the mothers who said they would feel very bad, scored higher in somatization, depression, anxiety, phobic anxiety, and psychoticism, and those who said that it would not affect them scored higher in hostility and paranoid ideation.

8. Three years have gone by since this story began. Your daughter is now 9 years old. Could you think over what you could have personally done to avoid this rather unfortunate situation for you? The question demands a reflection on how to act in the future, given that the mother in question lost contact with her daughter. Of the two alternative answers, 14.09 percent of mothers said they would trust in justice, while 85.91 percent

would make use of tricks to disobey. Those who chose to disobey presented a higher level of obsession-compulsion and of phobic anxiety.

In summary, this study presents a case that re-creates the situation faced by mothers after discovering that their son or daughter has been being sexually abused and decide to file a complaint against the other parent. The findings of the study demonstrate how, when faced with a similar situation, all the mothers decide to file a complaint, expecting the justice system to protect their son or daughter by avoiding contact with the father. However, after filing the complaint, most mothers become aware of two circumstances: First, that because abuse happens in intimacy, while the abuse itself can be proven on several occasions, it is not easy to ascertain who the abuser was; second, that there are psychologists, judges, and district attorneys that adhere to an unscientific doctrine—Gardner's Parental Alienation Syndrome (PAS), which will be discussed in a later chapter—that accuses the mother of fabricating nonexistent aggressions and instilling hate in their children against the noncustodial parent (normally the father); this enables the father to invert the complaint process through false statements in such a way that the mother is turned into the manipulator of her children, the one who instills hate in them against the father, and even convinces them to harm themselves with the intention of breaking the relation with him. Thus, the focus of the judicial process shifts from investigating the alleged abuse, to trying to prove that the mother, sometimes called "malicious mother," is guilty. From that moment on, the mother begins receiving a number of impositions from the justice system, intended to ensure the continued contact of the child with the father, despite the mother's certainty that her children are still being abused.

As part of this chain of events, if the mother refuses that her children have contact with the noncustodial parent, the threat from within the system may go as far as warning her that her custody may be taken away, that her children may be admitted to a center to re-educate them, and that she may even end up in prison. That is what Gardner called the "threat therapy." Obviously, this is institutional violence, exercised by the justice system, that originates in the father's complaint, which nullifies that of the mother, turning her into a suspect, allowing the investigation for the alleged sexual abuse to come to a halt, and putting the assaulted child in the hands of the aggressor. Eventually, the one who filed the complaint becomes the perpetrator.

Such circumstances trigger the first moral dilemma of the mothers, who have to choose whether they are to obey or disobey the law; all the mothers that participated in the study decided not to comply with the visitation rights, but taking two evenly distributed options: to disobey, but with excuses making it easily understood that it is not their wish to disobey the court orders, or to overtly disobey, without any attempt to hide it.

The following step in the story is that in fact the daughter is separated from the mother and the latter is forbidden from any contact with the former. Faced with this dilemma, most mothers disobey, that is, they do not abide by what the judge has determined, although the mothers who take that decision present higher levels of paranoid ideation—they feel suspicious of being followed and being treated in an unfair way. In other words, they experiment a reaction that is in all respects compatible with their suffering after being separated from their children, and upon not being able to defend them from possible abuse. The system has not only accused—and still accuses—the mother; it goes beyond that, putting the child in the hands of his or her aggressor.

As I already mentioned, this story is based on true facts; therefore, it would be unlikely that a hearing takes place to determine if the condition of separation of the children from the mother should be revised after two years have gone by. Mothers are then asked how they would react in that hearing. Once again, reactions were divided into two evenly distributed groups: the mothers who remain calm, in control, and accept the situation, and those who show sadness, lack of control, and confrontation with the court.

Unfortunately, after two years of being separated from their mothers, the children usually show in public their preference for the parent who has abused them. For this reason, the following question was how a mother would explain that situation. Most of them thought that that manifestation was the consequence of the coercion that their children had been through, as well as of having had to adapt to the new situation to survive. But a third of the mothers thought that the cause is different—the fact that they hate their mothers, on interpreting that they were abandoned; their mother, in whom they had placed their trust to free them from a very problematic situation, had failed them, and they do not understand that the mother had no other option whatsoever.

After having impatiently waited for the moment to recover her child, how would the mother feel upon hearing that the child wishes to remain with the father? The majority say rather badly, but almost 25 percent of them state that it would not affect them. On this occasion, there are variables of personality that differentiate the two ways of feeling. The judges and district attorneys usually interpret that women who lose control in a court hearing are expressing a mental disorder, which shows their incapacity as mothers; these judges and attorneys obviate the fact that that reaction is normal for a mother who is sure of her children being assaulted by the father, and that the mere fact of filing a complaint and therein requesting help from the justice system, has made them guilty and separated them from their children. There could be two possible explanations for this way of thinking of the judges and the district attorneys: For the judges, a woman who, in their presence, cries and screams, accusing them of committing an injustice for not protecting their children, is in most cases bothersome, it makes them uncomfortable for putting them in a moral problem; the second explanation might be that, if they believe in the PAS doctrine, that behavior concurs with the explanation that they are dealing with a malicious and manipulative mother who will never be able to collaborate with the justice system. Both explanations are likely to occur simultaneously.

Lastly, participants were asked if they had reached any conclusion as to how to behave in the future in a similar situation, after having practically lived it through the questionnaire. In this case, most mothers expressed that they would look for ways of disobeying the justice system, thus avoiding the suffering infringed upon them by the system itself, while 14 percent of the participants expressed that they would trust in the justice system, to avoid further difficulties.

Although this data could not be verified, the experiment seems to demonstrate that the decisions that mothers took, owing to the justice system, clearly deteriorated not only the mental health of the mothers but also that of the children.

This research suggests how women who are separated from their children are accused of presenting a syndrome that is not a syndrome, nor does it even exist, nor has it been proven scientifically, present the same behavior that any mother would express by simply defending their children (Clemente, 2013a; Clemente and Padilla-Racero, 2015a, 2015b, 2016; Clemente, Padilla-Racero, Gandoy-Crego, Reig-Botella, and Gonzalez-Rodriguez, 2015; Padilla-Racero, 2013, 2015, 2016; Saunders and Oglesby, 2016; Shaw, 2016).

Other works have also explored the issue of institutional errors and harassment. Silberg and Dallam's work, for instance, studied twenty-seven cases in which judges granted the custody to the father on the grounds that the mother was lying about the maltreatment of the child by the father. Afterward, it could be verified that the father had abused the child and that the mother's accusations were correct. Unfortunately, judges authorized the children to spend 3.2 years on average with the abusive father. Besides, it was found that the justice system wrongly considered that the mothers had some type of mental illness. Unfortunately, Gardner's arguments are frequently used within a judicial context in several countries.

That is the topic of this book. Firstly, it examines the issue of violence and assaults within the couple; next, it explores the topic of the ideology of the role, and of machismo; lastly, it examines the issue of child sexual aggression.

Chapter 1

Intimate Partner Aggression

AN EXAMPLE

The story that serves as an introduction to this book begins with a mother's suspicion that her daughter is being abused, but it could just as well begin when the relationship is beginning to fail. In most cases, those who assault their children have previously assaulted their couple; and yet, they do it so gradually, and to someone who was so agreeable with those aggressions, that the victim, usually a woman, is not conscious that she is being assaulted.

Intimate partner aggression is a social and a public health problem and one that, unfortunately, is rather common in our society. Data from numerous studies demonstrate that it occurs in almost all couple relationships. A recent study by Johnson and Moore (2020) demonstrates that aggressions affect 60–90 percent of couple relationships. These aggressions also have long-term negative psychological consequences. The phenomenon is also rather common in couple interactions over the Internet.

Let us illustrate it with an example that, again, resembles cases which we come across through our research; Maria and Robert are indeed fictitious characters.

Maria met Robert—who later became her husband—30 years ago, when she was 22 and he was 23. Maria affirms that the maltreatment began almost from the moment they met; initially, it was psychological in nature, such as him reproaching that she had not finished all her meal and that that was improper behavior. He gradually reprimanded her for more and more things until, eventually, almost every moment they spent together gave occasion to his discontent. He then started to insult her and to claim that he did everything for her, but she did nothing, implying that she was constantly in debt to him. When the psychological maltreatment became part of their routine, the physical maltreatment began. At the beginning it was mostly slaps, but Robert was a strong guy, so at times, Maria found herself on the floor; other times, it would be violent pushes, and every now and then he would grab her to bring her close to him—so violently that he would rip her clothes.

Maria affirms that Robert treated her with tremendous psychological and physical violence. She also comments that neither she nor anybody could speak while he was speaking, because otherwise he would slap or push her afterward. Maria asked her mother-in-law for help, but she played the issue down and replied that her son was "very good, but very difficult."

Maria also says that the very violent attacks—during which Robert would break anything in sight and physically and psychologically assault her—were followed by the phase when he would ask for forgiveness and express his deepest love to her, and then, little by little, recriminate everything (closing what is called the circle of violence, which begins with an accumulation of tension, continues with an explosion of violence, and ends up in a wooing phase). She realized that the emotions of her partner were false; he had no empathy, could manipulate everybody, and only cared about his own interests. Day after day, Maria realized that her partner's emotional expressions were always false; he knew how to express himself when others were around, but he felt nothing. Maria also comments that when others besides her and her family were around, he became the most marvelous person on the planet, that is, what worried him most was to maintain appearances (later on we will explore the issue of the dark personality).

Robert was sent to New Zealand for work, and the mother-in-law of Maria begged her to go with him. Once they were there, he told her that she was not educated, and that he would educate her. The education, as Maria recalls, consisted in spanking and slapping her; he would only calm down when she asked to be forgiven for having done everything badly, and accepted to continuously engage in sexual acts against her will. As he was her couple, Maria did not consider it as rape. The sexual act calmed him down, and Maria yielded so that he would stop physically assaulting her. She mentions that he always blamed her for not doing it every time he wanted to, using expressions such as "you humiliate me," "you belittle me," and even "you are a prostitute." He called her a prostitute on the grounds that he was the one who paid for everything, when the truth is, he was also the one who stopped her from working out of the house.

Robert asked Maria to marry him; seeing how extremely violent his behavior was, she initially said no and gave him the runaround, but eventually gave in. Maria affirms that she saw him as a person with many qualities, who did various positive things; while he was "so special," she did not know how to do anything and was a nobody. She confesses that she had been completely overshadowed by him. In the end, they got married.

Maria recalls her honeymoon as a "horror movie." They went to Italy, and he kept yelling and insulting her throughout the whole trip with expressions such as slut, selfish, bitch, liar, rude, cruel, or manipulator. He constantly demanded apologies from her, for having behaved badly, or for being arrogant.

Some of the most troubling events that Maria mentions were when they went to visit Robert's family. Robert was obsessed with going to his hometown, she explains, and he and his family were proud of and obsessed with their family background. After the honeymoon, they went to the family home of Robert's parents, where Maria told him that she wanted to separate. In Maria's words, Robert "went crazy": He shoved a sock in her mouth, pushed her, insulted, and hit her, took away the bedding, and began to pour ice cold water into her ear, saying that if she did not apologize, he would kick her out of his parents' house. Maria had to go and sleep in the vehicle in which they had travelled, fearing that if she did not, he could very well kill her; she then left the house at four in the morning, bearing the ear pain caused by the cold water. The next morning, she returned home, but she is unable to remember what happened. Although she has completely forgotten about the remaining part of the day (due to post-traumatic amnesia), she suspects that she went to ask for forgiveness, because if that had not been the case, she figures that he would not have let her in.

Maria's relationship was based on fear, she goes on, and only today does she understand that she had been completely erased, and that her entire day revolved around her efforts to not make him angry, to not do anything that she knew he would not approve. And that, whatever she did, nothing changed, he would reproach her for everything, continuously. Furthermore, Robert exercised control over her throughout the entire day, even when he was not with her at home, by constantly calling her on the phone.

Maria says that she asked her mother-in-law for help, but she defended Robert, justifying and "normalizing" the situation, and explaining to Maria that everything that went on was normal. She said that "he is not crazy, he is difficult, but not crazy," and added that she "must have done something wrong."

After the wedding, Robert was sent to work to Sydney, and Maria went with him; she spent the morning doing household chores and going to the university in the afternoon. She explains that Robert would beat her up quite badly, and constantly assault her (for example, when he woke up in the morning, he would wake her up by pulling her hair); he would not allow her to meet up with anybody (not even with friends) if he was not there, and he did not even let her say that she missed her parents. Furthermore, he slept with a stick under his pillow to hit her with, in case she did not behave herself.

Maria's reaction to the maltreatment was to either become blocked or leave and go outside, but then she would later have to apologize to him, after hearing yet some more reproaches, and agreeing to lay with him against her will. Maria never filed a complaint against him, saying that she was overcome by fear, and she did not return to her country, as she thought she would never know how to explain to her family and friends what was going on.

Maria said that Robert constantly demanded that they had sexual relations, and if she did not agree all of the time, he would blame her, telling her things like "you have not complied."

When Maria came back from Australia, she was convinced that she had to find a job and get divorced. However, as soon as they got back, Robert was sent to Lisbon to work for six months—initially at least. Once they moved there, Maria sent out her resume and found a job in a bank; when she told Robert, he broke down and, crying, begged her to please not take the job. Robert—says Maria—is a "super manipulator" and wanted time to manipulate and persuade her. Maria worked for about four months, but ultimately, Robert convinced her to quit and live together again. From that moment on, everything went back to being as it had been before.

Maria also comments on some situations caused by Robert's extreme jealousy. She says that she was happy when there were more people around because he would keep up appearances and would, therefore, not attack her. In Maria's words, Robert does not have feelings like other people do, he does not feel anything for anybody, and if he seems caring it is because he imitates other's behavior, and because, knowing about the importance of social etiquette, he lies all the time. She comments that he is extremely tidy and organized, which he also uses to continuously torment her.

Maria became pregnant, and they shortly returned to their country. Maria says that she lived divided between the happiness of the pregnancy and the sadness of the maltreatment; she kept telling him that Judith, their future daughter, was bound to be born with problems, as Maria did not stop crying over the entire pregnancy. She could not tell him that she was in pain or complain about anything, because that would infuriate him.

When Judith, the first child, was born, Robert did not allow Maria's family to visit her in the hospital—not until he found it appropriate; and if the girl cried, he would not let her console her, it had to be him who did it. They later had a second child, Adam, who was born with grade four kidney reflux and an unclosed urethra. Maria states that he needed to have an operation, but the doctor refused after a very heated argument with Robert, and she had to talk to the doctor and apologize so that he would agree to the operation. After that, Peter was born, while Adam was in the hospital.

Raising children brought María to do whatever necessary, next to impossible, so that they would not perceive the existence of problems. After their fourth child Elisabeth was born, Maria did not have time for anything, as she had to take care of the house and four children; and yet Robert demanded that they continuously have sexual relations, reprimanding her that she did not pay attention to him anymore, and that she did not attend to her sexual obligations.

In complete defenselessness, Maria recorded a conversation with her husband, and asked a friend to listen to it and verify that she was not crazy. The friend said that, after hearing how badly he treated her, she could not sleep, and that she should go to a specialist, recommending her a psychologist. Maria began therapy with that psychologist in 2011. Later, Robert became jealous of the mental health professional, and María had to hide that she was still in therapy with him, to avoid problems.

Robert controlled Maria to the extent that he did not let her leave the house alone on the weekends, taking away the keys to the house and the cars. She was so convinced that the problem was hers that, when she went to the psychiatrist for the first time, she said: "I have a problem with my husband, I want to know if I am a monster." In fact, that Christmas season, as a New Year's wish, she asked to make her husband happy.

Other issues that Maria recalls refer to aspects that reveal the existence of economic maltreatment. He gave her the only money she had, according to the calculations that he himself made, which always amounted to just the necessary for the errands she had to run or the specific things they needed to buy. She always had to show all sorts of proofs of purchase or receipts. It seems, even, that Robert financially owned María's legal representation, in such a way that he obliged her to sign the sale of her shares in trading companies and declare that the money was exclusively his.

Other issues that Maria gives account of, which might help understand the situation that she was living, are the following:

- She had to go to the hospital, and he got angry saying that everybody in the hospital probably saw her "ass."
- She had allergic asthma attacks and he refused to take her to a hospital.
- Every day he would go over everything that she had done or not done and blamed her for the little she had worked and the poor condition of the house.
- At mealtimes, he was the only one to speak, and the others had to listen.
- At mealtimes, he was served first, and the others later.
- She affirms (in the presence of their children) that men should have relations with prostitutes, and women should accept it.

As Maria states, their children perceived the situation. She comments that Judith once asked her why her father treated her as if she was his daughter, rather than his wife, and Alfonso, when he was 13 or 14 years old, began to come between them in the verbal attacks and defend his mother. Maria forbade him to defend her, because his father would punish him, oblige him to get into the bathroom and hit him.

Maria convinced him to go with her to her psychologist once, and says that that session was extremely disagreeable; he was continuously defending himself, and very nearly came to blows with the professional. After that visit, he told Maria that he would no longer speak to her, and for several years, when he had to communicate something to her, he would leave notes around the house.

As the children grew older, whenever he wanted to physically attack her, he told her to get into the bathroom with him, he would take away her cell phone and would begin to hit her; the situation would remain the same until she asked for forgiveness and agreed to lay with him, something that she accepted in order to save the situation with the children and to avoid that he continue hitting her.

Lastly, five years after beginning the treatment, and partly thanks to the psychology sessions, she told him that she was "breaking up" with him, and that—after him insulting and yelling at her—she refused to lay with him again.

THE MAGNITUDE OF THE PROBLEM: THE EPIDEMIOLOGY OF MALTREATMENT

While this story is based upon real cases, it is but a mere example, and does not reveal other aspects of the issue, such as, for example, that this social problem is becoming even worse among young people. That can be seen, for instance, in a study by Okeke, Rothman, and Mumford (2020), carried out with 723 participants who were tested twice (2013 and 2016). The study emphasizes the relationship between being an adolescent woman with economic resources and residing in areas with social inequality, showing that those women are more prone to being assaulted by their partner.

One of the many ways of assaulting someone is by using their children. One of the reasons is that when a couple splits up, there are less chances that they attack each other, but if they have children, they need to continue to be in touch. Furthermore, there is a myth in our society that all parents love their children, and yet, while it tends to be true, in some cases it is nothing but a social desire. In fact, there are parents that, when the couple relationship ends, they also end the relationship with their children. There are also some parents that, when they have a new child with a new couple, no longer wish to know anything about their children from any previous marriage; and, unfortunately, there are parents who are never going to forgive their ex-partner who had ended their relationship and are going to use their own children for their personal revenge, perhaps perpetually.

When a couple separate, the one who wants to keep the children more is the one who loses out in the economic agreement, because they do not care about the money, they just want to live with their children. The parent who has no interest in their children has other worries—namely, to pay the least possible monthly amount of money for them or not to pay anything at all.

The most drastic form of assaulting the couple, when that person loves their children, is to kill them. We will explore that in the chapter about the dark personality with an example; let us now concentrate on the couple's relationship in itself.

What may be considered as intimate partner aggression? The answer is of vital importance in our research, since the inclusion of actions under that term that are not clearly identified might call into question the validity of the studies that are undertaken concerning the issue. This is acknowledged by, for example, Johnson and Ferraro (2000); in the most cited review article on this subject, they state that there are two major problems when studying intimate partner aggression: the distinction between types of violence, and the study of the control problems between the couple as a key explicative factor of the process.

Mazza et al. (2020) establish that partner violence (intimate partner violence, or IPV, is similar to intimate partner aggression, or IPA, and are terms that are used indistinctly) can be classified into four categories: physical violence, sexual violence, emotional abuse, and harassment. They also show that while those four types of violence are in most cases suffered by women, men may also experience them. Their study is one of the few that has gathered information in these times of pandemic, verifying that during the lockdown imposed by COVID-19, the home was at a high risk of becoming a very dangerous place for the victims of domestic violence.

Hayes and Kopp (2020) categorize physical violence, coercive control, reproductive control, psychological aggression, and sexual victimization as abuse. The problem with typologies is that the fewer categories that are established, the easier it is to leave out possible aggressions, and the more categories one contemplates, the less operative they are. In any case, as Hayes and Kopp (2020) suggest, the typologies provide an analysis of the victimization—despite the fact that data is collected from self-reports.

THEORETICAL CONCEPTS

When intimate partner violence occurs, it is important to consider how to explain it. Some theories suggest that intimate partner violence is influenced by—and is the result of—a high level of certain variables in the aggressor, such as impulsivity, stress, or the subjective interpretation of the situation (Johnson and Moore, 2020). However, there is evidence that intimate partner violence is not significantly associated with a deteriorated physical or mental health of the aggressor (Hayes and Kopp, 2020). In this respect, a study by Coccaro and Lee (2020) determines the prevalence and the correlatives of the intermittent explosive disorder—according to its definition in the DSM-5 (2014)—and of aggressive behavior. These authors analyzed the data collected by the National Comorbidity Survey Replication (NCS-R) and Adolescent Supplement (NCS-AS), resulting from the interviews of 10,148 adolescents and 9,282 adults (data was collected between 2001 and 2004). The results indicated that approximately 17 percent of the adolescents and 8 percent of the adults claimed to have a pattern of recurring aggressive outbursts at least once a year. These individuals are much more aggressive and impulsive than those of the control sample and are more likely to attack their couple, to carry and use a weapon, and to have been previously arrested by the police.

An explicative factor which has been analyzed from a more psychosocial point of view is how one of the members of the couple exercises control over the other. In their review of the literature, Johnson and Ferraro (2000) highlighted the fact that several studies focus on the explanation of violence as being typically exercised by men (who, in the context of couple relationships, use it to control women), suggesting the need for a more comprehensive analysis of the connections between violence, power, and control in the couple relationships.

In this sense, through a dyadic analysis of partner violence, Johnson's study (2006) notably identifies four types of intimate partner violence: intimate terrorism, characterized by the fact that one of the members of the couple is violent and controlling but the other is not; violent resistance, in which one of the members of the couple is violent but not controlling and the other is both violent and controlling; situational couple violence in which one of the members of the couple is violent but the other is not, and neither of the two is controlling; and lastly, mutual violent control, in which both individuals are violent and controlling. Johnson points out that this last type of violence is what is usually reflected in intimate partner violence statistics.

Lastly, we found that the use of the classification proposed by Capaldi et al. (2012) is of particular interest. After reviewing 228 works (170 were samples of adult participants and 58 of adolescents), Capaldi et al. concluded that what they define as risk factors (which may be considered as explicative variables here) can be classified into three large groups: first, the sociodemographic characteristics of the members of the couple; second, their individual and psychological characteristics; third, the characteristics of the interaction between them.

In view of this approach that analyzes psychosocial variables to explain violence in the couple, Dutton and Goodman (2005) took French and Raven's model of social power, which states that power may be conceptualized according to five different sources: coercive, reward, legitimate, referent, and expert. Later, they added the informational power (Raven, 1992). Dutton and Goodman focused on the conceptualization of coercive control that is generated in intimate couple relationships in which violence occurs. The model encompasses the following elements: social ecology; setting the stage; coercion involving a demand and a credible threat for noncompliance; surveillance; and delivery of threatened consequences. All these elements come spiraling and are superimposed, establishing a general situation of coercive control.

SELF-REPORTS AND TOOLS ON
INTIMATE PARTNER AGGRESSION

The degree to which intimate partner aggression occurs may only be determined through the application of self-reports, and for that information to be minimally valid, it is necessary to use large samples. For this reason, some of the research previously mentioned centered on the analysis of the data that was collected by large nationwide surveys. One example of the use of a wide range of samples but applied to specific research is Kuijpers's study (2020), with a sample of 1,183 heterosexual couples (i.e., a total of 2,366 subjects). Another possibility consists in extracting data from more general surveys such as the study of the National Intimate Partner and Sexual Violence Survey, undertaken in the United States in 2010, and elaborated with a nationwide representative sample of 13,699 men and women (Hayes and Kopp, 2020).

However, it is important to take into account the existence of a notable methodological bias, as the studies reveal that women and men do not respond to the surveys in the same manner. Thus, for example, when the perpetrator is a woman, she is more likely to openly admit it than male perpetrators (Kuijpers, 2020).

With regard to other instruments, perhaps the most widely known is Forms and Functions of Intimate Partner Aggression (FFIPA), by Halmos et al. (2018). The participants were 341 heterosexual couples who drank excessively (N = 682) and had a recent history of psychological or physical intimate partner aggression. The instrument describes how one person assaults the other (means at their disposal) and what motivates them to assault. The model pinpoints four dimensions: open, relational, proactive, and reactive. Results also indicated women perpetrated significantly more overt and relational aggression than men (Halmos et al., 2018).

WHO PERPETRATES INTIMATE PARTNER VIOLENCE: STEREOTYPES AND REALITY

There are several studies that describe intimate partner violence as perpetrated unilaterally by dominant and aggressive males toward vulnerable females. This unidirectional conceptualization has contributed to developing a stereotype of who is the perpetrator and who is the victim in domestic violence. Authors such as Hine et al. (2020) have found that the creation of these stereotypes—which are not but gender stereotypes—prompts society to ignore groups of victims that are unrelated to those stereotypes. This may happen to male victims, or to homosexual couples—few people infer that couples are not always heterosexual.

However, empirical research and the prevalence data suggest that the most common type of violence is bidirectional, that is, both members of the couple are victims and perpetrators (Hine et al., 2020). This idea is clearly expressed by Kaufman and Kimmel (2011) who, after a literature review, pointed out that it may not be concluded that domestic violence is perpetrated by men against women, as there are many empirical studies which show that the rates of domestic violence of women and men are equivalent. This idea, in line with Hine et al.'s (2020) notion of "bidirectional violence," also shows the importance of analyzing not only the general rates of violence of women and men, but how that violence manifests—clearly alluding to the fact that men and women perpetrate violence differently.

Authors such as Whitaker et al. (2007) suggested the use of a similar term, "reciprocal violence," or violence perpetrated by both parties, in opposition to the nonreciprocal. Their study was based on the data provided by the 2001 National Longitudinal Study of Adolescent Health, which gathered information about couple violence according to the self-reported answers of 11,370 individuals in the United States, all of them between 18 and 28 years old. Whitaker et al.'s analysis demonstrated that some sort of violence occurred in almost 24 percent of the couple relationships, and that almost half of the aggressions (49.7 percent) were reciprocal. It is interesting to highlight that in the case of nonreciprocal violent relationships, women were responsible for over 70 percent of the cases—that is, the reciprocity was associated more often with females than with males. However, in the case of physical aggressions, males were shown to attack females more often. Furthermore, when reciprocal violence existed, the levels of aggressiveness were higher, regardless of the aggressor's gender. The authors concluded that the reciprocity of violence is a good predictor of the severity of the aggressions.

As a matter of fact, one of the problems of statistic research is that the findings clash with the stereotypes. Hine et al. (2020) created hypothetical scenarios of intimate partner aggression and asked 178 university students to assign tags of "victim" or "perpetrator," assess the severity of the committed actions, and suggest how the issue should be resolved within the justice system. The results showed that in all scenarios the participants were tagged on very few occasions as "male victims" or as "female perpetrators." The participants recommended calling the police to men on less occasions than to women. In general, the data revealed how stereotypes of intimate partner violence and of gender are extremely powerful and clearly influence the perceptions of bidirectional violence.

Another study (Wilson and Smirles, 2020) explored how the perceptions of the severity of the abuse and the responsibility of the perpetrator differ according to factors such as the gender of the perpetrator and the victim, the type of abuse (physical vs. psychological), and the form of abuse (personal vs. phone text messages). The results demonstrated that participants perceived the abuse to be more serious when the perpetrator was a man than when it was a woman. Physical abuse was also conceptualized as worse than psychological. On the other hand, the abuse carried out by men was considered to be more serious, regardless of whether it was carried out in person or virtually, most likely because the participants attributed more responsibility to men than to women—and to those who committed physical abuse.

RISK FACTORS

Studies seem to demonstrate that some people are more prone to be assaulted in a couple relationship. Breiding et al.'s research (2014) exemplifies this. In a study that included only university women, the authors conducted surveys repeatedly over a period of four years (the same surveys were administered for a total of five years). Their data indicated the existence of two large predictors of sexual assault for university women: first, that previously (while studying in secondary school) they had been physically assaulted (without a sexual component being necessarily involved); second, that they had previously suffered some sort of sexual attack. Thus, for instance, Breiding points out that for women that were physically assaulted when they were adolescents, the relative risk of being victimized again in their first year at university or college was 2.96 times stronger than those who were not victims. Therefore, it was concluded that victimization during adolescence is the best predictor of victimization during their university years, and it was indeed a more accurate predictor than if the victimization had happened during childhood.

Risk factors can also be analyzed from the perspective of those who assault their couple. In fact, Paulhus and Williams (2002) suggested the term dark personality triad (Machiavellism, narcissism, psychopathy) to refer to personality traits related to detrimental behavior toward others. Later, they would add one more trait, sadism. We will explore dark personality in another chapter in more detail; concerning IPV, Kiire (2017, 2019) remarks that while the three classic traits (Machiavellianism, subclinical narcissism, psychopathy) are associated with those who show some type of IPV, psychopathy is the only one that predicts all types of aggression to the partner.

DIFFERENCES BETWEEN WOMEN AND MEN: SEXISM

An issue that has been widely debated is the extent to which the assaults— perpetrated or received—vary according to the gender variable. Several studies demonstrate that in minor disputes and when the type of assault is physical, women are more likely to acknowledge being perpetrators than men (Kuijpers, 2020). In serious and very serious assaults (of a sexual kind, for instance), there is no difference in the degree of acknowledgment of their actions between men and women (Kuijpers, 2020). In general, results indicate that women assault their partners in a more direct way (and recognize that aspect), while men usually use more indirect assaults, and they are less likely to acknowledge it (Halmos et al., 2018).

The female-male distinction brings us to the existence of sexual roles, which in itself incites violence. Philipp (2013) points out that violence manifests not only as a physical, verbal, psychic, or sexual phenomenon but also as a structural situation that operates symbolically. Thus, violence may be said to be ingrained within the structure of society. Galtung and Fischer (2013), for instance, distinguishes three types of violence; direct (in which the perpetrator and their direct implication in the committed violence is evident), structural (that originates and is reproduced in the structure of society, and can be found in all those norms and values that favor the marginalization and exploitation of individuals), and cultural (which is hidden in the culture of a society, legitimizing the consolidation of certain attitudes). As stated by Galtung in his theory of the "Violence Triangle" (2013), direct violence is visible, but the structural and cultural are not. Moreover, cultural violence (Philipp, 2013) includes legitimization, as well as cultural repressions and their symbolic representations. One of the main differences between structural and cultural violence is that the former acts subtly through different forms of power such as political or economic, while the latter acts through more direct actions.

Can psychological treatment provide a solution for this situation? Some studies focus on the possibilities offered by couple therapy. Jarnecke et al.'s paper (2020) is interesting in this respect, as it shows that the situation barely changes after family therapy, probably because the couple has had problems for several years. The authors studied a total of ninety-seven heterosexual couples, and their results indicate that the problems that couples face before seeking treatment vary widely—from problems that originate in the couple's own dynamic, to those arising from other external sources. Furthermore, it usually takes between 4 and 7 years for a couple to seek help; their attempts to solve their problems usually lead to a deterioration of the relationship, and it is more common that women take the initiative to seek help.

IN CONCLUSION: THE LIMITATIONS OF IPA STUDIES

All studies about IPA tend to show the same limitations. First, almost all the studies focus on heterosexual couples. Furthermore, although this should be imperative, it is almost impossible to include both members of the couple in the study (Kuijpers, 2020). The prevalence data and the research suggest that bidirectional violence is, in fact, the most common pattern in couples—that is, bidirectional violence occurs in situations in which the roles of "victim" and "perpetrator" can be attributed to both parties (Hine et al., 2020); therefore, it would be necessary to collect information from both members. In general, this type of research is hindered by the typical problems of self-report studies. Lastly, to what concerns intimate relations, online interaction is nowadays combined with simultaneous real interaction (Cantu and Charak, 2020).

Let us also highlight that violence is affected by culture. As a result, violence in the couple is more common in Asian cultures than in Western culture (Nam and Maxwell, 2020, among other authors); also, in the general population of Israel, for instance, verbal assault between couples is more frequent between Jewish couples than between Muslim ones (Sowan-Basheer, 2020).

Some researchers—among which our team is included—have differentiated two possible ways to obtain information about respondents of self-report studies. The first one is to inquire about the actions that the interviewed persons thought were more problematic for them (subjective or imagined criteria) or that they had suffered or currently suffer (objective or experimented criteria). The results shed light on the issue:

- Both men and women considered that to break the coexistence pact of the couple is the most problematic assault from the other member of the couple. That is, what is least tolerated in a couple is disloyalty, that the other member is not supporting, that they do not understand the other, that they cannot be trusted; and, of course, infidelity, lying and betrayal, and a general lack of communication. In other words, although the couple still exists de facto, it has been broken in its conception.

- The second aspect that is considered to be most serious is psychological abuse (which comprises threats and the manipulation of the other), and is feared more by women than by men. Being physically attacked appears as the third of the fears, with a much higher percentage of women than of men. It is interesting that the results are rather similar in the aggressive actions suffered and exercised by the couple.
- With respect to the differences between men and women, women contemplate being victims of different traumatizing behaviors to a larger extent than men. The results show that in the case of sexual abuse and physical aggression, such negative expectations are translated into real victimization.
- What is the response of the assaulted member of the couple against the array of traumatizing actions carried out by the perpetrator? The most common response, in men as well as in women, was to abandon the relationship (this response appears more often in women), followed by the attempt to dialogue (which is more common among males). Apart from abandoning the relationship, it is normal that couples speak about what happened. Another interesting data is that men are more likely to not know how to react in the face of an aggression from their couple. This tendency is not shown in sexual abuse on women, in which it is more common that abandoning the couple is accompanied by filing a case with the police or judicial system.
- Men score higher in Machiavellianism, subclinical narcissism, and subclinical psychopathy, and women in asking for forgiveness.

Physical violence within the couple is, unfortunately, higher than what had been expected, and it is inflicted by both but more often by men. Women tend to be more jealous than men, and both men and women complain that the other member of the couple usually breaks the pact of coexistence—which implies that almost all of them agree to not have relations with other people. All this reflects the changes that are taking place in our society. For that matter, our belief is that society should continue working to achieve that all forms of violence—in this case intimate partner violence—are minimalized as much as possible.

Unfortunately, intimate partner violence usually occurs due to the socialization that we receive when we are children, which is based on patriarchy. Therefore, the perspective of gender is a topic we felt important to address in the following chapter.

Chapter 2

Sexism, Machismo, and Patriarchy

Gender perspective may serve as a framework to understand terms such as sexism, machismo, feminism, misandry, misogyny—and many others. In our case, we prefer to focus on misandry and machismo as the opposite sides of a similar concept. There are several definitions of gender. For example, the World Health Organization defines gender as "the social concepts of norms, behaviors, activities and characteristics that each society considers appropriate for men or women" (WHO, 2015). It is generally accepted that there is a differentiation between sex and gender, the former referring to biological characteristics and the latter to cultural categories. But the truth is that one is not conceivable without the other; the existence of sexual differences has created sexual roles (gender), and gender determines the perception of the sex. This idea is expressed, for example, by Benhabib (1990, p. 125), when he affirms that "the sex-gender system is the essential mode that is not contingent upon anything else, in which the social reality is organized, symbolically divided, and lived as an experiment—understood as a sex-gender system the symbolic constitution and the socio-historic interpretation of the anatomic differences between sexes." Cobo (2008), states that "sex is an anatomic reality that historically would not have had a political or social significance if it hadn't translated into social disadvantage," revealing how cultural variations between women and men have created inequalities, as a result of which women find themselves in an inferior situation to men (see also Cobo, 2005). These differences were originally based on biological differences, but resulted from social structures. That is how the WHO conceives it, adding to the aforementioned definition that "the different norms and behaviors may generate gender inequality, that is, differences between men and women that systematically favor one of the groups" (WHO, 2015).

And yet the WHO criteria have developed over time; therefore, according to the UN Report on the protection against violence and discrimination motivated by sexual orientation or gender identity, all individuals have a sexual orientation and a gender identity. Sexual orientation consists of the sexual attraction and feelings that a person may develop toward another, while gender identity refers to how the person identifies with their gender—which might be different from the gender they had when they were born.

The UN report also acknowledges the five types of gender identity that are designated by the acronym LGBTI—lesbian, gay, bisexual, transgender, and intersexual. Intersexuality refers to those who have atypical sexual characteristics.

According to the UN, the ten most common gender identities are:

1. Heterosexuality: attraction to persons of the opposite sex.
2. Homosexuality: attraction toward persons of the same sex. Traditionally male homosexuals are referred to as "gay" and women as "lesbians."
3. Bisexuality: attraction toward persons of the same sex as well as to the opposite sex.
4. Demisexuality: attraction toward a person of the same sex or another gender that happens in some cases in which there is a strong emotional or intimate bond.
5. Pansexuality: attraction toward people (as persons)—meaning, independent of their gender identity.
6. Autosexuality: attraction toward oneself, without necessarily being a synonym of narcissism.
7. Lithsexuality: are those who feel attraction toward other people, but do not wish nor do they feel the need to be corresponded.
8. Asexuality: persons who do not feel any sort of sexual attraction.
9. Polysexuality: attraction toward specific groups of people owing to their gender identity.
10. Antrosexuality: those who want to explore their sexuality without being classified in any of the previous descriptions.

Hence, the traditional notion of gender as a binary opposition between male and female proves insufficient and gives way to the term non-binary gender (or genderqueer). Non-binary identities are usually included under the umbrella term of transgender identities, although there are non-binary persons who do not feel identified with it. The term genderqueer should not be confused with queer, which designates any type of sexual dissidence under the parameters of the LGBT identities.

After this brief revision of contemporary gender identities, let us go back to our original question: What are gender roles? In essence, as Cobo (2008) points out, gender roles are stereotypes: "The first ideological mechanism, crude but efficient, that points to reproduction and reinforcement of gender inequality, is the stereotype; stereotypes may be defined as a set of simple ideas—but strongly rooted in the consciousness—that escape the control of reason." In other words, gender roles are preconceived characteristics of a society that are assigned to men and women, in conformity with the functions that each of them are meant to fulfill. There are different interpretations as to how these roles might be differentiated, but the most widely accepted classification is that which divides those functions in to instrumental and expressive. Males are assigned instrumental roles (they should be good leaders, intelligent and efficient), while females are assigned expressive roles such as caring for others, for which they should be caring, expressive, and comprehensive. Sánchez and Iglesias (2008, p. 132) affirm that "male stereotypes are related to professional activities, to the public sphere, to power, and are characterized by words and expressions such as activity, aggressiveness, authority, braveness, risk, competition, leadership skills, aptitude for science, and the love of risk. Female stereotypes, however, are linked to notions of caring, privacy and lack of power, which show peculiarities such as passiveness, affection, submission, obedience, docility, fear, shyness, lack of initiative, a tendency to dream, doubt, emotional instability, lack of control, dependence, aptitude for words and weakness."

One characteristic of gender roles is that they are prescriptive—that is, they not only describe beliefs about how men and women are; they also establish how they "should be" according to certain social values. However, "proscriptions"—what a women or man "should not" be or do—are stronger driving forces in society, marginalizing all those who do not comply with social norms. Diekman's paper (2005), for instance, seeks to explain why women are less likely to achieve leadership positions, concluding that there is an imbalance between the stereotypical female characteristics (low competition) and the characteristics necessary to fulfil the role of a leadership position (high competition), which leads companies to overlook the leadership potential of women.

Roles are not biological, but culture-bound; they are highly sensitive to time and circumstance—even to age, and each society imposes them differently. Roles have served throughout history to reaffirm the role of the dominant males over females. As Philipp (2013) states, the imposition of roles does not correlate with a symmetric communication, but rather to an asymmetric one, in which some members of a group impose their definition of the roles even against the interests of the other members of the group. The same idea is mentioned by Perez, Paez, and Navarro (2001).

What about sexism? In the Ideological Feminist Dictionary (2002), Sau defines sexism as "a set of each and every one of the methods used in the bosom of the patriarchy to be able to maintain the dominated sex: the feminine, with an inferior situation, subordination, and exploitation." The gender roles mentioned earlier serve as one of the main tools that groups of power use to maintain the superior status of men, through the socialization groups (family, school, groups of equals, means of communication, et cetera.) that reward or punish the attitudes and actions of the individuals. As Moya (1998) suggests, we may say that there is an old and a new sexism; the old one, also called traditional sexism, is defined as an "attitude of prejudice, or discriminatory conduct, based on the supposed inferiority or difference of women as a group," and it is articulated through three ideas:

- Paternalistic domination: Women are weak, which legitimates male dominance to take care of and to protect them.
- Competitive gender differentiation: Women are biologically designed for the care of the family and are not equipped enough to be in charge of the politics or the economy of a country.
- Heterosexual hostility: Women are dangerous and have a great power of domination that stems from their "sexual power."

The new sexism is based on the theory of ambivalent sexism formulated by Glick and Fiske (1996), which encompasses hostile and benevolent sexism. Hostile sexism comprises all direct attitudes which imply that women are inferior to men—and therefore less able to lead a community, or even themselves. In contrast, benevolent sexism shows a certain affective, positive tone that may be confused with a positive attitude toward women, yet still implicitly legitimizes the inferior nature of their role by treating them as a romantic, fragile object that needs protection from the male. This is considered the most dangerous version of sexism because while hostile sexism usually triggers rebellion, benevolent sexism is more accepted by society as a whole, and males who adhere to it are perceived as "gentlemen." Nevertheless, however positive the feelings that benevolent sexism arises from, it is still sexism, as it is also based on male domination and on conceiving women as weak. These dimensions of sexism are a pervasive feature in practically all cultures (Moya, Páez, Glick, Fernández, and Poeschi, 2002).

Galtung (1990) distinguishes three types of violence: direct, structural, and cultural.

- Direct violence is that in which the perpetrator and their relation with the violent event can be clearly noticed.
- Structural violence originates and is reproduced in the social structure, and is present in all those norms and values that favor the margination and exploitation of certain individuals.
- Cultural violence is hidden within the culture of a specific society, legitimizing certain attitudes over long periods of time.

Direct violence is visible, while structural and cultural violence are invisible (Galtung, 1990). Besides, cultural violence (Philipp, 2013) includes legitimizations, cultural repression, and symbolic representation.

One of the main differences between structural and cultural violence is that the former manifests in a subtle way under diverse forms of power (namely, politics or economy), while the latter manifests through more straightforward actions. Androcentrism manifests in the cultural and structural dimension, which encompasses a large network of symbolic mechanisms to guarantee ideological continuity.

Against the backdrop of these approaches (which revealed how the term machismo ossifies a male power structure), Kaplan (2011) defines misandry from a psychological point of view—and in relation to the notion of social role—as hate and aversion toward males. He also mentions the existence of a psychological tendency (especially of the cognitive type) to disdain the male as a sex, and everything that is considered masculine. Benatar (2003) refers to misandry as the "second sexism." In its most extreme manifestation, misandrists—usually women—consider males as socially damaging beings, toxic people, even useless, and they may even advocate for forms of conceiving children that exclude having sexual intercourse with a male. While we use machismo as an opposing term to misandry, in reality, its antonym would be misogyny.

The concept of misogyny differs from misandry in that the latter refers to the superiority of women over men. In other words, misandry denotes an authoritarian position toward males, and it seems difficult to accept its existence, as it does not seem to be compatible with the evident reality of a machista society, in which the patriarchy has historically exercised—and continues to exercise—control over women. And that control has not been, nor is it, exercised by women toward men. In fact, while violence is one of the elements upon which machismo is based, feminism has never been based on that; machismo kills and feminism does not; therefore, misandry in reality is nothing but an attack on feminism. Feminazi is another example of the terms that were created to attack feminism (see also, for example, Limbaugh, 1993), which expresses hate toward women and toward the attempt to attain equality (Kaufman and Kimmel, 2011).

MISANDRY

It seems that there is a socially accepted assumption that all of us are machista, leading to misandry, or the disdain of males being sometimes accepted, or at least, not criticized. Indeed, this is not the case when misandry is taken to an extreme degree. Thus, there has been an avalanche of criticism of the way of education advocated by Nel Noddings, a well-known feminist whose idea of educating in feminism has triggered feelings of misandry. In this sense, the title of Vandenberg's paper—Feminine Ethics or Materialistic Misandry? (1996)—seems revealing. The opposite view can be found in other studies such as the one published by McCormack (2011) that shows how high-performance programs intended for secondary education students may foster a new masculinity in males that reinforces equality between sexes.

Studies on misandry can be broadly grouped into the following areas:

- Racial studies—and more particularly, those that focus on the black population in the United States. In fact, Smith, Yosso, and Solorzano (2007) coined the term "black misandry" to refer to a pathological, exaggerated aversion to black males, an aversion created and reinforced by certain social and institutional ideologies which result in certain behaviors, ways of feeling and thinking, of the stigmatized collectives. Most of the studies of this type use a qualitative methodology, through the use of focus groups. For instance, Smith, Allen, and Danley's study (2007) interviews twenty-six black students to analyze misandry toward black males in the United States. The results indicate that the subjects that are victims of misandry show a permanent state of hypervigilance and the necessity to control the situations out of fear. This is one of the few studies that introduces the concept of stress from fatigue when facing racial conflict and demonstrates how the Afro-American population of students suffer those specific symptoms. Racism in schools has been regularly analyzed, albeit it normally refers to misogyny, as demonstrated, for example, by Garcia (2015), Isoke (2014), and Nyika (2014).
- Misandry is also suffered by individuals who are intellectually disabled. Wilson, Parmenter, Stancliffe, Shuttleworth, and Parker's study (2010) explores ways in which the social system treats males and females differently, and shows how, in the case of intellectually disabled individuals, males are more often discriminated against than females.

MISOGYNY

In most cases, studies on misogyny are based on rape myth and its social acceptance. The acceptance of rape myths surfaces as a result of certain ideas and rape myth statements such as "This cannot happen to me"; "She had it coming"; "It is better not to go out at night, or walk down dark streets"; When a woman says "no" it often means "yes," et cetera. Among other authors, Burt (1980) points out that those who accept rape myths show antagonizing sexual beliefs, are usually more tolerant toward interpersonal violence, and hold more rigid gender stereotypes.

Rape myths consist of a number of false stereotyped ideas that, disguised as objective facts, are incorporated into the construct that we call reality, undermining it, and making the lie more real than reality itself; as the Thomas Theorem suggests (and the theory of symbolic interactionism perfectly explains), "If men define situations as real, they are real in their consequences."

Rape myth ideas stem from five false beliefs that affect women from the very moment in which they are attended after being raped, as they are beliefs held by police officers, healthcare workers, judges, members of juries—that is, a large part of society, if not as society as one entity. These false beliefs are:

1. Most sexual aggressions are committed by a stranger. The media have contributed to popularize the idea that women are assaulted in dark alleys. However, in the real world, it is much more common that rape and sexual aggressions happen within the home, and that they are committed by someone the victim knows.
2. A survivor of sexual aggression reports rape immediately. The data indicate that less than half of the victims of sexual assault, even in the case of rape, file a complaint with the authorities within the following 24 hours, and that around 15 percent of them take more than six months to do so. This delay is even longer if the victim is a child. Some studies estimate that, in the United States, two out of three sexual aggressions are not reported.
3. If the aggression is reported immediately, it is relatively easy to investigate the case and find the alleged aggressor. However, and despite the physical exams that are undertaken on the victims, the aggressor is not always caught or condemned, and the cases are not always investigated. In the United States, only 18 percent of the reported rape cases conclude with an arrest, and only 2 percent with a prison sentence.
4. If somebody, normally a woman, did not really wish to have a sexual relation in the first place, she would have struggled. This is a completely false statement. People vary enormously as to how they respond in the case of rape or sexual aggression. And yet, it is necessary to consider that several women undergo "dissociation"—a phenomenon that consists in feeling that the assaulted person abandons their body, and therefore feels that the terrible actions are not affecting them, but to the person who remains in that body.
5. The assaulted person might be confused about what happened. Several people who have been raped or sexually assaulted affirm that they have memories with vivid images, sounds, and smells associated to the

attack, even if it happened decades ago. However, when they are asked to recall the exact time and day in which it took place, or where they were at a specific time (the type of details that police officers and the district attorney's office usually concentrate on to establish the facts of a crime), they may have difficulties in doing so, or they may contradict themselves, undermining their own testimony. Unfortunately, the police and the judicial system do not commonly believe those women, when it is evident that they have been assaulted.

Thus, it is particularly important to verify the different ways in which men and women interpret rape myths (Lonsway and Fitzgerald, 1995), and to understand that misogyny is precisely one of the interpretative keys of this differentiation. Reilly, Lott, Caldwell, and De Luca's study (1992) delves into this perspective, adding specific variables to the analysis of victims. Curiously, women who have been victims of misogyny of a male are the ones who behave more equally; a study by Dall'Ara and Maass (1999) offers thorough research into that perspective, using a highly ingenious laboratory experimental methodology. This type of harassment can also be virtual (see, for example, Citron [2009], or Jane [2015], in which the concept of "e-bile" is discussed). The truth is that misogyny may be considered a pandemic, as Bitzer (2015) clearly explains.

Let us now analyze some of the contexts where extended misogyny—or, as we prefer to call it, machismo—is more likely to occur.

- Misogyny in the workplace has been extensively studied. Among other authors, Miner-Rubino and Cortina (2007) demonstrate both women and men are more likely to leave companies with misogynist environments. This shows that a misogynistic working environment may have negative effects on all the employees. Earlier, these authors (Miner-Rubino and Cortina, 2004) had already highlighted the existence of hostility toward women within the work environment, and they created indexes of hostility detection. They proposed the concept of working contexts with perceived misogyny. Of course, the study of companies within the financial business field can be set apart, because in those companies, competitiveness—which is embedded in misogyny—defines the way of acting of workers and also of students within the field (Chui and Dietz, 2014; Phipps and Young, 2015). Misogyny also happens among women in the work environment; Mavin, Grandy, and Williams (2014) use the term "micro violence" to refer to that, revealing an interesting aspect of the issue upon examining how women in managing positions treat other women that work for the same corporation with more misogynist values than them.

- Some sectors are particularly suitable for the analysis of misogyny. This is the case of nursing, for example. Usually, the personnel in Nursing is mostly composed of women and characterized by their lack of power before doctors, who are the ones that make the decisions and, at least a few years ago, are mostly men. This situation of inequality means that within the healthcare sector, men do have power, but women do not. This phenomenon has been investigated, for example, by Farrell (2001). Misogyny occurs in almost all areas related to health (see also, for example, the study by Silva and Lemos, 2015, concerning cardiovascular surgery).
- Perhaps the largest area of investigation of misogyny to date is sports; certain sports have traditionally been associated with masculinity and represent the idea of male superiority, since men are usually the ones engaged in the sport, while women are relegated to spectators or cheerleaders. Thus, a hierarchy is established in which the male is superior, and the role of women is residual, accompanying the male as decoration. This might be the case of rugby (Schacht, 1996). Some studies (Robertson, 2003) analyze the topic of governmental campaigns that encourage misogyny when promoting some sports. There are several team sports that only integrate males and create homo-social environments, limiting and avoiding contact with women, while also fostering a concept of masculinity in opposition to women. These characteristics imply attitudes that can be reverted if actions are taken, creating sports in which women are also integrated, as Anderson (2008) shows.
- The presence of misogyny in music has also been subject to study. The genre that has been more typically analyzed was rap. Thus, while Eveland and McLeod's study (1999) did not offer any conclusive results regarding the defense or attack of misogyny from the analysis of the lyrics, a work carried out later by Weitzer and Kubrin (2009) demonstrated how rap encourages misogyny (see also Oware, 2014). Indeed, the media are responsible for the diffusion of these messages, as Easteal, Holland, and Judd (2015) or Shoebridge (2014) show, and the media constantly create new ways of perpetuating violence against women, reinforcing patriarchal structures. Also, the use of the Internet to participate, for example, in collective games (MMOGs, or Massively Multiplayer Online Games) fosters misogyny (Braithwaite, 2014).

From a social viewpoint, the problem of gender violence equally arises from male and female attitudes. There are several women who are involved in situations of gender violence but are unaware of it, and when they are, they tend to underestimate their victimization to the extent that they justify the violence exercised on them (García-Díaz, Fernández-Feito, Rodriguez-Diaz,

López-González, Mosteiro-Diaz, and Lana-Perez, 2013; Rodriguez-Castro, Lameiras, Carrera, and Vallejo, 2012, 2013). Another problem is that women do not often acknowledge nonverbal violence when they suffer it (Pazos, Oliva, and Hernando, 2014). And yet, the number of women who do acknowledge that violence has been inflicted upon them is rather significant (the report by Diaz-Aguado and Carvajal (2011) in Spain, states that the number of both percentages in the case of adolescents is 14 percent and 10 percent, respectively).

SOME DATA FROM RESEARCH

Our research team has tried to determine if there is an attitude of rejection toward misandry, since misandry, as well as machismo, should be considered discriminatory attitudes. We tried to determine whether machismo is more often rejected than misandry or vice versa, or even if misandry is considered a positive attitude. We asked ourselves whether it is possible to differentiate the defining characteristics of machismo as opposed to misandry. In all likelihood, misandry is mostly associated with positive visions of humanity, and machismo to negative visions. These are some of the conclusions of our research team:

- People usually reject misandry as well as machismo, but misandry is more commonly accepted. The fact that 17 percent of the subjects of our study present a positive attitude toward misandry is worrying, although it is even more worrying that 9 percent defend attitudes in favor of machismo.
- Misandry is more pleasing to most; it is closer to the way each person thinks (their ideology) and produces more affection and conviction. However, machismo produces humiliation and anger.
- People who show an attitude that favor misandry stand out for their elevated femininity or for the value they place in the expressive aspects of behavior, but they hold a machista idea of intimate relationships, generally supporting the culture of honor—hat is, the existence of possessive couple relationships in which women are subjected by males. This notion of subjection does not include the work environment, as it is accepted that women at the workplace may work at nontraditional roles. Furthermore, violence is rejected.
- A machista attitude clearly implies the legitimization of violence.

While misandry is associated with kindness, grace, personal ideology, friendliness, and conviction, machismo is only associated with negative elements such as humiliation and anger.

Apparently, the general conceptualization of misandry and of machismo greatly differs from what is understood in the literature. It seems as if the idea that couple relationships in which exerting control over the other—specifically, when the male is the dominant and feels that his honor is offended whenever anyone addresses her—is not considered to be a sign of machismo. And yet misandry, as much as machismo, excludes violence. On the other hand, there is an emerging view of misandry which assumes that misandrists (female or male) show a positive attitude, on the grounds that they are expressing an antimachista way of being. Despite all these findings, the high number of people that accept and value machista attitudes is still worrisome.

ULTRAMACHISMO

We have examined different sexual orientations, showing how some of them imply a resurgence of attitudes of intolerance and a lack of respect toward others. Let us now mention the existence of an attitude—*ultramachismo*—that also implies a confrontation within society.

Against the idea that society advances toward the elimination of machismo, a movement has emerged that supports ultramachismo. Those (usually males) who are extremely machista may be referred to as ultramachistas. These types of individuals defend, for example, the legalization of rape within private property. There is a blog in which the author asserts that the result of instructing men not to rape is that women then refrain from taking protective measures from being raped.

The blog intends to create a movement that brings together "tribes of men," a concept that, according to the group, symbolizes a place in which "men can be men." Its promoter is the US writer Daryush Valizadeh, better known as Roosh V, who created the machista blog "Return of Kings." To participate in this movement, one must be a male and heterosexual.

Valizadeh speaks of "neomasculinity" and attacks equality because it generates "the loss of power in traditional men" and because "the value of women depends largely on their fertility and beauty, and that of men on their resources, intelligence and character." He also states that "the elimination of traditional roles unleashes promiscuity in women and other negative behaviors that hinder the creation of a family."

Regarding suffrage, he asserts that "women should not vote, since they are intellectually inferior; they do not have a sense of justice."

Sheriff Aderigbe describes the seven big lies that women usually tell men throughout their lives. Aderigbe alleges that they invent these answers with the objective of getting their way and getting the support of men.

1. Age: "forever Young." Perhaps this is the most common lie among women, and the reason is not absurd, states Aderigbe. The author explains that oftentimes women take off between two and three years from their real age because men feel more attracted to younger women and avoid those who are a few years older than them. It is said that love has no age, but it is also said that, while women get older, men become more mature and attractive.

2. Claim to be single (when they are not). When there is an annoying guy who is trying to score with them, many women allude to an invented boyfriend, so that they can be left alone. On the other hand, there are also those who momentarily forget that they have a couple when they come across someone whom they see as attractive. Some not only leave that information out, but go beyond, even introducing themselves as single.

3. "We are only friends. He is not interested in me." The "yes but no" game is not an exclusively feminine fallacy, but when a woman alleges that a male is only her friend it is because it is not a typical friendship, and she knows it. In the opinion of the author, messages such as "I miss you" or "You look really sexy in that pic" are clear indications that the two persons could be interested in each other and, so to say, try to freeze time just in case. Several people flirt simply to raise their ego or to demonstrate that they still know how to manage themselves on the market. Aderigbe expresses that woman reserve some men around them as a sort of security backup. They chat with them and keep them close in case their current relationship does not work or to have a "shoulder to cry on" when they argue with their boyfriends or husbands.

4. "No way. I'm not flirting." The author takes the premise that the definition of flirting is somewhat ambiguous. For him, it does not mean a simple talk, but actually getting close and showing interest in a person who we know is attracted to us. Once again, the author is convinced that women are much smarter: "Women are very good at reading body language and may easily deduce if they are flirting with somebody or someone is flirting with them." In his opinion, the majority of women make good use of the art of flirting to kill boredom and, as explained before, to have alternative plans in case their current relationship does not work out.

5. "I have never done this before." Aderigbe specifically refers to when women end up at the house of a one-night stand. He comments that it is

normal that they say that they never do those things, to appear innocent and make others think they are "good girls" grabbing the opportunity to begin a relationship. It is clear that in their environment, there are few women who may be willing to remain single, and most of them want to desperately find a husband.

6. "It has been a long time since I had a sexual intercourse." Most women say that the last time they had sexual intercourse was between six and eight months ago. Unfortunately, four out of five times, this is not true, says Aderigbe. The author insists on the idea that what they want is to marry and, of course, it is much better to seem prudish for a good husband that may rescue them from a life of chastity and innocence.

7. The number of sexual partners they have had. In the same line as what has already been mentioned, Aderigbe insists that women want to give the image of "good girls" and prefer not to confess the number of males they have slept with, in order to hunt a good man.

Indeed, according to Aderigbe, behind the fact that women worldwide are ashamed of their sexual and private life and feel practically obliged to hide it, there is a positive and comforting message: All those lies mean that they are seriously interested in men.

Whatever the reasons be, it may be true that there are a series of common lies that almost all women tell at some point of their lives when they want to begin a relationship; but does that not also happen to a large percentage of men? The ultramachistas are only interested in pointing out how women are liars, perverse, manipulative, without admitting that men may also act the same way.

These men define themselves as "beta men," in opposition to their hated "alpha machos"; it is better to be the victim than the executioner. All of them believe that women are marginalizing them in society, and they are being meek little lambs when, in reality, all women are "bitches" that want their money and to take them to the altar, to drain them of their last drop of life. These males have created the MGTOW association (Men Going Their Own Way), and they say they hate women. So much that it is difficult to find any reference on their page of whether they feel attracted to women, but they do not identify themselves as gay.

Against these forums and associations that only admit males, there are other forums and associations of women machistas, like those of "Women Against Feminism," who support the ideas that we just exposed.

Proponents of the so-called ultramachismo have coined the term feminazi to discredit feminism and all women who vindicate equality. The term was used for the first time in 1992 through a radio host, Rush Limbaugh, although other authors attribute it to Thomas Hazlett, an economy professor.

Ultimately, social movements gather their followers through a common mentality, which provokes a clash against other movements. The best-known dichotomy is that of machismo opposing feminism, but as we have seen in this chapter, the reality and classification of ideologies is enormous. The problem is that some of these ideologies are pernicious and attack those who are not like those who belong to that approach. One of those ideologies is the Parental Alienation Syndrome (PAS), which will be analyzed in the following chapter.

Chapter 3

Child Sexual Abuse

The introduction of this book was the account of a mother's suspicions that her daughter was being sexually abused, which raises the question: To what extent are children sexually abused? Are these relatively isolated incidents, and the story simply served its purpose for this book—to illustrate institutional harassment? We trust that this chapter allows for some answers.

The chapter revolves around one of the most terrible scourges of our society. As scientists, we are often equidistant in the analysis of social issues; we try to separate the emotional dimension from the purely scientific, placing ourselves at a vantage point from which we may supposedly be objective. However, not all social issues require the same scientific contributions, and scientific research should provide a component of "value," that is, of usefulness, to build a fairer, more humane, and civilized society. Child sexual abuse is an issue against which society must demand resources from science for detection, treatment of abused children, action concerning abusers, and above all, for its prevention. Sexual abuse of children should not leave anyone indifferent—and that includes social scientists. This is a brief reflection on the problem of child sexual abuse: how to detect the problem and how to provide the justice system with objective evidence of its existence so that appropriate action may be taken. Let us hope that this may help professionals to find more appropriate lines of action for the protection of children, and provoke thought and awareness to those who must deal with this issue. Indeed, children who are victims of sexual abuse—fewer have a higher need of protection than they do—will appreciate it.

CHILD ABUSE

Child sexual abuse is a form of maltreatment; maltreatment is, therefore, a good starting point for this chapter. Generally speaking, child mistreatment can be framed within the so-called battered child syndrome (BCS).

Unfortunately, the battered child syndrome is a worldwide phenomenon (see, for example, García-Piña and Loredo-Abdalá, 2009); BCS manifests in several ways, including negligence, physical maltreatment, psychological maltreatment, and of course, child sexual abuse (CSA).

From a psychological and psychosocial point of view, the term maltreatment is as broad as that of BCS, and it also encompasses CSA. For this reason, the next logical step seems to be to define—and reflect on—child abuse, and subsequently analyze a case study of child maltreatment: child sexual abuse.

Over the past few decades, the orientation of research on the causes of child abuse has gone through substantial change. Lameiras (2002) and Palacios, Moreno, and Jimenez (1995) review these changes in detail in their respective research papers. A few years ago, Palacios, Moreno, and Jimenez revealed how science and society, when conceptualizing maltreatment, have evolved from clinical-psychiatric explanatory theories to the most recent, more multivariate and interactionist approaches. In accordance with these authors (Palacios, Moreno, and Jimenez, 1995) we may distinguish four major approaches, which are set out below:

- Clinical-psychiatric approach: Initially, the causes of maltreatment were linked to parents' personality disorders, assuming that those who maltreat are mentally ill and emotionally unadjusted. The sheer amount of literature backing the approach is overwhelming, which contributes to the ideas that "everything is inherited" and that "everything is genetic," while facilitating reasons to give up the battle on a social level when facing a problem. Certainly, factors of this kind are at times present in people who maltreat, and studies show how the abused, like their abuser, show high levels of depression, anxiety, low levels of self-esteem, a tendency to impulsivity, difficulties in controlling their behavior and in being able to anticipate the consequences of their acts, low levels of tolerance to frustration, etc. These studies often identify the abuser with the parent (usually male) and the abused with the child, which clearly justifies the use of a genetic explanation. However, as Palacios, Moreno, and Jimenez (1995) point out, while these factors are commonly present, that does not mean they alone can explain the phenomenon of maltreatment. It is common knowledge that several people who maltreat do not suffer from any pathology, and others who suffer from different pathologies never mistreat children or anyone else. The widely popular idea that people who maltreat girls or boys must have been maltreated during their own childhood, clearly expresses this position, which is not proven by all studies—that is, sometimes it is confirmed, sometimes it is not. Therefore, the idea of intergenerational transmission of child abuse is but a myth. Powell, Cheng, and Egeland's studies (1995), which are also cited by Palacios, Moreno, and Jiménez (1995), report a number of investigations that do not confirm the idea of intergenerational transmission.

- Social approach: According to this approach, the responsibility does not fall on those who mistreat, but on the social conditions that affect families (unemployment, overcrowding, lack of social support, marital tensions, etc.). The number of studies that scientifically demonstrate that adverse social conditions are related to mistreatment is immense. Palacios, Moreno, and Jiménez (1995) point out some factors such as serious instability in partner relations, social isolation, prolonged unemployment, poor housing conditions, overcrowding, among others, that illustrate this approach.

- Cognitive approach: This perspective emphasizes the personal maturity and the psychological complexity of the aggressor, since those who maltreat are often considered immature individuals whose development was stunted at stages previous to maturity (Palacios, Moreno, and Jimenez, 1995). One of the consequences, for instance, is that what they perceive or expect concerning child behavior is incorrect, leading them to analyze children's behavior as if the children were older than they indeed are, attributing them an intentionality that they cannot possibly have, and expecting too many things—and too soon—from them. As a result, these people develop immature ways and mechanisms of reaction, often characterized by impulsivity. As Palacios, Moreno, and Jiménez (1995) argue, Crittenden's (1993) and Milner's models (1993) are perhaps the most representative of this position.

- Child vulnerability-centered approach: Lastly, the focus of this approach in not on the characteristics of the adult perpetrators, as in the previous approaches, but on the reasons that explain why certain children are more prone to become victims than others. According to Palacios, Moreno, and Jiménez (1995), the three factors that are more commonly referred to in studies are age, health, and behavioral characteristics of children. Some studies show that the likelihood of being maltreated is higher among children than in teenagers; in children with health problems (due, for example, to prematurity or to some kind of deficiency or physical limitation) or in those who present behavioral disorders (e.g., hyperactivity, impulsivity, etc.).

Perhaps, as Palacios, Moreno, and Jiménez (1995) set forth, the problem with the previous approaches is the pretention that the factors each of them analyzes are the only ones that provide an explanation to the problem. However, as it seems, there are no specific causes for child maltreatment, nor are the causes equally necessary or sufficient in all cases (Belsky, 1993). For this reason, when seeking the causes of child abuse, it is increasingly common for researchers to turn to interactional approaches of multiple, concurrent causality. There are different versions of these approaches, three of which are highlighted by Palacios, Moreno, and Jiménez (1995): the transactional model of Cicchetti and Rizley (1981), the transitional model of Wolfe (1987, 1991), and the evolutionary-ecological model of Belsky (1980, 1993).

As it would be impossible to explore all of them, we will only analyze the latter, since it seems that the ecological model has the characteristic of being more inclusive, considering the existence of four levels of mutually interactive influence:

- Ontogenetic level: the psychological characteristics of the person who is maltreating, such as their personal history, mental health, level of development, perception and feelings toward the child, etc.
- Microsystem level: family characteristics, such as the size of the family and that of their home; characteristics of the child—level of maturity, difficulties they may present, problems of conduct they may have, etc.; characteristics of conjugal relations—strong disagreements, type of family structure.
- Exosystem level, such as the work situation, relations with other relatives, relations with neighbors or colleagues, social support networks, etc.
- Macrosystem level, such as attitudes and social representations concerning children and their upbringing, the general level of violence in society, the social attitude to various forms of violence, etc.

The advantage of this model is that it allows for the combination of these levels. Let us look into one example (Palacios, Moreno, and Jimenez, 1995): A father with a poor evolutionary level, who shows inadequate expectations regarding the child's behavior, and interacts with a problematic child with eating disorders or hyperactivity (microsystem level), in the context of a family life marked by difficulties such as poverty, unemployment, and social isolation (exosystem level), and in a society within which violence is present in some family traditions, of a certain style of interpersonal relationship, and of the contents of the mass media (macrosystem); that would be the most comprehensive set of interacting factors.

On the other hand, Cicchetti and Rizley's model (1981), as well as Wolfe's (1987), offer the advantage that in their analysis of the causes of maltreatment, they consider vulnerability and protection factors. Thus, while the factors that trigger maltreatment and destabilize good adult-child relationships lead to risk situations, the compensatory factors mitigate tensions and protect against those risks. Vulnerability factors may include all those mentioned at any level of the ecological analysis and may be either permanent or transient in nature. The same can be said about protective or compensatory factors, which entail characteristics such as marital and social support, improvements in living conditions, social support programs, community support, therapeutic interventions, the acquisition of new skills in relation to the children and in controlling their behavior, and so on.

The advantage of these models is that they afford a new insight into the typical contradictions of scientific studies, such as conflicting data showing that certain personality traits of parents are associated with maltreatment, while on other occasions suggesting that it is the absence of such a relationship that is associated with it; or the common contradiction between research showing that certain childhood issues (prematurity, hyperactivity, health problems, etc.) increase the likelihood of abuse, against other studies that have been unable to document such a stance. Perhaps maltreatment is a rather intricate phenomenon, resistant to investigation, analysis, or treatment with simple, monocausal, and unidirectional models (Palacios, Moreno, and Jiménez, 1995), and that is the view that should guide us in further analyzing, and reflection upon, this phenomenon.

DEFINITION OF CHILD SEXUAL ABUSE

After this broad analysis of the concept of abuse, let us now focus on the subject of this chapter—the specific phenomenon of child sexual abuse.

The American Academy of Pediatrics (1999) has defined child sexual abuse as the practice of physical or visual contact committed by an individual within a sexual context; by means of violence, deception, or seduction, the child is unable to give consent by virtue of their age and difference of power. Therefore, in order to have a more clear idea of the elements involved in the dynamics of child sexual abuse, there are several factors to consider:

- Coercion. The perpetrator uses their position of power or strength to interact sexually with the child; that includes threats, deception, seduction, physical strength, or a combination thereof.
- The difference in age and level of development. The disparity of these factors between the aggressor and the victim prevents freedom of decision or consent from the latter; there are differences in their experiences, their degree of biological maturation, and their expectations. Thus, when analyzing these elements, the ages of the victim and the perpetrator should be considered.

- Experiences between girls or boys, and adults. It is usually understood that if there is sexual interaction between girls or boys under the age of 12 with an adult 18 years of age or older, there is child sexual abuse.
- Sexual encounters between girls or boys, and adolescents. It includes sexual experiences between girls or boys under the age of 12 and another person who is under 18, but is at least four years older.
- Sexual experiences between adolescents and older adults. Sexual interaction between adolescents 13 to 16 years of age and adults who are older than the adolescent by 10 years or more.
- Sexual experiences between children of the same age. Physical or emotional coercion is sufficient criteria to establish the diagnosis of child sexual abuse, regardless of the age of the aggressor; this includes peer abuse.
- Type of sexual conduct. This is another aspect that needs to be analyzed. We must differentiate between normal practices, or sexual play, which occur between children of similar ages, and abusive behavior, in which age or developmental difference and coercion often make a difference. Sexual play usually occurs in preschoolers and early school years and is normal behavior.

Let us proceed to review, specifying and analyzing some of the aforementioned characteristics.

Among other authors, Echeburúa and Del Corral (2006) have defined the term and provided some examples. These authors state that child sexual abuse refers to any sexual conduct between an adult and a child; that is, they exclude that the perpetrator may be another child. Furthermore, they point out that while age matters, lawfully, a relationship may be consensual, according to the diverse legislation of different countries, if the minors are at least 13, 14, or 16 years of age. The asymmetry of power within the relationship of those involved and the existence of explicit or implicit coercion bears more importance than difference of age in itself.

Another possibility in defining the term is to focus on the operational aspect—using, for instance, the elements that psychological scales include in this regard. One of the possible definitions of this type, perhaps the most common, is the one that makes the term operative through the Traumatic Life Events Questionnaire (TLEQ), by Kubany and Haynes (2001). In this questionnaire, sexual abuse is defined as unwanted sexual contact:

- Between a child under the age of 13 and someone at least 5 years older,
- Between a child under the age of 13 and someone of similar age by coercion, and

• Between a child under the age of 18 and another individual, against the will of the former.

PREVALENCE

There are several statistical data on prevalence, and, as one may expect, they do not match. The examples we include here give us an idea of the relevance of the problem. Taking as an example the data obtained by Pereda and Forns (2007), the prevalence of sexual abuse is as follows:

• 17.9 percent of cases happen before children reach the age of 18 (14.9 percent before the age of 13, and 3 percent between the ages of 13 and 18).
• 15.5 percent of men and 19 percent of women report having gone through this experience.
• The high percentage of penetration, both in men and in women, before the age of 13 (26.7 percent and 42.1 percent, respectively) and after this age (27.3 percent and 25 percent), is noticeable.

The first national survey on the history of sexual abuse in the United States, conducted in adults, showed that 27 percent of women and 16 percent of men retrospectively recognized having been victims of sexual abuse as children. The prevalence rate of serious sexual abuse, with clinical implications for affected children, is significantly lower (around 4 percent to 8 percent of the population). Victims are usually more often female (58.9 percent) than male (40.1 percent); they are between the ages of 6 and 12, but cases increase as the age comes closer to puberty. Girls predominate among the victims of the so-called intrafamily abuse (incest), with an earlier age of onset (7–8 years), and a greater number of boys suffer abuse outside the family (pedophilia), with a later age of onset (11–12 years).

Data from Echeburúa and Del Corral (2006) show that in 20 percent of child sexual abuse cases, the perpetrators are other children; this undermines the notion that child sexual abuse always involves an adult perpetrator and an underage victim, on which they themselves based their studies. On the other hand, while abuse is always thought to involve physical contact (genital, anal, or oral), there are also noncontact cases in which victims are used as an object of sexual stimulation, and perpetrators are mere spectators.

But let us not let the data mislead us; these statistics are false because one of the main problems in ascertaining the actual incidence of child sexual abuse is that it normally happens within a private environment (usually the family), generating a feeling of helplessness in several children that struggle in revealing the abuse. Besides, it is widely thought that, while cases in developing countries are extremely frequent, they are not recorded or reported; and if the perpetrator is a person outside the family, it is the family that takes care of it, usually taking justice into their own hands and attacking (sometimes killing) the perpetrator. All these factors lead to the assumption that prevalence figures are in fact higher than those shown in the studies. The following conclusions can be drawn on child sexual abuse, according to the 2014 UNICEF report "Hidden in Plain Sight: A Statistical Analysis of Violence against Children," which collects information from 190 countries.

- Sexual violence: Approximately 120 million girls under the age of 20 worldwide (about 1 out of 10) have experienced forced sexual intercourse or other forced sexual acts, and 1 out of 3 adolescent girls aged 15 to 19 who were once married (84 million) has been the victim of emotional, physical, or sexual violence by their husband or partner. The report does not show data on males.
- The prevalence of intimate partner violence is 70 percent or higher in the Democratic Republic of the Congo and Equatorial Guinea, and is close to or above 50 percent in Uganda, the United Republic of Tanzania, and Zimbabwe. In Switzerland, a 2009 national study involving girls and boys aged 15 to 17 found that 22 percent and 8 percent, respectively, had suffered at least one incident of sexual violence with physical contact. The most common form of sexual violence for both sexes was victimization on the Internet.
- With regard to homicide, one fifth of homicide victims worldwide are children and adolescents under the age of 20, which amounted to about 95,000 deaths in 2012.
- Homicide is the leading cause of death among males aged 10 to 19 in Panama, Venezuela, El Salvador, Trinidad and Tobago, Brazil, Guatemala, and Colombia. Nigeria has the highest number of child homicides, at 13,000. Among North America and the Western European countries, the United States has the highest homicide rate.

FORMS OF MANIFESTATION OF ABUSE

In most cases (see Echeburúa and Del Corral, 2006) child sexual abuse is perpetrated by someone within the family (parents, older siblings, etc.)—it is the definition of incest—or by persons related to the circle closest to the victim (teachers, coaches, monitors, etc.). In both cases, which amount to 65–85 percent of the total and are the longest-lasting situations, it is not common to find associated violent behavior. Sexual abusers, who often show a problem of sexual dissatisfaction, are tempted to look for sporadic sexual satisfaction with children who are closer to them and who are less able to resist. When perpetrators are interviewed, they often show cognitive distortions to justify themselves for their behavior (a phenomenon we will address when tackling the issue of dark personality and moral disengagement).

Incestuous situations usually follow a similar pattern (Echeburúa and Del Corral, 2006): They start with caresses and continue by resorting to masturbation and oral-genital contact; with girl victims, vaginal intercourse occurs only in exceptional cases, often at later ages, when the girl has reached puberty. Being able to legally act from the outset is rather difficult, when the only testimony is that of the child and there is no evidence of physical contact; the problem lies in that if one does not legally act at that time, the perpetrator will move toward the stage of penetration.

In other cases, the perpetrators are unknown. Logically, this type of abuse is often limited to isolated occasions, but it may, however, be accompanied by violent behavior or threats. And yet, violence is less frequent than in the case of nonconsenting relationships between adults, because children usually do not offer resistance.

On the other hand, children with a higher risk of becoming victims are those with reduced ability to resist or to talk about the situation, such as those who do not yet speak, and those who show developmental delays, or manifest physical and/or mental disabilities. Also, children who do not feel loved within their family are at high risk, since they may initially be hailed by the attention they are subjected to, regardless of whether, eventually, this pleasure produces a deep sense of guilt in them (Echeburúa and Del Corral, 2006). For this reason, it usually takes months or years to discover that a child is being abused.

INDICATORS OF ABUSE

But abuse can be detected; and, depending on its effects, it can be ascertained whether we are facing a recent aggression or whether it has been occurring for a long time. Let us begin by describing the short-term indicators.

Short-Term Effects

One of the most used classifications for determining short-term effects is the one created by Echeburúa and Guerricaechevarría (1998), which organizes the indicators according to physical, behavioral, and/or sexual effects in sexually abused children. Sexual indicators are probably the ones that more closely address possible traumatic experiences. In any case, indicators should be assessed holistically and together, as no direct relationship can be established between a single symptom and the occurrence of abuse. However, the most effective strategy is to pay close attention to the sudden changes that take place in the child's life.

There are classifications of the most at-risk family situations associated with the initiation of sexual abuse (Echeburúa and Guerricaechevarría, 1998). The main short-term consequences of sexual abuse in children and adolescents can also be classified into physical, behavioral, emotional, sexual, and social; there is also a classification of the main psychological sequelae in adults who were victims of sexual abuse in their childhood (long-term effects).

After conducting a comprehensive bibliographic review of these short-term effects, Pereda (2009) suggested a classification of the various immediate symptoms of child sexual abuse, grouping them into five categories: emotional problems, cognitive problems, relationship problems, functional problems, and behavioral problems. These are the main symptoms corresponding to each category:

- Emotional problems: fears and phobias, depression symptoms and anxiety, low self-esteem, feelings of guilt and stigmatization, post-traumatic stress disorder, suicidal ideation and behavior, and self-harm.
- Cognitive problems: hyperactive behaviors, attention and concentration problems, poor academic performance and a worse overall cognitive functioning, attention deficit disorder, and hyperactivity.
- Relationship problems: problems of social relationships in general, decrease in the number of friends and less time to play with them, and high social isolation.
- Functional problems: sleep problems (nightmares), loss of sphincter control (enuresis and encopresis), eating disorders, and somatic complaints.
- Behavior problems: sexualized behavior, compulsive conformity, and disruptive and dissocial behavior.

Long-Term Effects

One of the most frequently used strategies to explore the long-term effects on people who have suffered abuse during childhood is to ask adults—usually university students, as the research is conducted among a captive population—to fill out a questionnaire and rely on the truthfulness of the self-report data and of the accuracy of their memories. While anyone who has been abused remembers it perfectly, determining specific details is much more complicated, especially due to the emotional burden it entails for victims. One of the studies that uses this technique is Pereda and Forns (2007), with data obtained through the application of the Traumatic Life Events Questionnaire (TLEQ) by Kubany and Haynes (2001).

Echeburúa and Del Corral (2006) also highlight that not all people react in the same way to the experience of victimization, nor do all experiences share the same characteristics. The emotional impact of sexual assault is modulated by four variables:

- The individual profile of the victim (psychological stability, age, gender, and family context).
- The characteristics of the abusive act (frequency, severity, existence of violence or threats, chronicity, etc.).
- The existing relationship with the abuser.
- The consequences associated with the discovery of abuse.

The first of these factors is clearly related to how victims cope with the situation they have suffered. The study conducted by Cantón and Justicia (2008) is one that addresses the issue of coping as a possible way to minimize long-term effects. In this study, participants who were victims of child sexual abuse had significantly higher scores in depression and lower scores in self-esteem when compared with those in the control group. The analysis of coping strategies revealed that only the use of avoidance strategies was related to psychological adjustment, showing that participants who make use of them show higher depression scores and lower self-esteem scores. The results confirm the idea that the adjustment of the victims of child sexual abuse can be affected to a greater or lesser extent, depending on the coping strategies they use.

The severity of the sequelae is generally dependent on the frequency and duration of the experience, as well as the use of force and threats or the existence of a rape (vaginal, anal, or oral penetration). Thus, the more chronic and intense the abuse, the greater the development of a sense of defenselessness and vulnerability, and the more likely the appearance of symptoms (see again Echeburúa and Del Corral, 2006).

With regard to the victim's relationship with the abuser, the degree of kinship between the two is not as relevant as the level of emotional intimacy that exists. Thus, the greater the degree of intimacy, the stronger the psychological impact, which can be aggravated if the victim is not supported by the family or is forced to leave the home. On the other hand, regarding the age of the abuser, sexual abuse by adolescents is generally less traumatizing for victims than that committed by adults (Echeburúa and Del Corral, 2006).

There are two major models that explain the appearance of long-term effects: the model based on post-traumatic stress disorder, and the traumatogenic model, which is the following topic of discussion.

Model Based on Post-Traumatic Stress Disorder

It can be argued that the main problem of people who have suffered child sexual abuse is post-traumatic stress disorder (PTSD). Results from Martin and de Paul's research (2004) clearly support the hypothesis that those who suffer a traumatic event are rather likely to develop post-traumatic symptoms. The findings also show the relevance of some variables as predictors when a person is diagnosed with PTSD after a traumatic event. In this regard, the analysis of the gender variable in the diagnosis of PTSD shows that after experiencing a traumatic event, women are more likely to meet the diagnosis criteria than men, which means they have a greater vulnerability (as also indicated by Green [1994]and Norris [1992], for instance). Martin and de Paul's findings (2004) also indicate that experiencing certain traumatic events such as rape, sexual assault, or child sexual abuse, victims are specifically at risk to meet the PTSD diagnostic criteria (which has also been argued by authors such as Corral et al. [1992], or McLeer et al. [1992]). This was particularly evident among rape victims, as all of them were diagnosed with PTSD. In the case of child sexual abuse, 33 percent of people reported PTSD symptoms.

Some authors have tried to explain the effects of sexual abuse through the post-traumatic stress disorder model (Wolfe, Sas, and Wekerle, 1994). Sexual abuse in childhood does actually meet the "trauma" criteria of the DSM-IV and DSM-5 classification for the diagnosis of this clinical disorder. DSM stands for *Diagnostic and Statistical Manual of Mental Disorders*; it is the manual used by the American Psychiatric Association (APA) and includes descriptions, symptoms, and other criteria for diagnosing mental disorders. A sexual assault, and even more, a rape, generates, at least in most victims, the characteristic symptoms of the disorder (Echeburúa and Guerricaechevarría, 2005), which are:

- Intrusive thoughts
- Avoidance of stimuli related to the aggression
- Sleep disorders
- Irritability
- Difficulties in concentration
- Fear
- Anxiety
- Depression
- Feelings of guilt

Unlike in adults, this clinical disorder in children may take the form of unstructured or agitated behavior and manifests with physical symptoms such as stomach aches, headaches, and the like. The disorder manifests if the trauma remains in the child's active memory, based on inadequate information processing and if adequate cognitive mechanisms are not used to recover from it (Hartman and Burgess, 1989, 1993).

Among other advantages, this model provides an operational description of the symptoms derived from the abuse and allows a diagnosis that all professionals can understand (Echeburúa and Guerricaechevarría, 2005; López, Hernández, and Carpintero, 1995).

However, according to Boney-McCoy and Finkelhor (1996), Finkelhor (1988), and Vázquez-Mezquita and Calle (1997), this model shows some limitations in its application to the area of child sexual abuse:

- It can only be applied to some victims.
- It does not allow for a clear explanation of the relationship between the traumatic event and the clinical disorder, as it does not explicitly refer to the stages of development.
- It does not include all symptoms, especially those related to cognitive and attention dimensions (for instance, the tendency to make negative or hostile attributions). In fact, fear (for the future or from threats), depression, guilt (referring to family disintegration generated by the revelation of the secret), sexual problems, and a state of confusion and distortions in beliefs about oneself and others are the most frequent sequelae in these types of victims (Echeburúa and Guerricaechevarría, 2005).

Traumagenic Model

As an alternative to the previous model, Finkelhor (1988) proposes the more specific traumagenic model, which draws on the following reasons to explain the psychological impact:

- Traumatic sexualization
- Loss of trust
- Powerlessness
- Stigmatization

These four variables constitute the main cause of trauma, as they distort the victim's self-concept, their vision of the world, and their affective capabilities. In turn, these factors are associated with the child's development of an inadequate coping strategy and to the emergence of behavioral problems (Finkelhor, 1997; López, 1993; Cortés and Cantón, 1997). Let us analyze each of these variables (Echeburúa and Guerricaechevarría, 2005):

- Traumatic sexualization refers to the interference of abuse in the child's normal sexual development. They learn to use certain sexual behaviors as a strategy to gain benefits or manipulate others; they also acquire distorted learning of the importance and meaning of certain sexual behaviors, as well as misconceptions about sexuality and sexual morality.
- The loss of trust might not only be exclusive to the relationship with the perpetrator, it can also be extended to relationships with the rest of the family or with others, because they have failed to save the victim from having these experiences.
- Stigmatization is felt as guilt, shame, loss of value, and the like. These negative connotations are part of the child's self-image.

The feeling of powerlessness becomes a child's belief in their own inability to react to situations and in their little control over themselves and over what happens to them. All of this arises in the victim a sense of helplessness and a fear of what might happen to them in the future, provoking attitudes of passiveness, unassertiveness, and retreatment.

On the other hand, the abused person, especially in the case of males, usually suffers what is referred to as the sexual abuse accommodation syndrome, initially detected by Summit (1983) and later analyzed by Redondo and Ortiz (2005) among others. The five stages of the syndrome are:

- Secrecy
- Helplessness
- Entrapment and accommodation
- Delayed, scarcely convincing disclosure
- Subsequent retraction of revealed abuse

MEASURING TOOLS

Pereda and Arch (2012) conducted one of the most comprehensive reviews of forensic tools for detecting child sexual abuse, including a table with each specific tool. After analyzing eighty-two papers, the author concluded that 71.9 percent of them focused on clinical tools based on psychological and emotional indicators, while 28.1 percent were based on analysis of the credibility of the testimony.

The most commonly used witness assessment system today is European; while the use of clinical indicators that are created in the United States is obviously widespread, European countries are more active in the development and adaptation of tools for assessing the credibility of witness testimony. The main tools are:

- Adolescent Dissociative Experiences Scale
- Child Behavior Checklist
- Child Dissociative Checklist
- Child Sexual Behavior Inventory
- Children's Impact of Traumatic Events Scale Revisited (CITES-R)
- Children's Impact of Traumatic Events Scales (CITES)
- Trauma Symptom Checklist for Children and Young Children
- Traumatic Life Events Questionnaire (TLEQ)

Game Analysis:

- Unsexual anatomical dolls
- Various gaming systems

Statement Analysis Systems:

- SVA system for evaluating the validity of the statement
- Criteria-based Content Analysis (CBCA)

Interview systems:

- Various types of semistructured interviews

Pereda and Arch (2012) confirm how much progress has been made in recent decades in the field of child abuse in general—and particularly, in its assessment. However, due to the complexity of the phenomenon, the psychological assessment of children and adolescents who are victims of sexual abuse is still a challenge for professionals. It is essential to continue working on the improvement of the existing assessment tools in order to transfer the resulting empirical data into clinical and forensic practice; this will allow for a more accurate detection and for a better psychological and legal treatment of the abused child, while also reducing the risk of becoming a victim once again (re-experiencing abuse due to the attitude of people who are in contact with the victim) associated to these cases.

Let us now discuss the main problems that arise within the judicial field regarding the use of specific techniques and their impact, trying to determine the most appropriate action, that is, the one that acts most adequately in the best interest of the child.

THE CREDIBILITY OF THE TESTIMONY

Many judges and prosecutors, as well as those accused of abuse, state that children lie and that their testimony is therefore unreliable. It is precisely for this reason that an assessment of testimony credibility is necessary. Over time, the stereotype that children are liars has emerged, or that they lie because they are influenced by one of the parents, usually the noncustodian, to give testimony against the other (the so-called Parental Alienation Syndrome, or PAS, which will be discussed later). Is that premise based on evidence?

The answer is no (Clemente, 2013b; Echeburúa and Del Corral, 2006). Children do not tend to lie when they make a report of sexual abuse; it is ill-advised to think otherwise. In fact, only 7 percent of testimonies have been proven to be false (a simulation phenomenon), although some authors claim that false testimonies may increase when allegations occur in the context of a conflicting divorce (Echeburúa and Guerricaechevarría, 2000, 2006). A study by Clemente et al. (2015) showed that children do not lie but sometimes interpret reality differently, leading adults to claim that they are lying (this issue will be discussed later).

What is relatively common in some children is the withdrawal of a complaint due to family pressure (the phenomenon of dissimulation). Most complaint retractions are false. In fact, it is not uncommon to retract, as the child fears the abuser's retaliation, or realizes the significance of disclosing what happened on a familial, social or judicial level. In general, children are more likely to deny experiences that have occurred to them—and that are perceived as traumatic—than to make false statements about those experiences. If the child denies the abuse from the outset of the judicial process, an expert assessment may not be conducted, or it may be conducted inappropriately. The disclosure of traumatic events is dependent on reaching an appropriate period in which a climate of trust is created, so that the child can feel safe and reveal an event that would otherwise be kept as a deep secret.

The most negative consequence of retraction is that it causes others to doubt the child and to allege that the child is constantly changing their opinion, so their initial testimony is branded as false, leading to the defenselessness of the victim.

The timing of the complaint with respect to the events that took place is an important element to bear in mind. The closer the complaint is filed to when the sexual abuse took place, the more credible the testimony is (Echeburúa and Del Corral, 2006). When much time has gone by, the effect of forgetting and the interference from other interviews that have taken place (by parents, police, psychologists, etc.) detract from the credibility of the testimony (Masip and Garrido, 2001, 2007).

The issue of testimonial credibility becomes, in fact, a problem because in cases of child sexual abuse, there are not usually bodily injuries or witnesses to what happened; therefore, the only evidence is usually the testimony of the child. Furthermore, the child's evolutionary cycle may impose restrictions on their memory capacity or on how they perceive reality—that is, it may facilitate fabulation, which involves confusing fantasy with reality, as well as encourage the induction of a witness account tainted by an adult (Canton, 2003; Canton and Cortés, 2003; De Paul, 2004).

There are several tools in the forensic field to assess the credibility of children's testimonies, among which CBCA is widely accepted by scientists and other professionals for its reliability. The procedure consists of applying a set of criteria to the verbal transcription of the interview that corroborate the truthfulness of the child. The Criteria-Based Content Analysis (CBCA) is based on the hypothesis that statements made by a child about events they have in fact experienced differ quantifiably from false claims or fantasy product—that is, from those that may have been induced by a parent or another adult.

However, it must be clearly stated that the existing psychological procedures for the analysis of the credibility of statements do not constitute a valid technique for detecting lies, since lie detectors, however much literature there is about them, do not exist (Manzanero, 2001; Manzanero and Diges, 1993). To date, as we have pointed out, the most elaborate and seemingly valid procedures for determining the truthfulness of the testimony of child victims of sexual assault are the SVA and the CBCA (Raskin and Esplin, 1991a, 1991b). At least this seems to have been demonstrated by many years of the application of such procedures in Germany and other Western countries, even though some authors have advocated for the need of more research to allow for their empirical validation (Wells and Loftus, 1991). In any case, it seems that this technique is more advantageous than others that evaluate variables such as the degree of anxiety of the witnesses (as is the case with the lie detector known as polygraph) or behaviors or personality traits that do not have to inevitably be associated with sexual assault.

Furthermore, as Manzanero (2001) points out, we cannot speak of the accuracy or the truthfulness of a statement in a specific case. Not only it is impossible to assess the veracity of a memory or of a description of something remembered, but it would also be impossible to do so in legal terms.

In any case, we should reiterate that there are no reliable lie detectors, and that the various techniques that can now be used to assess the credibility of a statement are subject to error; for this reason, we always refer to the likelihood of credibility (Manzanero, 2001).

These procedures are relatively new, but since they first appeared in 1991, they have become common in the field. Their use has been applied to different types of sexual offenses against children, and judges and courts of justice have readily welcomed them. Moreover, their recent use does not exclude cases of children of a specific culture or nationality; as there are no cognitive differences between people of different cultures, the techniques do not require an adaptation to different populations; it can be said that memory functions in the same manner throughout all populations.

Lastly, it should be clarified that the application of these procedures requires extensive knowledge of how memory works, from the point of view of cognitive psychology, and from the factors affecting the memory of witnesses (Manzanero, 2001).

Another problem that has been less analyzed and seems more complex to address is that despite the existence of specific evidence, children hide the abuse or reveal it only partially (Ceci and Bruck, 1995), which makes it advisable to practice a psychological expert test on the credibility of their statements. In other words, it is a question of determining whether the child correctly perceives reality and properly remembers it, whether they distinguish fantasy from reality well and whether they tell the truth without any external pressure (Alonso-Quecuty, 1995; Diges, 1997; London, Bruck, Ceci, and Shuman, 2005).

PSYCHOLOGY AND LAW: DIFFERENT VIEWS OF THE PROBLEM

Psychology and law are different disciplines, with different methodologies and different visions of reality. In fact, whenever two scientific fields use different methodologies to analyze reality, they will generally find it difficult to share information. This creates a disagreement, which is particularly easy to notice in the following aspects.

Different Meanings of Child Sexual Abuse

There is no direct connection between the psychological and the legal concepts of sexual abuse. The psychological concept of sexual abuse—which closely parallels that of nonspecialized language—refers to children. Criminal codes, however, often refer to unconsented acts that, without the need for violence or intimidation, threaten a person's sexual freedom, regardless of whether that person is older or younger (Echeburúa and Del Corral, 2006).

In fact, only 50 percent of child sexual abuse cases are revealed by the children (Echeburúa and Del Corral, 2006); only 15 percent of cases are reported to the authorities; and only 5 percent are analyzed by the courts of justice (that is, the bottleneck effect occurs). Because children show many limitations on reporting sexual abuse and unequivocal physical manifestations are not common (due to the type of sexual behavior that may be performed—caresses, masturbations, etc.), it is rather difficult for a case to come to trial.

It is worth mentioning that the assessment of child sexual abuse is probably one of the areas within the clinical-forensic field that has generated greater controversy and technical difficulties. As Pereda and Arch (2012) state, the assessment in this area focuses on ascertaining the credibility of the testimony of the child through various techniques. However, some of the tools used to conduct this assessment have not been standardized (for instance, the playing procedures—see Murrie, Martindale, and Epstein's review, 2009); many specific tools are not validated and, in cases where standards exist concerning this tool, appropriate validity studies have not been carried out (see Canton and Cortés, 2000). One example of significant works regarding this matter is Bustos, Rincón, and Aedo (2009), which perform the validation of the Child PTSD Symptom Scale (CPSS).

Another typical problem is the lack of knowledge on the part of the professionals of the most appropriate assessment techniques, which poses a risk of the child becoming a victim for a second time. In these cases, the psychological distress of the assessed is higher owing to the misuse of credibility assessment procedures by the professionals involved in the process (Conte, 2001).

Different Professional Roles of the Forensic Psychologist and the Clinical Psychologist

With regard to actions before the courts of justice, it should be noted that clinical intervention with a victim is not compatible with acting as a forensic or legal expert in the judicial field (Echeburúa and Subijana, 2008). Therapists who conduct interventions on a child must not take part in the expert reports of their patients. What may happen is that upon court injunction and after having been authorized by the victim, the clinical psychologist may write a clinical report (but not an expert report) and even take part in the oral hearing as a witness to provide evidence exclusively on the facts which came to surface over the course of the therapeutic assistance and that are relevant to the judicial process (Del Rio, 2005; Recover, 2006).

Unlike clinical psychologists, forensic psychologists serve justice and are not subject to professional secrecy, a matter which must be communicated to *those subject to the expert testimony* (or in the cases of children, to the adult responsible) to obtain their informed consent relating to the various interventions (interviews, video recordings, etc.). In turn, forensic psychologists (or psychologists who, without being legal experts, intervene as such in a case), cannot conduct therapeutic interventions in that same case (Martín-Corral, 2002). In summary, professional interventions in the clinical or psychosocial field are incompatible with acting as a legal or forensic expert in the judicial field (Echeburúa and Guerricaechevarría, 2000).

Ways to Avoid Secondary Victimization: The Child before Justice

The fact that abused children must come into contact with the judicial and police systems is always negative for them, yet inevitable. To mitigate the impact the incorporation into the judicial process may have on them, new approaches have recently begun to be developed. Secondary victimization precisely refers to the negative emotional consequences of the contact of the victims (in this case, sexually abused children) with the judicial system (Ferreiro, 2005). Let us not forget that being involved within the judicial sphere always increases the child's level of stress, while also decreasing their ability to provide accurate evidence. The report and the subsequent judicial action—more particularly, the repeated interrogations and examinations, and the delay in the trial—can add to the abuse itself, aggravating the psychological—and even physical—consequences for the children. Let us remember that what the child fears most is not being believed (Echeburúa and Subijana, 2008).

Echeburúa and Subijana's study (2008), based on Montero and León's research (2007), is a critical review of the methods currently used in two fundamental aspects of the judicial field (the expert report concerning the credibility of the testimony of sexually abused children, and the child's performance in the oral trial), and it suggests alternative proposals in line with the actual possibilities—and not always used—that the current Spanish legal system offers.

The fact that children provide courtroom testimony, especially when they are victims of sexual abuse, poses a challenge for criminal justice (Hernández and Miranda, 2005). Victims may feel abandoned in a system that is established upon the presumption of innocence of the accused, making it sometimes easy to forget that a fair trial must integrate the victim; not by excluding who is already protected in the system (the accused), but to ensure the inclusion of the child (the victim), who is not, and should be. The intention should be to guarantee the rights of the accused (intangible) and to provide the victim with a specific legal status based on four pillars: information, participation, assistance, and protection (Beristain, 2001).

We must bear in mind that, as sexual abuse is a crime, the intervention of justice is unavoidable. The objective is to make the judicial framework compatible—which is circumscribed to the clarification of the facts and the imposition, when applicable, of the sentence—with the psychological framework—which focuses on protecting the health of the child. From different perspectives, both frameworks must have the common objective of attaining the *preeminent interest*: the protection of children (Canton and Cortés, 2008).

The psychological framework should provide detailed evidence of the child's ability to communicate information and specify the type of psychological impact that their participation in court proceedings might have. In turn, the judicial framework should adapt the necessary measures to ensure that the participation of the child in the court case is limited to the strictly necessary. There should also be guarantees that in cases where the participation of the child is deemed necessary, the intervention may be executed in an adequate context, avoiding psychological damage to the child that would add to what had already been suffered with the crime (Echeburúa and Subijana, 2008).

The interaction between the judicial and the psychological frameworks enables the existence of various alternatives, always aimed at avoiding secondary victimization, which is the main objective when it comes to children (Echeburúa and Subijana, 2008):

- The nonparticipation of the child in court proceedings. This alternative is based on two assumptions: the child's cognitive or emotional inability to testify at trial, or the significant risk of causing serious psychic damage in the case of testifying. In the first scenario (i.e., if the child is not old enough and lacks the minimum capacity to understand or explain the sexual abuse suffered, or has dissociative amnesia regarding what happened), the child's participation in the oral trial would be pointless as the source of the evidence (the child) is not able and does not serve the purpose (to provide meaningful information of what is being judged). Besides, forcing the emergence of painful memories in a child when there is dissociative amnesia can be detrimental to the psychological recovery of the child. In these circumstances, judges must use other testimonies. In the second scenario, the child's intervention can be counterproductive when, even if they are able to describe the sexual abuse, their participation in the oral trial can provoke a serious imbalance if they have an emotionally unstable personality or severe mental disorders caused by the traumatic event from which they have not yet recovered.
- The participation of the child in the court proceedings, but before the oral trial. Since oral trials are frequently conducted long after the abuse occurred, it is possible to make the statement before the judge at a psychologically appropriate time, when the least harm can be caused to the psychological evolution of the child. Conducted in such way, the practice of testimony in a pretrial procedural phase allows psychological demands to be integrated with legal imperatives. Thus, *conducting the testimony* in advance can better respond to the psychological situation of the victim, reduce the number of interrogations, and avoid the

detrimental consequences of making a statement in a public hearing, without undermining the procedural rights of the accused. Another possibility is that the child testifies to questions from a psychologist in a one-way crystal room, enabling the judge, the prosecutor, and the lawyers to follow the interview; even the psychologist can receive, via some audio device, information from the judge or the prosecutor to try to investigate any aspect related to the testimony.

• The participation of the child in the oral trial. In this case, when the child did not give testimony prior to the trial, and there is no psychological contraindication, the testimony is given in the usual format: The child answers the questions posed to them in the oral trial. Regardless of the format used, it is advisable that the child gives testimony only once for three reasons: It minimizes the risk of secondary victimization; it preserves the quality of testimony, avoiding contamination or the settling of false memories of abuse in memory; and it allows the future life of the child not to be permanently conditioned by the need to evoke the traumatic event suffered.

There is yet another problem related to what some health professionals have called Parental Alienation Syndrome (PAS), which will be discussed in a different chapter.

A work by Pereda and Arch (2009), which does not criticize the PAS, does, however, provide some indication that the PAS is indeed a fallacy, and that it is possible to properly detect the occurrence of child sexual abuse.

Pereda and Arch (2009) highlight the existence of indicators with a high discriminatory power that allow us to differentiate between real cases of sexual abuse and possible false allegations—for now, let us avoid the use of the term PAS—based on a system of evaluating the credibility of the child called Criteria-Based Content Analysis (CBCA).

In professional practice, it is also common to consider what we call clinical indicators, or behavior patterns of the child; there are some specific behaviors which have been observed in several victims of sexual abuse, such as sexualized behavior (also called eroticized behavior), which can be measured, for example, through the Child Sexual Behavior Inventory, but also through the study of the distorted attributions and perceptions of the child (assessed by the Children's Attributions and Perceptions Scale of Mannarino, Cohen, and Berman), or by observing the post-traumatic symptoms associated with sexual abuse, through the Trauma Symptom Checklist for Children (Pereda and Arch, 2009).

All these criteria can facilitate the assessment of these situations and help the professional differentiate between a case of real sexual abuse and an induced witness case, that is, false allegations.

However, the actual problem lies in the difficulty of evaluating very young children with a low capacity for expression and understanding. Sometimes, it is rather difficult for the child to understand the issues raised by the evaluator throughout the interview, as well as for the evaluator to understand the language used by the child; on the other hand, the testimony of such young children may not contain sufficient data to assess the credibility of their statements.

With regard to the PAS, little can be argued, precisely because of its unscientific nature (Clemente, 2013b; Padilla-Racero, 2013; Rozanski, 2013). Richard Gardner never proved his claims and could not demonstrate the existence of the syndrome he defined.

Pereda and Arch's study (2009) sets out the relevant criteria that would allow us to identify whether we are dealing with a case of child sexual abuse or false allegations.

In short, we may conclude that justice is only fair if it is based on scientific principles, and only by listening to the child's testimony can their rights be protected and act in their best interest.

CONCLUSION: TOWARD A REDEFINITION OF CHILD SEXUAL ABUSE THAT DEFENDS THE CHILD

Child sexual abuse is a scourge to society; it is also a drama for an extremely high number of children (some statistics indicate that 20 percent of children might have suffered it), and indeed for parents and family members who face this problem. It is a social problem that remains largely silent, firstly because it usually occurs within the intimate family environment; secondly, because those that are affected by it usually try to keep it hidden; and thirdly, because sometimes the abuse is neither known by others nor is it reportable by the victim—when they are very young children or disabled. Precisely due to these characteristics, disclosure of the problem and persecution of the perpetrator must become a fundamental task of society, which must be tackled from different angles:

- From within the families, being aware of the clinical picture of the abused child (or, more generally, maltreated), resorting to immediately separating the child from their abuser and rapidly proceeding to file a report (within this chapter, in addition to the described general characteristics, it has been pointed out how to find the charts that allow to determine whether it is necessary for a possible case to be investigated).

- From the juvenile prosecutor's office, since we deal with children, a population which is particularly vulnerable and has no resources to defend itself.
- From the health system, similarly, proceeding to file a report before the court, when faced with the slightest doubt of possible abuse.
- From the school system, preventing and avoiding cases of abuse by older children to younger children.

But the biggest problem arises when the child sexual abuse is covered up, based on the fact that the reporting it in itself could be explained and/or perpetuated owing to an alleged judicial struggle between the parents.

This is how Gardner, a psychiatrist accused of being a pedophile, labelled the so-called "parental alienation syndrome" (PAS), arguing that many reports of maltreatment or even sexual abuse from mothers who hold the custody of their children against the fathers are not due to the occurrence of the abuse itself, but to the desire of the custodial parent (usually the mother) to harass the noncustodian (usually the father) with false allegations. There is no data to support this theory, and even less from a scientific point of view, as has been demonstrated in this chapter. But the fact that the justice system, legitimizing the supposed PAS, presumably continues to allow an abuser to maintain contact with their children causes a situation that:

- Leaves the child in defenselessness, suffering such abuses with the permission of—and in collusion with—a system of justice that legitimates the existence of a nonexistent syndrome.
- Condemns the custodial parent to a mental imbalance and a state of despair; since sometimes it is the police who pick up their child for visits, they feel helpless as they see that they can do nothing to prevent the other parent from abusing the child (there are mothers who have even been imprisoned for refusing to comply with the visitation order).
- Causes rather serious sequelae in the child, exacerbating a post-traumatic stress disorder that is extremely difficult to overcome over time.
- Seriously damages the rights of persons before the law, and in particular, the right of any person to report when they are aware of a crime, because the crime is assumed to be an invention of the custodial parent, and not as a reality, and is therefore not investigated.

All of this is possible due to the subtlety of child sexual abuse; if it was abrupt and obvious, it would be impossible to hide; but as it is subtle, the guarantees that the accused has within the justice system protects them from being sanctioned as such. As a result, if a girl is returned by the father with her panties soaked in blood (or cut to pieces with scissors), or with the vagina full of paper wipes, or with redness in the anus or vagina, if the hymen has not been broken and there are no anal tears, the legal question is raised of whether the child—who states that the parent sexually manipulated her—is right, or if the explanation given by the parent is the truth, who says that the child continually touches her genitals until they bleed, or that she does not know how to clean herself well and fills her vagina with papers, and that the testimony of the child is not true, for what she expresses is the manipulation of the mother and a false allegation.

What could the solution to this dilemma be? How should the system act? The system must, of course, act to protect the child first and foremost, and therefore:

- It should never start from the assumption that children lie. As has already been mentioned in this chapter, it is rather infrequent for such behavior to occur in sexually abused children, being much more common for the child to retract their statement because they perceive that it creates a serious family problem. The starting point must always be the fact that the child says the truth.
- Furthermore, there is an obvious fact that we must always bear in mind: To determine the truthfulness of a child's statement, such statement must be listened to and recorded. That is, it should not be done as in many procedures, where everything is reduced to the statement of one parent and another, and the child never gives testimony. Unless the child's inability to speak makes it impossible (and yet, an attempt should be made to verify by other procedures whether a situation of insurmountable fear has been created in the child), it should be mandatory by law to collect the child's statement (under appropriate conditions and by qualified professionals, of course).
- In order to verify whether the child effectively recounts what has happened to them, scientific procedures must be used to determine the truthfulness of the testimony. As also stated in this chapter, verification procedures today have limitations, since no tool has been invented that has the capacity to actually detect truth and lie. But even with the existing limitations, some procedures are more reliable than others, and the SVA system, which integrates CBCA, is the most appropriate to date.
- Neither judges nor prosecutors are trained to ascertain whether a child lies or tells the truth, nor those professionals who, without applying any scientific evidence, decide according to their own determinations in their reports whether such truthfulness exists.
- Only legal psychologists trained in this regard, specialized in this task, are suitable for such determination. And they are the ones that can give validity to the child's declaration.

- And of course, one of the parents should never be blamed of being guilty of the abusive behavior that the child reveals. This fact implies an attempt—accepted by the justice system—to exculpate the accused, rather than an attempt to seek the truth.

To date, the justice system has not found an adequate way to deal with child sexual abuse. In this chapter we have analyzed whether it is appropriate for the child to declare in the courtroom or not, and we dove into the problem that no person who has treated the child may act as a forensic expert in their case. Moreover, we have seen how the mere intervention of the justice system with children today generates secondary victimization—that is, further victimization of the child. For that matter, it is common to encounter cases of children who were sexually abused, and until turning 18 (age), did not escape the judicial labyrinth, practically created from the time of their birth. In its intervention, the system does not always protect the child, and generates such tension in those who suffer it for years that it creates serious health problems later in the child and in the parent accused of manipulating (migraines, fibromyalgia, cervical or lumbar pains, etc.), sometimes to the point of making their working life impossible (there are women who are continuously reported by the other parent for alleged breaches of the visitation arrangements so that they have to go to police and judicial offices more than thirty times throughout the year, and they cannot maintain their work activity or a normal partner relationship).

We are certainly facing unresolved issues, which must be approached from different angles; from the judicial and police investigation, to obtain reliable and objective evidence that detects abuse and protects the child, while fostering a new form of action, which is beyond the scope of this chapter. From psychology, developing ever more reliable and valid systems of witness credibility. From society, clearly betting against child sexual abuse and all forms of abuse, thus protecting children. Let us hope that, together, we will succeed.

Chapter 4

Influences on Gardner's Ideas

Sigmund Freud, the doctor who coined the term and founded psychoanalysis, was born in the Moravian town of Freiberg and died in London, but he will always be associated with the city of Vienna, where he lived for almost 80 years. Had the Nazis not occupied Austria in 1937, forcing him to seek refuge in England, Freud would have spent his whole life in the Austrian capital—except for his first three years. When Richard Gardner was born, on April 28, 1931, psychoanalysis was already a sensation in Europe, and echoes of it were resounding in the United States, his homeland. Gardner died at the age of 72; although his death was officially ruled as a suicide, it stirred much controversy.

Freud's long life (1856–1936) encompasses one of the most fruitful periods in the history of science, the years when Gardner forged the knowledge which, in fact, led him to pursue the career of his alleged master (medicine, and later psychiatry), working at Columbia University since 1963. But let us return to those early years in Freud's life that laid the foundations of Gardner's thought. Darwin's *The Origin of Species* was published the same year that 3-year-old Freud was brought to Vienna by his family; the book would revolutionize the notion of humankind forever. Before Darwin, the human species was differentiated from the animal kingdom in that humans have a soul. After the theory of evolution, humans became part of nature—an animal among animals. The assumption of such a radical view meant that naturalistic approaches were apt for the study of the human being. The human being became an object of scientific study, no different from any other form of life, excepting the complexity (Clemente, 2010).

Some scholars suggest that Gustav Fechner founded the science of psychology the year after the publication of *The Origin of Species*, when Freud was 4 years old. In 1860, this formidable German man of science and philosopher of the 19th century demonstrated that the mind is subject to scientific study and that findings about it can be measured quantitatively. Ever since, psychology has taken its rightful place among the natural sciences and is not just considered a mere branch of philosophy.

These two men—Darwin and Fechner—greatly influenced Freud's intellectual development, as well as that of many young people of that time and beyond.

During the second half of the nineteenth century, there was a growing interest in life sciences and in psychology. Louis Pasteur and Robert Koch established the science of bacteriology through their major study on the microbial theory of diseases, and Gregor Mendel founded modern genetics through his experiments on pea plants. Life sciences burst into full force.

Freud was also heavily influenced by the new discoveries on physics. In the mid-nineteenth century, the great German physicist Hermann von Helmholtz developed the principle of conservation of energy, stating that, like mass, energy is also quantity and that it can be transformed but not destroyed. When energy disappears from one part of a system, it must appear elsewhere within the same system.

The study of energy changes in a physical system led from one breakthrough to another in the field of dynamics. Those 50 years which spanned from Helmholtz's claim on energy conservation to Albert Einstein's theory of relativity could be said to be the age of energy. Thermodynamics, electromagnetic fields, radioactivity, the electron, quantum theory, are but some of the milestones of that crucial half-century. Figures such as James Maxwell, Heinrich Hertz, Sir Joseph Thomson, Marie and Pierre Curie, James Joule, Lord Kelvin, or Dmitri Mendeleyev were literally changing the world with their discoveries of the secrets of energy. Most of the inventions that save us time and make our lives much easier today arose from the great horn of plenty that was nineteenth-century physics. We are still reaping the benefits of that golden age. But the age of energy and dynamics did not only provide humans with electrical appliances, television, automobiles, airplanes, and atomic and hydrogen bombs; it also brought a new conception of the human being, one that was based on natural sciences (Clemente, 2010).

As a young man of science committed to biological research during the last quarter of the nineteenth century, Freud did indeed feel the influence of those new trends. Energy and dynamics became part of every laboratory and of the minds of scientists. As a medical student, Freud had the good fortune to be a student of Ernst Brücke, director of the Physiology Laboratory at the University of Vienna and one of the greatest physiologists of the century. His Lessons in Physiology, published in 1874—a year after Freud entered the School of Medicine—put forward the radical view that a living organism is a dynamic system that is subject to the laws of chemistry and physics.

Freud held Brücke in high regard and soon accepted the doctrine of that new dynamic physiology. Twenty years later, he claimed to have discovered that the law of dynamics could be applied to the study of the personality of human beings as well as of their physical aspect. Once that discovery was made, Freud went on to create dynamic psychology, which explores the transformations and exchanges of energy within the personality.

CREATION OF DYNAMIC PSYCHOLOGY

Freud studied medicine and received his diploma from the University of Vienna in 1881, but he never intended to work as a doctor. He wanted to be a man of science. With this goal in mind, he joined the Faculty of Medicine at the University of Vienna in 1873. Contact with patients served as a stimulus to think in psychological terms. When Freud began practicing medicine, given his scientific background, it was only natural for him to specialize in the treatment of nerve disorders, a branch of medicine that was underdeveloped. Not much could be done for those who suffered from mental aberrations. In France, Jean Charcot would achieve some success in his treatment of hysteria through hypnosis. Freud spent a year in Paris (1885–1886) learning the Charcot method. However, he was not satisfied with hypnosis because he thought that its effects were only temporary and did not fully address the causes of the problem. From another Viennese doctor, Joseph Breuer, he learned the benefits that could be derived from cathartic therapy or from overcoming problems by telling them. The patient spoke while the doctor listened (Clemente, 2010).

Similarly, after studying medicine, Gardner did not show a great interest in psychiatry in a broad sense. As a volunteer, he dedicated himself to writing expert reports, especially in cases of family breakdown; in 1985, after conducting a series of interviews with parents and children who had experienced family breakdowns, he devised the concept of "Parental Alienation Syndrome" (PAS), which, drawing on psychoanalysis, seeks to explain the difficulties that, at times, one of the parents has in trying to stay in touch with their children. By the time of his death, Gardner had written approximately 40 books and 250 articles about the syndrome.

Charcot, who was one of Freud's masters, had a strong influence on Gardner's ideas through the works of Freud; both Charcot and Freud claimed that women are characterized by the manifestation in their personality of a disease that they called "hysteria" that held no known biological rationale, but because it usually disappeared after the removal of the female genitalia, it was attributed to women. Medicine, as in other moments throughout history, became sexualized, distinguishing between male and female diseases. It was now commonplace to characterize women as having a "medical" disease, as unlikely as that indeed was, as there was no detectable biological rationale.

The discovery of hysteria runs counter to any scientific demonstration, since it has no specific location or definition; it was only demonstrated by the effects of the removal of an organ, and yet, it all too easily sank into the collective imaginary of society, associating the fact of being a woman with being "hysterical."

In those days, social science—and more particularly, psychology and social psychology—could not come close to explaining what later became obvious: That no hypothesis can be called scientific if the researcher verifies the original theory, independent of whether it is supported by evidence or not. There are some scientific theories that are readily accepted at certain historical times, regardless of their scientific value (an example of this today would be neurosciences). Thus, Freud introduced the unscientific concept of denial, according to which, if the subject's behavior did not conform to the theory, they were, in fact, corroborating—even more clearly—the theory, as the subject was either rationalizing, denying, or making use of any other defense mechanism, implying that the psychoanalyst was always in the right.

The ideas of psychoanalysis are but that, mere ideas. No scientific analysis reveals a minimum of truthfulness in their conclusions. Karl Popper's arguments are widely known in this regard. In his works on philosophy of science (1959, 1962), Popper criticizes psychoanalysis on the grounds that the theory is based on hypotheses that are not falsifiable, and for questioning evidence, when it does not confirm hypotheses, by resorting to what is unfalsifiable. In his model of demarcation of science, Popper explained psychoanalysis as an example of pseudoscience, in contrast to Albert Einstein's theory of relativity. Popper observed that while the conditions of refutation of Einstein's hypotheses were accurately determined (and Einstein was willing to reformulate them if they were not supported by evidence), Sigmund Freud's theories were unfalsifiable, allowing him to reinterpret the evidence in order to uphold the hypothesis, despite the lack of empirical support. And yet, not all scientists acknowledge that psychoanalysis is unfalsifiable. Grünbaum claims that psychoanalysis is only unfalsifiable in its analytical phase, due to the circular reasoning generated in its explanations of unconscious desires. He suggests that the theory can be falsifiable and that, as it turns out, it is clearly false. In the 1960s, Hans Eysenck collected and criticized all existing studies on the effectiveness of psychoanalysis, concluding that psychoanalytical treatment does not better the rate of spontaneous remission (without treatment) of neurosis. Thus, Eysenck (1952) stated that Freud "was, without a doubt, a genius; not of science, but of propaganda; not of rigorous examination, but of persuasion." To bring matters to a head, Freud was also criticized for having falsified the results of his own research.

WHAT IS PAS? THE SUPPOSED PARENTAL
ALIENATION SYNDROME

We have qualified the term PAS with the adjective "supposed," precisely because of its unscientific nature. Let us now explain the concept of the so-called Parental Alienation Syndrome to the readers by quoting Padilla-Racero (2013), which states that (p. 58):

"The term parental alienation syndrome (PAS) was described in the United States by psychiatrist R. Gardner. Gardner was a well-known advocate of pedophilia who self-published a work imbued with misogyny. Based on the extrapolation of the American legal precedent (where, from 1985 to 1997, conflicts over the legal custody of children were resolved by drawing upon a syndrome that had not been validated), Gardner himself defines his fabricated PAS as a disorder, a psychiatric syndrome that causes a child, induced by his mother, to lie about the father, defame him, and completely reject his company. The mother would indoctrinate the child to defame the father, but the child's own contributions in this campaign of discrediting the 'alienated' father is what makes the signs and symptoms qualify as syndrome. For Gardner, these contributions of the son or daughter are the test of the existence of psychosis or madness—shared delusions between mother and son or daughter—that will be extended to all those professionals and people who, drawing on scientific knowledge from different disciplines, and using reliable and contrasted sources, might try to protect the child."

The PAS equally relies on the notion that children inherently lie (which has already been refuted in a previous chapter and will also be again in a later chapter), as well as in the unsubstantiated fact that mothers manipulate their children against the noncustodial parent, thus sexualizing custody issues, as the father is never recognized as a manipulator. Both aspects are reflected in the paper (Padilla-Racero, 2013, p. 58):

"Among other arguments, the PAS is based on the 'inherent falsehood in children' (which means that children should not be given credit if they accuse their father of maltreatment, abuse and/or neglect), and on the idea that the mother makes use of the legal system to separate the child from the father, using the manipulative, perverse, vengeful nature that is inherent in the female sex; as a result, Gardner's theories were soon at odds with the movements in defense of children and women, as well as with those of the scientific community worldwide. As a purely incidental example, since the newspaper archives are riddled with Gardner's misogynistic statements and cases for pedophilia, let us point out that the title of one of Gardner's works is *Sex Abuse Hysteria: Salem Witch Trials Revisited.*"

CRITICISM OF THE EXISTENCE OF THE PAS

Following the same methodological rationale, Escudero et al. (2010, p. 12) point out how the supposed PAS was questioned as a valid concept, due to several facts:

1. The two major classification systems for medical and psychological disorders accepted by the scientific community and by official international bodies—the *International Classification of Diseases*, or ICD-11, and the *Diagnostic and Statistical Manual of Mental Disorders* (DSM 5)—have repeatedly refused to acknowledge the PAS.
2. Other institutions that are of significant relevance in the field have also rejected it. Even the US Supreme Court (Escudero et al., 2010) ruled that all testimonies must comply with the standard system established after the Daubert case (in which the Court reexamined the standard previously established in the Frye case), and the PAS does not comply with the new standard.

Gardner's way of showing who is alienating their children when a parental alienation syndrome occurs is indeed a vicious circle. But Gardner also touches on the rather serious concept of child sexual abuse, with his initial assumption that any report filed by a divorced or separated parent about alleged sexual assault on their child by the other parent is false, therefore attempting to demonstrate how the plaintiff, who is also usually the legal custodian, tries to prevent the defendant from having contact with their children.

Strictly speaking, Gardner acts prior to the justice system itself, since, on the grounds of his own argument, exercising the very right of any citizen to go to court would imply that the parent is an alienator of their children; and what is even more serious, such an argument prevents the judicial system from even considering whether there is maltreatment or sexual abuse on the part of the noncustodial parent, as it tends to automatically understand that the claim is false, avoiding an investigation.

As Escudero et al. (2010) remark, the supposed PAS originated in the hypothesis that when a parent is accused or reported by another parent—and by a child, if their verbal ability is properly developed—of maltreating or abusing the child, the supposed PAS has the scientifically tested capacity to discriminate if there is falsehood in these reports and what the real motives are and to propose the change of custody under strict control measures between the child and the diagnosed parent. Therefore, what is at issue is the possibility of removing custody from the custodian parent if they ever report the other parent. The exercise of the right to report is thus impeded, and a situation of defenselessness occurs in cases where sexual abuse or maltreatment does exist, by threatening the custodial parent with the removal of their status. If this were the case, it would precisely be an abuser who could claim the supposed PAS and the child would be given to them in custody by the judicial system (Escudero et al., 2010). Some of the services that can rule on reports regarding the existence or not of violence or abuse—and therefore, the intention to make a false allegation—subscribe to the theory of the supposed PAS, and this establishes an obvious deterring measure for Gender-Based Violence Complaints (which, as such, usually happens when the victim has decided to initiate a process of separation from the abuser); if the supposed PAS falls short of fulfilling its proposed discriminatory capacity, the allegations may be declared false, and the children may be given in custody to the abuser. This, in turn, implies a situation of even greater vulnerability for the child, while also posing a threat to the generic principle that justice should protect the child, because it would give the legal custody to a parent reported for maltreatment or sexual abuse without verifying or clarifying whether these have actually occurred.

Oddly enough, the way psychologists who adhere to this trend—or to be more precise, psychoanalysts or dynamic psychologists—pin down the existence of the so-called syndrome is simply by relying on the conclusion they draw from the interview with the parents. And that again brings us back to Freud himself. Although the Viennese doctor would later develop other therapeutic techniques, the method of "relating" or free association turned the room where he treated his patients into his laboratory, his couch into his only piece of equipment, and the digressions of his patients into scientific data. No laboratory, no scientific verification, only the words, and he as an interpreter and as a verifier of whether the hypotheses he created in his head were fulfilled or not.

Perhaps one of the major scientific errors that Freud committed—which Gardner would reproduce—is that he began an intense analysis of his own "unconscious" forces—as he himself named it—to verify the material provided by his patients. Based on the knowledge acquired through treating his patients and himself, he began to lay the foundations of a theory on personality. The evolution of this theory occupied his efforts for the rest of his life. Similarly, after creating the supposed "parental alienation syndrome," Gardner spent the rest of his life reflecting on it.

REPERCUSSIONS OF THE PAS THEORY IN PRACTICE

Statistics show that mothers are awarded custody more often than fathers. Therefore, it is also more common that they report the possible occurrence of maltreatment or sexual abuse from the other parent—that is, the male; as a result, the problem is sexualized, the PAS is sexualized, and it often becomes an offensive weapon against women, who normally hold custody. The situation creates the idea of falsehood as inherent to women in the collective imaginary.

While most social stereotypes have an empirical basis, there are some which do not (see, for example, Clemente, 1992b). In addition, stereotypes tend to remain, even when their lack of scientific support is obvious, and that is precisely what happens with the PAS. If it is true that custodial mothers often make false allegations to male parents accusing them of maltreatment or sexual abuse to children, this is something for the judicial statistics to detect.

Therefore, there is no scientific evidence to claim that false accusations are inherent in the action of mothers to avoid their children's contact with the other parent.

It is generally admitted that parents are always able to act in the best interest of their children, protecting them as much as possible from the consequences of family breakdown. For this reason, it is necessary to try to keep children out of court proceedings; they should live as complete strangers to the judicial universe. But if there is a case of maltreatment, it is impossible to keep them oblivious to the judicial system. And in such a situation, the PAS undermines the investigation with the assumption that the alienator parent (that is, the one who holds custody, and thus, to this day, usually the woman) has induced in the children a negative vision of the other parent; this would also imply that any statement coming from the child is supposedly influenced by such manipulation and does not express any truth; that is, it shows children as liars. Establishing the notion that children invariably lie seems already serious (especially, given that all children are socialized in telling the truth); but having doubts about possible sexual abuses or maltreatments on the grounds that the child is alienated, and that, rather than the truth, their account expresses that manipulation, is even more serious. The accusation of lying would pile up not only against the parent who denounces but also against the child. And yet, the determination of falsehood would now be made by means of diagnostic criteria. In other words, the evidence is the qualification of falsehood in the (clinical) trial performed on the parent who is the complainant, by a technical professional specialized in the diagnosis of the supposed PAS. Similarly, the final objective of the diagnosis—that is, the materialization of the withdrawal and change of custody arrangements—is defined as therapeutic, but at the expense of redefining the concept itself; this terminological reconversion now hides that fact that if it were not a (conventional) therapy, the arrangement would be a corrective measure (Escudero et al., 2010).

There are other circumstances that make the PAS even more ludicrous, such as the fact that, as an overarching principle, the justice system today alleges—with Gardner—that a violent person in certain contexts and situations is not necessarily a violent person with his or her children. From the psychological point of view, this is impossible, as it undermines the notion of personality itself, which is based on consistency; if there were no consistency in the behavior of individuals, in their ideas, or even between their behaviors and ideas on a regular basis, it would not be possible to study human behavior by analyzing thoughts and conduct. Not only that, but in cases when the mother has been maltreated by the father, and such maltreatment—of any kind—has been witnessed and experienced by the children, this maltreating parent is also indirectly maltreating his children. If, as a result of the experience of such maltreatment on the other parent, the child rejects the perpetrator, it is not because they are being manipulated, but because they repudiate violence and love the maltreated parent, usually the mother. It is not true that an abuser may be a good father; oddly enough, people who have abused their former partner are sometimes granted custody, even when the abuses have been witnessed by children (Clemente, 2011), and it seems even more shocking that, with that record, if there are also allegations that the parent who mistreated their former partner has mistreated the child, if they have not been proven guilty, they may be granted custody. The verification of intimate partner violence, and the tenacious, perverse manipulation of the abusive partner over the emotions of children who live in a situation of permanent uncertainty and ambivalence, should suffice to prevent them from holding the child's custody. Unfortunately, this is not the case. As it may happen to a woman who manages to get out of the abusive relationship and wants to stay as far away from the abuser as possible, these reasons are sufficient for the child who bears witness to the violence of their father, and who may be afraid and not wish to have any contact with him (Escudero et al., 2010).

There are several emerging sectors in society today that regard this fact as contrary to law and discriminatory against men; they claim that a man who is violent with his partner can nevertheless be a "good father" to the children of both. Along the same lines, two factors would corroborate such a claim: One of them is the supposed PAS, created by Richard Gardner from a position that reconciles parenthood and abuse; Gardner also holds the view that the child needs to be assisted to appreciate that, in our society, we have an exaggerated punitive and moralistic attitude about adult/child sexual encounters; the other is the deterrent effect to report that this construct exerts on women victims of violence.

Let us now address the issue of sexuality, which we have not explored yet.

SEXUALITY, INCEST, PEDOPHILIA

The reference to sexuality is, perhaps, the first of the elements that define Freud's structure of personality. The relationships that humans create, maintain, and end originate in sexual attraction. Freud states that friendship relationships are frustrated sexual relationships at their end—that is, we relinquish conceiving them as sexual and call them friendship. The same could be said about those that we consider leaders, or those who we simply get along with; a sexual desire—which we do not recognize—would always be hidden behind our appreciation to them. This lack of recognition can be understood through the Freudian conception of the psychic apparatus, which is composed of three elements known as the id, the ego, and the superego. There is an unconscious part, the so-called "id," encompassing the impulses and desires of each person, that counterbalances the "superego," a psychic structure that allows us to live in society, and that implies the renunciation of the sexualization of all social relations, a prerequisite for societies to be able to progress and advance. Everyone's behavior fluctuates between these two dueling forces, and our thoughts, which are called the "ego," are an element that is sometimes overridden by the id and sometimes by the superego. In order to survive as a species, and to prevent killing each other, guided by the vital need to eat and have constant sexual relations with everyone, we need a superego, through which we create social institutions, social norms, and culture—and therefore the law and the justice system. Such social norms imply the need to renounce the instincts, which, for psychoanalysis, are basically two: eros (or sexual desire) and thanatos (or drive for death, to destroy others and seek survival).

These notions afford an insight into the role of family as conceived by Freud, a social entity that seeks to channel sexual desires toward couple relationships; couples are meant to have children and to favor offspring, which is beneficial to society and prevents conflicts within and outside the family, but at the same time, it creates individuals who live "frustrated" throughout their lives. This sheds light upon classic psychoanalysis concepts such as the Oedipus complex (since Freud did not think of daughters, but only thought of the male sons, consequently, he only referred to the complex of Oedipus; this stirred some controversy among feminist groups, which later allowed for the emergence of the Electra complex), which is the desire of a descendant to kill the parent of their same sex and to be sexually involved with the parent of the opposite sex. This desire would also explain that most members of any association wish to "kill the leader" (for a patriarchal mentality, that would amount to killing the father) to seize power, which means also having sexual access to females.

We will later attempt a critique of these views; meanwhile, these arguments beg the question of whether to take a theory like this seriously or not. Gardner inherits this tradition and embraces it without introducing any original contributions or evidence; when he states that pedophilia is a normal practice in many societies (which, luckily for us as a society, is not), he is simply falling for the ideas of his master—the precepts of psychoanalysis dictate that every parent wishes to be involved in an incestuous relationship with their children, and that most of them repress the idea because the superego prevents them from even recognizing such possibility. Welcoming another of the most controversial Freudian principles, Gardner even claims that children are sexual beings who want to seduce other children and adults, thus turning them into sexual "provocateurs" of the parent of the opposite sex. He states, for instance, that "there is a bit of pedophile in each of us" (Gardner, 1991, p. 118), that "children are naturally sexual and may initiate sexual encounters seducing an adult" (Gardner, 1985, p. 93), or that "children should be helped to understand that in our society we have an exaggerated punitive and moralistic attitude toward sexual abuse against them" (Gardner, 1992, p. 572). In a nutshell, Gardner appears as a faithful disciple of Freud, a good follower of an orthodox psychoanalytic line.

Indeed, according to the same reasoning that prompted Gardner to assert the positive aspects of pedophilia, it could be argued that no child can be proven guilty to justice if they kill their parent of their sex, as this could be justified by the—also unscientific—Oedipus complex.

It is interesting to notice how, for Gardner (and for proponents of the theory of psychoanalysis), every single argument can serve the function of justifying previous theoretical claims, therefore emphasizing the unscientific nature of such claims. Thus, for example, with regard to pedophilia (or by extension, incest), Gardner states that, in many societies, relations between groups of relatives that are not confined to the group of members of the nuclear family are considered incestuous, but that this only confirms the universality of the prohibition and its strength. The underlying principle of the Oedipus complex is the prohibition of incest, a universal law that regulates marital exchanges in all societies. According to Freud, on an unconscious level, incest is always desired. Its prohibition inhibits two fundamental human tendencies: to kill the father and to marry the mother. But the anthropologist Bronisław Malinowski, in light of the results of the field research he conducted in the Trobriand Islands, criticized the Freudian hypothesis about the universality of the Oedipus complex, as well as its biological origin. In his book *Totem and Taboo*, Freud had proposed the existence of the complex in all human societies, but Malinowski showed that, in the matrilineal structure of the Trobriand people, as women were the ones who carried out economic activities, the presence of mothers in the lives of children was rather scarce, and their physiological role in procreation was unknown. The social roles of the parents were thus performed by the older sisters and the maternal uncles of the children. In this context, they generally developed sexual fantasies toward their sisters, and feelings of hate toward the maternal uncles. Thus, Malinowski demonstrates the nonuniversality of the Oedipus complex (Parkin and Stone, 2007).

It is common to claim that Freud discovered infantile sexuality, but before him, scholars such as Wilhelm Fliess and Albert Moll had already noticed the widespread existence of certain childhood sexual phenomena. One of the most acerbic critics of psychoanalysis was Albert Moll, who, in 1897, published a book that analyses the development of child sexuality; Moll criticizes Freud's method of inquiry, based on suggestion, and well as his attempt to investigate children's sexual life through the analysis of the accounts of adults. In Moll's view, the "demonstrations" of psychoanalytic theory are rather problematic (Moll, 1931): "Freud and his supporters subordinate clinical records to theory, not theory to clinical records." Freud tries to demonstrate his theory by psychoanalysis. But there are so many arbitrary interpretations on this point that we cannot speak of a demonstration. Sigusch (2012) describes extensively the disputes between Freud and Moll. It is grotesque that Freud accused Moll of plagiarizing his discoveries, when Moll's book on sexual development appeared eight years before Freud's work on sexual theory. Many doctors welcomed psychoanalysis. But as the psychoanalytic movement became a kind of religious sect, Freud's colleagues distanced themselves from analysis. The analogy with a religious community was used not only by adversaries, but also by supporters of psychoanalysis. Thus, says Wilhelm Stekel, that he became the apostle of Freud, "who was my Christ," and that the club meetings on Wednesdays at Freud's house were lived as a revelation (Tortosa, 1998, p. 434).

For years, Freud's statements about his isolation concur with his fiction of living as Robinson Crusoe on a desert island, but there is a fundamental difference between historical facts and the myth of the psychoanalytic hero. Reactions to his theories among his contemporaries were disparate: Some critics strongly rejected them for moral or scientific reasons; several of his colleagues welcomed his work with sympathy but expressed doubts on some points about his doctrine; finally, there was a group of enthusiastic supporters who took the words of the teacher as a revelation. After a few years, Gardner would certainly become one of them.

There is no need to insist on the lack of scientific basis—and validity—of Gardner's theories; his notions on sexuality are ill-founded, as they are based on psychoanalytic theories, which are also completely inoperative from a scientific point of view.

PARENTAL ALIENATION SYNDROME OR
PATRIARCHATE PERPETUATION SYNDROME?

With this question, Padilla-Racero (2013) highlighted that, while the relevance for humanity of the Declaration of Human Rights—as well as that of the other instruments relating to human rights—is undeniable, their origin has been strongly rooted on the image of humans as men; that is, the male sex was the only reference within these human rights, and males were considered the paradigm of humanity, with no consideration about the ways of feeling, thinking, fighting, and living of the female sex, which represents the other part of humanity, but has been made invisible by this androcentric model of society.

Over the centuries, there has been a pervasive patriarchal conception of the world that considers males as a paradigm of humanity. The situation has reflected in human rights and its language (let us not forget the strong influence that language exerts upon thought, and the fact that, eventually, ideas, values, customs, and habits end up being embodied in norms and laws). Since their reference is only one part of humanity (the male), women have only been placed in society through the feelings and thoughts of men, as inferior beings, submissive and dependent, without the right to their own gender identity.

The term patriarchy must be understood as institutionalized male supremacy. The PAS becomes a powerful weapon of patriarchy when the father of the family has inflicted violence, has neglected his children, has no parental skills, or does not accept marriage separation.

The PAS diagnosis responds to the subliminal mandate to reduce or eliminate reports of violence to women as well as to children themselves.

THE DIAGNOSIS

Faced with so much criticism, the supposed PAS adopts different names and masquerades under new labels to avoid its original nomenclature. Its proponents try to keep hidden some not so minor concepts and evidence associated to it. We have noticed that when the supposed PAS or some of its euphemisms appear in any judicial record ("parental alienation," "family alienation," "parental interference," "contact impediment," "fantastic ideation," "self-fulfilling prophecy," "false memory," "malicious mother," among others), all the records, the evidence, and the previously predicted and foreseeable consequences take a subordinate role (or directly disappear from the scene), and from that point on, the focus is shifted to the assessment of the plaintiff's behavior, who, having been the "victim" until that moment, is accused and named as aggressor.

The supposed PAS would arise from the concurrence of eight symptoms present in the affected child (Tejedor, 2006):

- A campaign of denigration of the targeted parent.
- A frivolous, weak, or absurd rationale for the denigration.
- A lack of ambivalence.
- The phenomenon of the "independent thinker."
- Reflective support for the alienating parent in parental conflict.
- Lack of guilt about cruelty and/or denigration toward the targeted parent.
- The presence of borrowed scenarios.
- Extension of hostility toward the friends and/or extended family of the targeted parent.

Gardner himself defined these symptoms, but they seem as ambiguous as his theory. With the intention of properly diagnosing the syndrome, he devised the "Sex Abuse Legitimacy scale" (SAL scale). Analyzing Gardner's ideas, Escudero et al. (2010, p. 30–31) suggest that "this scale is intended to allow a differentiation between 'bona fide' and 'fabricated' allegations by corroborating the presence or absence of certain characteristics in the cases." And yet, there is no evidence whatsoever to support the psychometric properties of the scale; therefore, it cannot be considered scientifically reliable or valid (Clemente, 1992).

Since it did not reach the minimum standards for a scale to be a valid measuring tool, Gardner's scale received such strong criticism that he himself stopped using it, avoiding any mention to it in his works after 1995. Gardner's own awareness of the scale's uselessness led him to suggest the use of other tools that were not conceived to detect his "syndrome." Thus, as Escudero et al. (2010, pp. 34–35) point out: "To avoid error, Gardner suggests using the criteria of post-traumatic stress disorder alongside the symptoms of the supposed PAS. According to the author, the DSM IV description of this disorder would be close to the typical reaction of an abused child. Similarly, in an article published in 2004, Gardner proposed relying on the criteria described in the 'False Memory Syndrome' (FMS) to help (the supposed PAS) distinguish true from false allegations."

Therefore, there is no diagnostic tool to detect the syndrome conceived by Gardner. Let us bear in mind that if we take psychoanalysis as a starting point, it is impossible to derive any plausible and demonstrable hypothesis from theory, or to create any measuring tool.

CONCLUDING REMARKS

Psychoanalysis has achieved a deep impact on modern society, especially in the field of culture. There are many trends and directors in the film industry that bring the concepts of psychoanalysis into play—David Lynch, Kurosawa, Buñuel, or Woody Allen, to name a few. An example that easily comes to mind is Alfred Hitchcock's *Psycho*, in which Norman Bates states that a man's best friend is his mother, obviously referring to the Oedipus complex. Besides, no one doubts the influence of the seventh art in both collective and individual psychology. In music, the example of Mozart—to which we owe great productions that he composed in an almost delirious state—is particularly illustrative; he was obsessed with the anonymous character that commissioned him the *Requiem*. His opera *The Magic Flute* is bristling with oneiric symbols, and scholars still find connections with Freemasonry in it; in short, the inner reality of individuals—and all the repressed instincts that show through—is a common topic in all arts. Some artistic movements are in fact built around Freud's theories. Let us take, for instance, the example of a painting by Dalí or of any surreal painter (Clemente, 2010).

And yet, society cannot—and must not—accept the ideas that derive from psychoanalysis. Thus, Freud has received harsh criticism from several feminist movements for his explanation of women as "men without a phallus" and for the notion of "envy of the penis." Other movements also criticize his theory for considering homosexuality as a perversion; the huge cultural impact of Freud's theories on psychosexual development—and possibly a lack of rigor or objectivity in its interpretation—popularized the idea of homosexuality as a disease, which, in the first half of the twentieth century, led to an increase in the number of admissions of homosexuals in mental health centers. Psychoanalytical treatment was used for several decades to try to "cure" homosexuality.

In addition, as Escudero et al. claim (2010, p. 22), if "there is no such validation of the methodology, and the creator of the supposed PAS cannot guarantee in any way whether allegations are false or not; if there can be several plausible explanations for the hostility of the child toward the parent that cannot be discarded by the supposed PAS; if the possibility of false positives (erroneous determination that a child suffers from a supposed PAS when it is not the case) is so high that, in such a case, the measures taken in custody proceedings can actually pose a risk and harm, impossible to handle by the child; and, if it can be proven that the foundations of the supposed PAS were constructed by distorting the terminology used, and establishing a logic to justify any *a priori* results, could a system of protection, such as the judiciary, allow itself to continue with its use?"

Probably, if only for the purpose of adhering to the ontological simplicity of Ockham's razor principle, we should first accept any much simpler
explanation than those established by Gardner. Many are the failures resulting from the model. From a more technical point of view, a serious problem
in Gardner's theory is the fact that it does not contemplate the evolutionary
development of "alienated" children. Escudero et al. also comment on this
(2010, p. 38): "The omission of the role of child development in the description of behaviors; on the contrary, the set of eight symptoms of the supposed
PAS is considered valid at all ages."

But Gardner does not limit himself to making persuasive claims about the
existence of the PAS; in an attempt to establish mechanisms to prevent the
manifestation of the so-called syndrome, he takes a step further by creating
the "Threat Therapy," which he stipulates as the therapeutic treatment that
would act on the supposed pathogenic mechanism of indoctrination or incite-
ment. The therapy consists of separating the custodial parent, who allegedly
wishes to stir hostility in the child against the other parent; taking custody
away; and forcing them to enter treatment. The mere denomination of a "therapy" as a "threat" goes against psychological and medical codes of ethics.

The threat itself primarily gravitates toward a permanent change of custody: "The threat of taking custody away can also be a convenient reminder
for those mothers 'to cooperate.'" Thus, as Escudero et al. (2010, p. 49) point
out, "the argument is that only a justice that effectively makes good on its
threats can proceed with the measures of the supposed PAS." For Gardner,
this represents almost a struggle against the primitive instincts he found in
women: "Throughout the animal kingdom, mothers will literally fight to
death to safeguard their descendants, and women are still under the influence
of the same genetic programming." In many cases, periods of imprisonment
or hospitalization will be recommended for both the mother and the child as
a reminder of the court's executory capacity. The relationship between punishment and disapproved behavior is clear in this fragment: "Another option,
especially for younger children, would be for them to temporarily reside in
a foster home or in a shelter for abused children. This is obviously punitive
and could help such children rethink their decision of not visiting the noncustodial parent."

The report by Escudero et al. (2010, pp. 64 et seq.) also refers to the terminology used by Fink—president of the Leadership Council on Child Abuse
and Interpersonal Violence, and former president of the American Psychiatric
Association—about how pseudoscience or "junk science" originated in the
1980s: "Science tells us that the most likely reason for a child to reject a
parent is the behavior of that parent. Labels such as the supposed Parental
Alienation Syndrome (PAS) serve to divert attention from these behaviors.
. . . Children suffer when the law accepts a syndrome only because someone

who calls himself or herself an 'expert' creates an elegant phrase. [. . .] increasingly, courts are deciphering the pool of the alleged PAS and refusing to allow trials to be used as a theater for the promotion of junk science."

What is even worse, the consequences are often fatal. The application of Gardner's theory has provoked disputes of child-custody in some court cases in which the father filed for custody alleging the existence of the supposed PAS, leading to the suicide of adolescents; the admissibility of the supposed PAS in judicial proceedings must therefore be called into question. The truth is that from a scientific point of view the PAS has not been acknowledged nor does it matter.

To conclude, let us briefly highlight some conclusions about the meaning of the PAS from a psychological point of view.

The supposed PAS is an attack on science for the following reasons (Clemente, 2013b):

- It is based on the unscientific psychoanalytic theory; the hypotheses of the psychoanalytic theory are unfalsifiable, and there is ample consensus today that it constitutes more of a philosophical trend, and a way of considering life, than a psychological or scientific theory.
- It is not based on substantial theoretical principles and cannot be verified; therefore, there is no possibility of creating any diagnostic tool. While Gardner himself "elicited" a test, it cannot be scientifically verified, and therefore it has no reliability, validity, sensitivity, or specificity.
- The PAS falls into the category of the so-called projective psychological tests, which have no reliability but "dependability," and their interpretations depend on the assessor's own unscientific "personal opinion."
- There is no adequate diagnosis (and therefore, no effective treatment), so it is impossible to ascertain whether the treatment would affect the person who manifests the supposed syndrome or others.
- Indeed, Gardner's "threat therapy" is not a therapy as such, but only a threat. In fact, it is based not on the application of psychological procedures, but on the use of the systems of social control (the justice and police systems) to bring the threatened subject to a standstill.
- Threat therapy (which, as already mentioned, is not actually a therapy) is not equipped with a mechanism to verify its effectiveness. And yet, in any case, even after a supposed therapy, there is the risk of the suicide of the child (forced to live with the parent with whom any type of contact was unwanted); thus, the only alternative therapy that remains is the radical elimination of the procedure itself.
- Furthermore, considering an intervention in the health area, action can only be taken on persons who agree to enter treatment and therefore

wish to participate in the procedure. Otherwise, all ethical principles, both scientific and professional, are violated.

- The scientific literature barely mentions the PAS as it lacks interest for researchers, which demonstrates its null scientific impact, and therefore has a virtually nonexistent interest generated within science.
- Lastly, there are so many deficiencies in Gardner's scientific ideas that a serious analysis of his theories is not even worth considering, much less question matters such as the justification of pedophilia, which are covered by most criminal codes. To question terms in a courtroom that are already covered as a crime within the law is quite incongruent, to say the least.

But the PAS is also an attack on the rule of law for the following reasons (Clemente, 2013b):

- It hinders victims from reporting possible crimes, thus undermining the right of any citizen to do so, as it establishes that filing a report, in itself, is one of the defining elements of the syndrome. Once again, the legal and psychological sphere could be mistaken for the other, and those whose rights have been violated and should report to the authorities are left defenseless.
- By avoiding reporting, the PAS favors that some cases of child maltreatment and abuse remain uninvestigated, thereby promoting the commission of crimes and turning the rates of these crimes into hidden figures.
- It creates a radical defenselessness of those affected; the greater the number of reports, the more passive the system becomes—which does not only eschew checking the veracity of the allegations, but even justifies its passivity by laying the blame on the victims.
- It involves an interference of the justice system in the private life of individuals—in this case, of the custodial parent, who is forced to take, for example, family mediation courses for a family that no longer exists, and therefore to continue in contact with a partner they are already separated from, and with whom no one should force them to remain in contact, except for matters relating to their children.
- In general, it violates citizens' rights. Moreover, science works for society enabling justice to be served between different parties, and to rely on nonscientific theories would be unjust to citizens.

It is also an attack on the children themselves, for the following reasons—among others (Clemente, 2013b):

- It identifies them as liars, on the premise of the child having given false testimony, obviating that all parents raise their children to tell the truth.
- It disregards scientific procedure applied toward children in so far as ascertaining the truth. By following the Freudian presumption that the child lies, science is neglected.
- It leaves children defenseless, as they are unable to accept the judicial determination of having to remain with a parent that maltreats them, which may lead to suicide.
- In less severe cases, it causes serious behavioral disorders in the child.
- It destroys the relationship not only with the parent who can harm them, but also with the one who is forced to observe the visitation arrangements, whom the child perceives as another abuser for not averting their suffering.

Lastly, the PAS is also detrimental for the parents because (Clemente, 2013b):

- The parent who knows that the other parent maltreats the child is forced to be a bad parent, or otherwise to disobey the court orders and judicial sentences.
- The parent who may be an abuser can maltreat their former partner by making them suffer through the child, but also generate even more hatred and bitterness in the child.
- The parent who is complying with a court order and with visitation rights, despite suspecting or knowing that abuse is taking place, must deal with the anxiety created that affects their mental and physical health, with long-term repercussions.

Is there a solution? Maybe two questions should be borne in mind: Justice is only so when based on scientific principle; and only by using the child's testimony may the best interest and the rights of the child be protected.

Chapter 5

The Moral Dilemma Posed by the False Parental Alienation Syndrome

Protect the Children or Obey the Justice System

As previously mentioned in the introduction, one of the several problems posed by a false theory such as the Parental Alienation Syndrome (PAS) is the ethical dilemma between defending the children or abiding by justice, when a judge determines that a parent, normally the mother, should hand over the child to the other parent, knowing that the child is being abused by them, when the justice system has not been able to corroborate the abuse. An ethical dilemma is a situation in which there is a conflict between two ethical imperatives, in such fashion that obedience to one implies the transgression of the other. Generally speaking, an ethical dilemma is presented in any situation in which an individual has reasons to choose between two (or more) actions, each of which favors a different principle and excludes the remaining ones. Thus, the individual will inevitably make a mistake: Regardless of their choice, they will do something wrong or will not comply with an obligation (McConnell, 2014). When it comes to legal precepts, ethical dilemmas may emerge as a result of a conflict between moral, ethical, or emotional guidelines, and legal regulations.

The dilemma that interests us is that which confronts ethics against the law (Mappes, Robb, and Engels, 1985; Pope and Bajt, 1988), knowing that the justice system has the resources to take children away from their mothers, if she denies access of the child to the father.

Regardless of the reasons that a father might have to deliberately attack his children (and consequently, their mother), attacking the mother with what is most dear to her (her children) implies a high level of sadism (a matter that we will explore in the chapter about the dark personality). It would be logical to think that the testimony of the child should suffice to avoid contact of the father with the child, even enough for him to be sentenced, but the procedural guarantees of legal systems prevent this from happening, in such a way that upon the father not being condemned, he may request contact with his child. These parents present a high level of Machiavellianism, subclinical psychopathy, subclinical narcissism, and sadism; they do not show any empathy or affection toward their children, and mostly concern themselves with attacking the mother through using the children, be it for having filed a complaint against them, or even before that, for having broken the couple's relationship.

These parents are Machiavellian (filing a complaint against a person who filed a complaint against them, fabricating reasons to explain that the children are capable of hurting themselves), usually narcissistic (this way of acting usually originates in that their former partner separated from them, often for having, as well as the children, suffered maltreatment), psychopaths (they have no empathy, and therefore can attempt and hurt others without the necessity of putting themselves in the place of the victim), and sadistic (they enjoy hurting their own children, and through them, their former partners). That is to say, they could be included in what we call the "dark personality" (Azizli et al., 2016; Berger and Caravita, 2016; Book et al., 2016; Garcia and Rosenberg, 2016; Malesza and Ostaszewski, 2016).

There are several studies that have empirically and theoretically refuted Gardner's arguments (Bantekas, 2016; Clemente, 2013b; Clemente and Padilla-Racero, 2015a, 2015b, 2016; Clemente, Padilla-Racero, Gandoy-Crego, Reig-Botella, and Gonzalez-Rodriguez, 2015; Erard, 2016; O'Donohue, Benuto, and Bennett, 2016; Padilla-Racero, 2013, 2015, 2016; Saunders and Oglesby, 2016; Shaw, 2016). And yet, unfortunately, Gardner's arguments are used on a regular basis in a judicial context in several countries.

From a sociopsychological point of view, the most important ethical dilemma studied to date was that set out by Milgram in an experiment of obedience to authority (Bantekas, 2016; Clemente, 2013a, 2013b; Clemente and Padilla-Racero, 2015a, 2015b, 2016; Clemente, Padilla-Racero, Gandoy-Crego, Reig-Botella, and Gonzalez-Rodriguez, 2015; Erard, 2016; O'Donohue, Benuto, and Bennett, 2016; Padilla-Racero, 2013, 2015, 2016; Saunders and Oglesby, 2016; Shaw, 2016). The results obtained by Milgram may be interpreted in several ways; as he himself explained, he had the idea of conducting the study when trying to explain how the Holocaust even took place, that is, that the Nazi troops killed around six million Jewish, and his statement might have contributed to create some confusion among those who tried to analyze his findings. The analysis of his archives—which includes the recordings of the participants' statements—show that Milgram did not intend to explain the Holocaust (Baumrind, 2015; Fenigstein, 2015; Mastroianni, 2015; Nicholson, 2015).

The question that Milgram set forth was simple: How is it possible that, by the mere fact of receiving an order from a superior, a sensitive and respectful human being is capable of killing other human beings? He thus explored a basic tenet in social psychology: Can the explanation be found in the fact that people doubt between obeying a person respected as a leader or following their own principles, opposed to those demanded by the leader? If that is the explanation, we may draw two important conclusions: Despite going against our principles, hurting (even killing) another person is something that anyone can do if they are guided by a paradigm which tells them to obey someone with authority in whom they trust; besides, behind that behavior, there is not an individual with a pathological mind, a psychopath, but a person who is confronting an ethical dilemma. In Milgram's experiment, two thirds of the subjects obeyed authority, that is, they administered false electric shocks—that they thought to be real—to their colleagues, even believing that they had killed some of them (Clemente, 2016). Milgram created the OTA paradigm (obedience to authority).

The main key to explain such a situation seems to be the diffusion of responsibility (I am not responsible, the researcher is) or, in other words, the attribution of the responsibility of what happened to others. And all this reveals something rather important: Previous ideas, what we call personality, do not hold the same weight as the circumstances, the surrounding environment. Obedience is the norm.

Milgram's experiment shows how official, bureaucratic institutions may nullify the values and beliefs of their users. Russel and Gregory (2011) applied Milgram's ideas to the verification of how public employees solve moral dilemmas in a work situation that had been organized through bureaucracy, in such a way that judges, as well as the justice system in general, could end up taking rather extreme decisions (such as taking the custody of a child away from one parent and giving that child over to an abuser) through the mere application of the law, which also implies a process of diffusion of responsibility.

The concept of diffusion of responsibility was later nuanced and amplified by two other concepts: that of "moral disengagement," created by Bandura (1990, 1999), and that of the "zone of organizational indifference," by Barnard (1938).

Barnard's study (1938) specifically explains how there are people who carry out their tasks and are dominated by an administrative perspective, more than a moral one. Barnard explains that individual values of loyalty, duty, and discipline derive from the technical necessities of hierarchy. Individuals feel that these are highly valued moral imperatives, but on an organizational level, they are simply the technical conditions necessary for the maintenance of an official institution, and once passed through bureaucracy it may annul the values and beliefs of the users. Let us not forget that Milgram, in addition to being a social psychologist, was a political scientist. As a matter of fact, Russel and Gregory (2011) examine a variety of factors in the laboratory work of Milgram that help to understand how civil servants can resolve a moral dilemma in a situation of work organized through bureaucracy.

This individual aptitude toward obedience is what Milgram (1974) calls "the agentic state" (AS): a state in which individuals stop acting and thinking by themselves, assuming that what a superior entity requires of them (in this case, the justice system) is what must be done, without the need to think. This procedure allowed Milgram to explain how a person would be capable of obeying, even as far as attempting on the life of another human being. The doubt is whether a mother would be capable of being in an "agentic state," no longer defending her son or daughter, and when that change would take place. If a person takes on an AS, they no longer hold responsibility, they simply obey authority. Who accepts the condition of AS becomes another element in the judicial chain, and their conscious becomes an element of acceptance of the conscious itself of the system—in this case, of the judges that represent the maximum authority.

Milgram argued that there were two main factors that favored that the subjects would assume an AS: the "binding factors" (BFs) and the "strain reducing mechanisms" (SRMs). The BFs are coercive binding mechanisms that help block the subjects when they assume AS. The SRMs are mechanisms that help compensate the participants for the strain they go through upon thinking they are hurting someone else.

The only exception to this general pattern was a variation that Milgram never published, possibly because it was not very ethical: what is called the relationship condition, which was published afterward by Rochat & Modigliani (1997). In this experiment, the participants were asked to bring someone to the laboratory who had known them for at least two years. Milgram instructed the friend how to imitate receiving electric shocks, in such a way that they were able to perfectly imitate being a victim of their friend's behavior (in the original paradigm in which they supposedly received the shocks, they worked with actors). Under these conditions, 85 percent of the participants constantly questioned the experimenter of the necessity to apply shocks, and 80 percent of them rejected continuing to apply shocks beyond 195 volts (in the normal condition, 63 percent obeyed until the end, applying 450 volts).

The key difference between the relationship condition and the other variations was that the victim was not a stranger for the participants, but someone they knew, which enabled them to overcome the fear of confronting the experimenter. In a similar way, Dolinski and Grzyb (2016) bring to the fore the rhetorical question posed by Gilbert (1981): Would a participant agree to administer high electrical shocks if they were asked to do so before the experiment?

The dilemma posed here is whether one would obey authority or defend a child, a situation whereby the circumstances for the relationship condition are more clearly met. Nearly all participants chose to continue inflicting more shocks—resulting in their passing the point of strain equilibrium and then having to experience what we call "learner over experimenter strain disequilibrium" (LESD)—that is, the point from which the learner's pained reactions surpassed the maximum strain the experimenter, using verbal prods, was capable of imposing on a defiant participant. The longer participants remained in LESD, the more likely they could not help but feel mostly responsible for the learner's painful experience. Their flicking of switches was clearly causing the learner's progressively tormented reactions to the shocks. Also, as the screams intensified, the first four verbal prods became increasingly implausible: It was clearly not "essential" that this experiment dangerously harm a person. There was obviously another "choice" available: to not seriously harm (or perhaps even kill) the learner. During LESD, participants typically became more agitated and nervous. Around this point of the experiment most of them were unsure of what to do, except that they neither wanted to keep shocking the learner nor to confront the experimenter. Consequently, most participants hesitated and, while enduring the intense stress associated with LESD, allowed themselves to be drawn a little further into inflicting more shocks.

One way of interpreting the results obtained by Milgram is through Barnard's Theory of Authority (1938) and through what he called the "zone of indifference." In fact, according to what Barnard suggests in his "theory of authority" (1938), Milgram's electric shock generator may be conceived as a "zone of indifference." For Barnard, subordinates blindly accept authority—that is, they accept an order because they trust that authority. According to this theory, the orders are accepted by the employees of organizations if they are within the zone of indifference. Only for a small minority (those that opposed the experimenter from the beginning), the zone of indifference had disappeared.

Parents are not public employees, yet as Russel and Gregory (2011) point out, Milgram's electric shock generator may be conceived as a metaphor for the zone of indifference. Practically all participants were initially indifferent to the orders of the experimenter, but almost everyone, sooner or later, questioned that zone of indifference and began to worry about the legitimacy of the researchers and the effects that the experiment could have on the subjects who were administered the shocks, despite the fact that they continued participating. Only a small minority—those who had opposed the experimenter from the outset—were situated outside of the zone of indifference.

Therefore, what Barnard established in his theory of the organization is akin to what Bandura (1990, 1999) calls the "selective separation of moral control," a mechanism through which people carry out routine activities that bring on personal benefit but at a great cost for others. Thus, it is possible to assert that Milgram's experiment aimed at broadening the "zone of indifference" of the participants. Milgram himself was conscious of how, the more malevolent or destructive the desired purpose was, the easier it was to design an organization to effectively get people to follow suit, refining the means through which the members can overcome more efficiently what we called LESD.

The concept of dehumanization of bureaucracy was introduced by Weber. Dehumanization is the main special virtue of bureaucracy. However, Weber never considered that the virtue in question might also be its biggest problem. Bureaucracy increases efficiency, allowing that people in organizations leave their own humanity aside and act as if they were insensitive parts of a machine. As Bauman (1989, p.155) states, "The more rational the organization of the action is, the easier it is to cause suffering and remain in peace with oneself." In fact, it is considered that the impartial exercise of authority is the defining characteristic of a good government (Rothstein and Teorell, 2008). However, unlike Weber, Milgram's experiment demonstrated that the human element is important to facilitate action.

In psychology, these ideas have been gathered by Bandura (1990) under the concept of "moral disengagement," or selective separation of moral control. According to Bandura (1999) people make use of social and psychological strategies to commit inhuman actions without having to feel guilty. Bandura calls those thoughts and judgments that people use to justify their behavior mechanisms of moral disengagement. Individuals develop moral standards with which they rule their lives. These standards are the moral principles that they know, assume as valid, and try to follow in their daily behavior, like, for example, respecting the life of others. These are moral standards because they imply the acknowledgment of the rights of others, as well as respecting their dignity as human beings. However, human beings are capable of using several "psychological maneuvers" that allow them to leave aside and act contrary to those standards. Usually, as Bandura asserts, individuals maintain a process of moral self-censorship—we have conversations with ourselves about the right and the wrong of our actions. However, on many occasions, this moral self-censorship may become disconnected from the wrong behavior, in such a way that we can take incorrect actions without passing them through our filter of self-censorship. Bandura proposes four types of cognitive mechanisms that serve as justification as to why someone might have committed an immoral act, and lets them explain how it was possible, despite knowing what was right, and that on occasions we act incorrectly: the reconstruction of the behavior in itself, in such a way that it is not perceived as immoral; the executer of the act in a way that the perpetrator can minimalize their role in the commission of the damage; the perception of the consequences that are derived from the actions, in such a way that these are minimalized; and the way the victims of maltreatment are considered, devaluing them as human beings or blaming them for what is done to them. Therefore, disengagement can be attained through redefining the damaging behavior as acceptable, through moral justification, the beneficial social comparison, or euphemistic language. It can be focused on the actor, so that the perpetrators can minimize their role in the production of damage, through diffusion or moving the responsibility. It can also involve minimizing or distorting the damage that follows harmful actions, so that the person no longer perceives the actions to be harmful. Lastly, disengagement can also include dehumanizing or blaming the victims of maltreatment. Therefore, the typology of the four major types of mechanisms of disengagement presented above is divided into eight specific mechanisms: moral justification; beneficial comparison; dehumanizing; blame placement; displacement of responsibility; diffusion of responsibility.

Individuals are socialized regarding the internalization of values that are instilled in them from the social sphere and that are necessary, for example, to maintain the justice system. This is how individually internalized values such as loyalty, duty, or discipline are derived from the necessities of the institutions to be kept up on a social level, yet at the same time are experienced by the individual as highly personal moral imperatives. Furthermore, the system has coercive procedures so that, in the case of disobedience by an individual, they can be obliged to revert and obey. According to what Russel and Gregory (2011) state, Milgram had created a context in which many of its participants were able, and prepared, to "morally detach" themselves of their obligations to face their LESD, using for that some of the "techniques" suggested by Bandura that Milgram called SRMs (Blass, 2004; Darley, 1992; Goodwin and Darley, 2008; Russell and Gregory, 2005; Zimbardo, 2007).

There are studies that suggest alternative explanations. Haslam, Reicher, and Birney (2016), for instance, focus on a third of the subjects that disobey, referring to them as committed followers. Some studies even seek to determine the areas of the brain implied in obedience to authority (Caspar, Christensen, Cleeremans, and Haggard, 2016).

According to Gardner's PAS theory, the mothers labelled as "malicious" should be punished by separating them from their children, as they are considered to be manipulators and instill hate in their children toward the father, making the one who files the complaint guilty, and in some cases, handing over the child to the abuser. Even in the literature there are scales intended to quantify the presence of PAS, curiously without considering whether that term is conceptually correct (Gomide, Cunha, Camargo, and Fernandes, 2016; Zicavo-Martínez, Celis-Esparza, González-Espinoza, and Mercado-Aravena, 2016). Furthermore, the literature is brimming with studies that, before verifying if a child was, in fact, being manipulated by their mother, consider that child as a future delinquent (Al Ghazi, 2016; Fermann and Habigzang, 2016). Yet perhaps the most problematic is to verify how trends have been created that unite law and mental health, converting the judges into executors of family psychological treatments (Walters and Friedlander, 2016) and creating new ways to award the custody of the children (Austin, Bow, Knoll, and Ellens, 2016; Baker, Asayan, and LaCheen-Baker, 2016).

Of the many problems set out by the example of a false theory such as the PAS, in this book we are going to focus on ethical dilemmas, specifically on the one posed between defending a son or daughter and obeying justice, when a judge determines that a parent, normally the mother, should hand over the child to the other parent, knowing that the child is being abused, but that justice has not been able to determine so. The PAS theory asserts that the mothers who refuse to comply with the court orders—that the fathers may have contact with their children—should be obliged to obey, and upon refusing, they should firstly be economically penalized and then separated from their children, and even jailed. And according to the PAS theories, a "normal" mother in that situation would obey the justice system and comply with the court orders. According to the justice system, despite the mothers initially being in an AS, as the pressure increases from the judicial bodies, they will break off from the LESD state, and will disobey.

This research examines how women who are separated from their children present the same behavior that any mother would show by simply defending her children (Bantekas, 2016; Clemente, 2013; Clemente and Padilla-Racero, 2015a, 2015b, 2016; Clemente, Padilla-Racero, Gandoy-Crego, Reig-Botella, and Gonzalez-Rodriguez, 2015; Erard, 2016; O'Donohue, Benuto, and Bennett, 2016; Padilla-Racero, 2013, 2015, 2016; Saunders and Oglesby, 2016; Shaw, 2016). In these cases, the paradigm of obedience to authority (OTA) of Milgram (1963, 1965a, 1965b, 1974) will not work, leaning on the results and the variant that Milgram did not publish, what is called the relationship condition, that was later published by Rochat and Modigliani (1997), and included the rhetoric question that Gilbert posed (1981), collected afterward by Dolinski and Grzyb (2016). The mothers mainly chose to protect their children, disobeying the justice system. Therefore, mothers do not usually experience what Bandura (1990, 1999) calls moral disengagement. We believe that these results should make the justice system reflect.

Chapter 6

Are Children Manipulable?

TRUE OR FALSE?

We have already discussed that Richard Gardner's theory of the PAS has exerted the most notable influence over the last few years on society as a whole and in particular on the Justice system, to establish the belief that women are manipulators (primarily of their children) and therefore, that children are manipulable beings, capable of lying as a result of having been brainwashed by their mothers.

Gardner (1985) was a professor of clinical psychology in the Division of Child Psychiatry, Columbia University, and began to use the term PAS in his article "Recent Trends in Divorce and Custody Litigation." He died in 2003 and is the main theoretical referent of the legal and psychological approach that is built around the PAS. Neither Gardner himself or those who support his theories have been able to scientifically demonstrate the existence of the mentioned syndrome, and none of his followers have become noted experts on the field.

Gardner used the term PAS to define the symptoms of rejection and denigration of children toward one of their parents after they have separated or divorced. In parallel, two American psychologists, Blush and Ross (2005), were using the term Sexual Allegations in Divorce (SAID) to describe false accusations of abuse during a family crisis (also see Blush and Ross 2005, as well as Ross and Blush 1990).

When Gardner defined the PAS, he drew on the notions of "brainwashing" and "programming" (Gardner, 1998), which started to be used as synonyms, further damaging the scientific entity of the PAS. According to Gardner, the PAS entails that the alienating parent programs the child, while the term "brainwashing" only refers to the changes of consciousness experienced by the child, without any specific explanation as to the nature of such changes.

These differences become particularly relevant when it comes to treatment: While an individual victim of a sect can leave the group if they have the will to do so, the treatment of child victims of PAS is more difficult, as they live with the alienating parent.

The term "campaign of denigration" (Gardner, 1998, 1999) implies the assumption that children generally lie. This is indeed one of the main problems of this supposed syndrome and originates in the notion that children do not tell the truth because they are being manipulated. Thus, if a child expresses an unwillingness to see their father, this can be explained because they are being manipulated by the mother, and she would be accused of being a manipulative mother. Nonetheless, the hypothesis of the child being maltreated or sexually abused by the father is not even considered, and therefore not investigated. In other words, the testimony of children who are being maltreated by their father is invalid because it is not given credibility.

On the basis of the premise that children usually do not make false statements, and that mothers would defend their children from a possible maltreatment, Clemente (2013a) explains that the PAS approach is based on psychoanalysis, an unscientific theory that attempts to explain human behavior, created by another psychiatrist, Freud, which is built around the idea that reality is determined by the criteria of the psychoanalyst and not from external criteria of truth.

Therefore, the key element to determine the existence of the syndrome is the child's statement, which, unfortunately, seems to be irrelevant, because the evaluator can all to easily claim that the child manifests the syndrome, on the grounds that they are lying, because they are being manipulated. But do children lie? Or, by the same reason, can children be easily manipulated? This is what we will try to determine. Let us briefly reflect on the concept of truth and falsehood.

We often think that there is a clear-cut distinction between what is real and what is imaginary, between the "truth" (what is real) and the "lie" (what is imaginary, the unreal). Conventionally, lying implies an intentional act to say something that one knows not to be true. In psychology, the term designates a different concept, that of the relativity of truth, which is in fact closer to the concept of imagined memory, a matter of great interest for us, and that Gardner (2004) also explored. The issue is present in the studies initiated by Loftus (see, for example, Garry, Manning, Loftus, and Sherman, 1996) or Diges (1997). Loftus asserts that 25 percent of the population is susceptible of creating imagined memories from external influences. She and her team conducted the following experiment: A group of persons were induced to believe that, when they were children, they had a wonderful day in Disney World, where Bugs Bunny had hugged them. They remembered the contact with the skin of the character, and even remembered how much fun they had

had petting his huge ears. More than a third of the children who participated in the experiment remembered the moment as if they had really lived it, which was impossible, not only because it was an imagined memory, but also because Bugs Bunny is not a Disney character. Thus, the term of imagined memory was originally created in experimental psychology, after the research undertaken by Loftus, Miller, and Burns (1978).

Perhaps, as some authors suggest, what we refer to with the word "lie" does not really exist. These authors state that lying is not possible because every attempt at communication is, in such, a lie that expresses a particular way of conceiving reality. The fact that language is metaphorical and instrumental only becomes a problem if it sustains a theory tailored to the truth. Against adequationism, there is a constructionist conception of truth. The truth should lead us to its pragmatic value. And yet, the undeniable pragmatic character of the truth should not be understood as just any utility, but as an objective construction that, ultimately, is free of subjective biases.

Lying might be consubstantial to society. La Rochefoucauld (maxim 87, see Willis, Bund and Friswell, 2005) said that "man would not live long in society were they not the dupes of each other" and Kashy and DePaulo (1996) assert that rather than an odd or extraordinary phenomenon, lying is a reality of social life.

As Gergen (1992) suggests, it might be interesting to explore what we shall call the step "from the self to a personal relationship." In a few words, the self, as an agent of moral conduct, is no longer a valid concept. In an ever changing, plural society, individuals must behave in different ways according to the interactional contexts in which they are involved. The idea of a "central agency," or of a substantial entity called "self," disappears. The postmodern individual is a plural individual. The "self" no longer exists. There are only relational aspects, networks in which a person is inserted (even when this insertion is not done by the "person," but by specific aspects of that person). The next step is to state, as Gergen (1992, p. 217) does, that the "good moral reasons" of an individual are inevitably derived from the reservoir of established precepts that are accumulated in culture. When individuals declare what is good and what is bad in a specific situation, they act as local agents of broader relationships in which they participate, and those are the relationships that speak for them.

As Escudero et al. (2010, p. 7) point out: "The supposed origin of PAS emerged from the assumption that when a parent is accused or reported by the other parent (and/or by a child, depending on the verbal capacity of their evolutive development) of abuse or maltreatment (without abuse) of the child, the supposed PAS takes a stance as having the scientifically endorsed capacity to detect if a falsehood exists within these reports, as well as the real motivation. Thus, if they adhere to the PAS theory, judges may recommend a change of custody under strict measures of control between the child and the diagnosed parent,"

There is no diagnostic tool to detect the syndrome fabricated by Gardner. Indeed, given that the syndrome is based on psychoanalysis, and that deriving any plausible or demonstratable hypothesis from the theory is impossible, the creation of such tool is also unattainable.

THE PECULIARITIES OF CHILDREN'S ACCOUNTS OF EVENTS

As they grow, boys and girls explore their environment and gradually activate the cognitive ability that enables the development of expression and communication. Let us focus on two phenomena, the acquisition of symbolic thinking and the stages of development.

Symbolic Thinking

The use of symbols enables human development. Symbolic thinking allows humans to create and manage diverse mental images, symbolic representations of reality that go beyond the experience or direct contact with the environment. Without symbolic thinking it would not be possible to acquire language, and language is the faculty which allows for the development of thinking. Symbolic capacity enables the transmission of information from one person to another (which facilitates cultural and social development), as well as the possibility to know and learn concepts without the need to directly experience them.

When children are born, they do not understand their environment, the objects or ideas that surround them; they do not know how to identify emotions either. Symbolic thinking begins to develop from the first year of life on. In this moment, children begin to think by means of images and symbols, understanding and representing objects or ideas through gestures, recognizing images, and uttering their first words. In the development of symbolic function, the bonding of infants with their environment is fundamental, as imitation will be the first way of learning how to develop that capacity.

Before reaching 1 year of age, it is impossible to obtain any information from the child, any attempt to get information is unfruitful. In fact, it is rather difficult to obtain any information from children until the age of 3.

What are the periods of cognitive development? We will briefly go over them in detail, following the classification created by Piaget.

Stages of Cognitive Development

In his theory of cognitive development, Jean Piaget divided the growth of cognitive capacities in childhood into four stages: sensorimotor, preoperational, concrete operational, and formal operational. We are only going to mention the sensorimotor stage, because it entails the stage from birth until 2 years of age; that is, the child has not yet acquired symbolic capacity, or that capacity is at its very early stages of development.

In the preoperational stage, children are characterized by having an egocentric vision of the world (everything revolves around them); they are still at the beginning of the development of their symbolic thinking, and they believe that all objects are alive. This is the stage of children between 2 and 6 years of age, and it is denominated preoperational because when Piaget conceptualized it, he thought that children at these ages were not capable of undertaking abstract mental operations, their thoughts being highly influenced by how they perceived immediate things. The preoperational stage presents advances with respect to the sensorimotor stage. Among the most important facts are, as one could imagine, the cognitive capacities such as using internal images, managing schemas, having language, and using symbols, which are fundamental in the development of one's own conscious. The main goal of this stage is for children to acquire a larger representative knowledge, improving on their capacity of communication and learning. They begin to use tools of persuasion to get what they want, such as toys or sweets. However, as they do not completely understand logic, they are still not capable of manipulating the information in such a way so as to ensure that their needs will be satisfied or to show the rest of the people their point of view. Information is much more attainable from children between 2 and 6 years of age if the matters we are citing are taken into consideration.

As children grow up, they undergo changes in their way of understanding and capturing ideas while becoming more able to express them better. That is, they build experiences around what is taking place around them, and a more coherent and logical thinking is progressively formed. Furthermore, they begin to be able to understand that something may represent something else—that is, they begin using symbols, transforming objects into other objects (for example, a piece of bread becomes a train), etc. And yet they still do not comprehend concrete logic, so they are still unable to manipulate the information mentally and take on someone else's point of view. This makes it impossible for them to lie; thus, when in legal contexts it is asserted that a child who is 6 years old or less is lying, this is a mistake. In the preoperational stage there are two substages: the symbolic and preconceptual substage (from 2 to 4 years of age) and the intuitive or conceptual substage (from 4 to 6 years of age). In the former, children make use of concrete images to understand the world but do not acquire abstract or generalizable ideas yet. Words have a meaning depending on the experience lived, and not depending on what they represent. They make use of preconcepts that are very close to their sensorial experience. During the latter substate (intuitive or conceptual), the mind of the child is dominated by immediate perception. Intuition plays a fundamental role in this stage, because intuition entails the interiorization of perceptions in the form of representative images that prolong the schemas seen; as a result, children intuitively dare to generalize what they already know.

Piaget attributes various characteristics to the children who are in the preoperational stage, which are briefly detailed below:

- Centration: The tendency of the child to concentrate on only one aspect of an object or situation at once. That is, children in this stage struggle to think in more than one characteristic and give heed to more than one simultaneously. The opposite situation—being able to shift their attention to a different aspect of an object or situation—is called decentration, which they progressively acquire. Furthermore, their capacity to deconcentrate varies depending on the type of situation. It is easier to change the focus of attention in nonsocial than in social situations.
- Egocentrism: Thought and communication of children in this stage are typically egocentric—that is, preoperational children assume that whatever they see, hear, or feel is what others are also seeing, hearing, or feeling.
- Play: Children between 2 and 7 years of age play, but their way of doing it is in parallel. That is, they often play, they can even do so with various children in the same room, but they do not interact, each one is absorbed in their own thoughts, and they rarely play collectively.
- Symbolic representation: Symbolic representation is the capacity to perform an action, either through words or objects, to represent something different. Whether through phonemes or graphemes, language is the peak of symbolic representation that enables humans to show their ability to represent objects, ideas, and actions.
- Symbolic play: Related to the capacity of symbolic representation, preoperational children are capable of role-playing something that they are not, such as superheroes, firemen, doctors . . . in other words, they can symbolically represent other people. They are also capable of turning objects into something else—for instance, they can take a broom and conceive it as a horse. They know what the object is objectively, but with the intention of having fun, they change it in their mind and act accordingly. This is also the age in which children can invent an imaginary friend. Thanks to symbolic play, children advance in their knowledge about how the world works, people, objects, and the actions that other

people can perform. Thus, they construct more and more sophisticated representations of the world through their experiences. As the symbolic game increases, the egocentric vision decreases.

- Animism: This is the belief that inanimate objects—namely toys, pencils, or cars—have feelings and human intentions. The natural world is alive and conscious and has a purpose.
- Artificialism: Refers to the fact that children in the preoperational stage think that certain aspects of their environment—such as clouds, stars, or animals—are made by people. It is a rather usual characteristic at these ages, resulting from the combination of children's lack of knowledge about how the world works and their natural interest in the surrounding phenomena and objects.
- Irreversibility: Refers to the fact that preoperational children are incapable of inverting the directionality of a sequence of events backward from the starting point. For instance, after having performed a series of actions with pieces of Lego or of any other type of similar toy, children would not be capable of taking the inverse steps to return to the starting point.

The third stage is that of concrete operations. This stage is developed between 7 and 11 years of age and is characterized by the development of organized and rational thinking. Piaget regarded it as an important point of inflection in the cognitive development of children, as it marks the beginning of logical or operative thinking. Children are now mature enough to use logical or operational thinking (i.e., the rules), but they can only apply logic to physical objects (i.e., it is a concrete operational stage). They acquire the ability of conservation (number, area, volume, orientation) and reversibility. However, although they may solve problems in a logical manner, they are usually not capable of thinking in an abstract or hypothetical way. Their account of events may be perfectly determined, and they begin to have the capacity to lie at will; accordingly, we should use, if necessary, techniques to detect the veracity of their testimony, as we will later see.

The stage of formal operations is the last one. Children are becoming adolescents and present a better capacity of abstraction, a more scientific thinking, and more ability to solve hypothetical problems.

Formal operational thinking is manifested from 12 years of age on until adulthood, and it is characterized by the fact that preadolescent children have a more abstract vision of the world and a more logical thinking. They can entertain theoretical concepts.

Throughout this stage, individuals use the hypothetical-deductive thinking that is characteristic of the scientific method.

Children are now not dependent on physical and real objects to reach conclusions, they can conceive hypothetical situations and imagine several types of situations without the need to have a graphic or palpable representation of them. Thus, adolescents may reason about more complex problems.

These are the fundamental characteristics of this stage:

- Hypothetical-deductive reasoning: Preadolescents can think in solutions to problems by drawing on abstract and hypothetical ideas. Through these hypothetical approaches, they may arrive to several conclusions without relying on physical objects or visual support. At these ages, they have the capacity to think scientifically, generating hypothesis and predictions, and trying to find answers to complex questions.
- Problem solving: At these ages, more scientific and reflective thought is acquired. The individual has a larger capacity to tackle problems in a more systematic and organized way, no longer limiting the strategy to trial and error. They can now plan hypothetical situations in their mind in which they question how things may evolve. Although the technique of trial and error may be helpful in getting benefits and conclusions, being able to have other strategies of problem resolution expands knowledge and experience greatly for young individuals. The problems are resolved with less practical methods, using logic that the individual previously did not count on.
- Abstract thought: Young individuals may think in hypothetical and abstract concepts without having to have previously experienced them.

LITIGATIONS BETWEEN PARENTS

It seems obvious that once a couple relationship is over, litigation between parents leaves them confronting each other for years on matters related to their children. The individual explanations of the parents coincide with what is sociably desirable: Each parent fights for what is good for their children. Unfortunately, reality dictates that there are parents who, far from being mostly concerned about their children first, take advantage of the justice system to attack the other parent. This is often done to the point of instigating the interruption of the child's home by the police to take away the custody, even when the child has expressed that the then noncustodial parent abuses them. Does a parent who loves their children and wishes the best for them use a system of justice for that? How is it possible that there are noncustodial parents who do not claim contact with their children, but then sanction or condemn the other parent? There are too many facts that demonstrate that some parents use the system to harass the other parent instead of using it to defend their children. There are too many cases, all of them supported by the concept that was previously known as the PAS and is now referred to as parental alienation. There are even programs designed to, after taking away the children from their parents, "re-educate" the children, separating them from the influence of the perverse mother and denying contact with both parents (Reay, 2015).

In an effort to defend the previous concept created by Gardner, some authors have published certain studies in which information is collected *a posteriori*, interviewing adults who come from families in which the parents could no longer live together (Baker and Verrocchio, 2015; Bernet, Baker, and Verrocchio, 2015; Verrocchio, Marchetti, and Fulcheri, 2015); their conclusions seem to show that all parents are manipulators and that children who were raised in broken families have all suffered parental alienation. It seems difficult to believe that they are right, especially given the fact that their data comes from self-reports of adults who lived in rather different periods of time. These authors also criticize those who do not support Gardner's views, to the extent that, in some of their articles, they suggest that research that does not confirm the idea that all mothers are manipulative should be banned. (see Bernet, Verrocchio, and Korosi's study [2015], which grossly criticizes Clemente and Padilla-Racero [2015a]; see also Clemente and Padilla-Racero's [2015b] reply to the article). And yet, almost all the assertions derived from the old PAS arguments are falsehoods, as Warshak (2015a, 2015b) demonstrates in his "Ten Parental Alienation Fallacies That Compromise Decisions in Court and in Therapy."

AN EMPIRICAL WAY TO VERIFY IF CHILDREN LIE OR NOT

This research team designed an experiment to verify whether children may lie as a result of being influenced by adults. The study was divided into two phases. In the first phase, the manipulation consists in that half of the children participants witness a verbal aggression (an accomplice of the researcher verbally attacks and humiliates another accomplice, when supposedly both are teachers who are preparing a theatrical activity with the children); in the other half of the classes (one class for each age, which meant working with every school level from 8 to 11 years of age) no type of supposed aggression took place between the accomplices. Therefore, there was a manipulation of a variable that is scientifically independent (the existence or not of a verbal aggression) and a variable that is scientifically dependent—which consisted in gathering the information from the children about whether anything problematic took place; children could supposedly tell the truth—that is, say that there was an argument between the teachers—or tell a lie—that is, if there had been an argument, not to say anything, or if there had been no argument, to invent that there had been one. The second phase consisted in simultaneously manipulating two independent variables: The first one is the pressure the children feel about the possible repercussions from reporting on what they saw—some are informed that the person who provoked the aggression will shortly be their main teacher (high pressure), others are not told anything concerning the matter (low pressure). The second variable concerns the image of the aggressor: Some subjects were told that that was a very good person (positive image), and the other half were told that that was a very bad person (negative image). That is, every fourth part of the total of participants received a combination of different information. After collecting the information, they were asked to disregard what they had said before, and then reflect and report whether they had seen a problematic situation. We then gathered the information concerning if they "lied" or if they "told the truth" once again.

Therefore, three variables were manipulated over the two phases: having witnessed an aggression or not, having received some information that connoted pressure that could have led the participants to change their mind, and receiving information that conveyed a positive or negative image of the person who had supposedly committed the aggression.

Lastly, the same design was applied dividing the participants according to the variables of sex and age.

The experience lasted a total of three sessions on three different days. During the first day, research assistants (that we called accomplices) went in pairs to two classrooms in each year of primary education (therefore, there was a group A and a group B for each school level), from the 8-year-old children to the 11-year-old children (12 classes in total). In the groups B of every grade, the two research assistants—accomplices of the researchers— interpreted a situation in which a verbal aggression took place between them, with the objective of letting the children perceive the existence of a conflict between the supposed teachers; one of them humiliated and looked down upon the other, in front of the children. However, in the groups A no situation of aggression took place. In order to justify that session, children were told that that group was to make a theatrical performance combined with games and activities.

The following day, two different accomplices returned to each classroom to interview the children individually and ask them if they had witnessed anything problematic. They recorded whether the children lied or told the truth. Thus, during that second day, the accomplices merely asked the children of both groups A and B in every year if they had seen anything strange during the class of the previous day. With regard to the children in groups A, they were asked if they had seen anything strange the day before, if they had observed any conflict between the two persons that had given them class, with the objective of detecting if, under the pressure of the question and of not having seen anything, they would make up their answer. However, children in groups B were asked if they had seen anything, to see if they would hide the fact that they had witnessed a conflict, or, on the contrary, if they would tell the truth.

The third and last day, the individual interviews were repeated, going back and asking the same question, but this time, the information that each child was offered was manipulated in the following way:

- Some of them (a fourth part) were told that one of the individuals who had carried out the activity (the one who manifested aggressiveness to half of the groups) was going to be their next main teacher (high level of pressure), and that he or she was a very good person (positive image).
- To others (a fourth part) no information was given concerning if that person in the future would have anything to do with them academically (low pressure) and that that person was a good person (positive image).
- Others (a fourth part) were told that that person was to be their main teacher (high pressure) and that he or she was not a good person (negative image).
- And lastly, to others (a fourth part) nothing was mentioned regarding whether that person would have something to do with them academically (low pressure) and they were told that that person was a bad person (negative image).

After having informed the children according to the manipulation of the two cited variables (pressure and image), they were asked to report, again, what they had witnessed, and the team recorded if they told a lie or the truth. Therefore, the information was gathered of what the subjects had supposedly seen on the two occasions.

Once the experiment was over, the teachers of every class were in charge of telling the children that it had all been a game, and that the verbal aggression was performed to observe how they would react.

Let us now analyze the results of the study. In phase 1, half of the children witnessed a verbal aggression, and the other half did not witness any aggression. The former told the truth in practically all cases. Therefore, out of the 154 participants who had witnessed that situation, all but eight (almost 95 percent) reported exactly what they saw—it can be stated that they told "the truth." However, when the aggression did not take place, over 40 percent of the participants reported that something strange had taken place, reporting that, in effect, they had realized that an incident had taken place when in fact it had not. Even though almost 60 percent of the children reported correctly, just implanting a memory of a problematic event, sparked the creation of that event in their minds. Overall, if one takes the manipulations out of the equation, three quarters of the children told the truth.

To what concerns Phase 2, after witnessing the aggression in Phase 1, when participants were subdued to high pressure there were barely any differences between those who told the truth and those who lied. The same conclusion was verified when the subjects were given the information about the person who committed the aggression as being a good or a bad person. Although most participants told the truth, those who supposedly lied were mostly the ones who received high pressure in this phase two (who were also told that the aggressor was a good person), followed by those who received a low level of pressure and were told that the aggressor was a bad person.

Regardless of the circumstances, children tend to tell the truth in most cases (94.8 percent of those who witnessed an aggression said so), even if they had been pressured by a "threat" that the aggressor would be their main teacher, or if they were told that that was a good or bad person.

In the case that participants had not witnessed an aggression in Phase 1 but invented that a problematic incident had happened (40 percent of the total within the subsample), they attributed the information that they had been given (pressure level and the negative or positive image of the aggressor) to a person who, in fact, had not carried out any problematic action. Thus, the results demonstrate that the percentages of telling the truth or lying do not rely on being subdued to high or low pressure. If we examine the possible difference according to the information received that the aggressor is a good or bad person, the percentages do not change much either; and yet, there is a small tendency that the subjects who receive the information that the aggressor is a bad person and suffer high pressure are the ones that tell the truth, that is, they assert that they had not witnessed any type of aggression. Most of those who lied were the ones that were subdued to low pressure and were given the information that the aggressor was a bad person. It can be said that the manipulation of the two independent variables did not imply a change in the children's statements.

However, the fact that those who scored higher in telling the truth did so despite having been told that the aggressor was a bad person, and despite the fact that they were under high pressure, demonstrates that children tend to tell the truth.

It is also worth noting that 58.45 percent of the children told the truth—that is, they did not report the existence of the aggression. Consequently, almost 40 percent of them invented an aggression, which confirms what had been determined in phase 1 of the experiment.

Upon analyzing the results according to the gender variable, no differences were found. Thus, 96.4 percent of male and 93 percent of female participants who had witnessed an aggression told the truth—that is, once again, practically all of them. Out of those who had not witnessed an aggression, 58.2 percent of males and 58.7 percent of females asserted that, in effect, no incident had taken place, that is, they told the truth. There is a greater degree of variation in results to what concerns the age variant; while practically all participants who had witnessed an aggression reported truthfully (even those of 8 and 9 years of age told the truth), out of those who did not witness an aggression, those who were more truthful were 7 years of age (91.7 percent of the truthful results), but only 24 percent of those were 10 years old or 45 percent were 6 years old. Despite that disparity, there is no tendency to tell the truth to a larger or lesser extent, according to age. The same as the sex variant, there were no significant differences between the different ages according to the type of information (positive or negative) given about the actor, nor according to the level of pressure (high or low) exercised.

CONCLUSIONS

Probably, if only for the purpose of adhering to the ontological simplicity of Ockham's razor principle, we should first accept any much simpler explanation than those established by Gardner.

As explained in a recent article (Clemente, 2013a), the PAS is an attack on science, on the rule of law, and on children and their parents. In fact, the justice system should not make use of an unscientific theory—which, in this particular case, goes against the best interest of the children.

This chapter seeks to verify whether children tend to fabricate their accounts of reality, and in that case, if two specific variables could be the explicative key for that: the first variable entailed that children were under pressure because they would be subjected to an asymmetric relationship of power in respect to the aggressor; the second variable was that children were told if the aggressor is a good or a bad person—which we have called "image."

The results clearly show that the children who witness an aggression (in this case, a verbal aggression) tell the truth—since only 5 percent of them do not say anything about what they had seen. That is, children who witness an aggression report that aggression without a problem. However, when children do not witness any type of aggression, in 40 percent of the cases they report that a problematic event took place, which means that, upon the request of the interviewer for them to report if anything problematic had happened, children may perceive that a problematic event did in fact take place. These results are consistent with our hypothesis that children who witness an aggression have no problems reporting it, and that implanting a memory of an aggression in their minds sparks the creation of that event.

On the other hand, it is worth noting that telling the truth or not barely relies on the degree of pressure exercised on the child, or on the fact that a positive or negative image of the aggressor is instilled on the child. These results, coming from phase 2 of the research, contradict our hypothesis, as it was expected that the participants would use the information to defend themselves from situations of asymmetric power, or that they would be influenced by the previous information that they had been offered.

Therefore, the ideas set out by Gardner are not supported by our data. It is rather odd for a child to lie about what they have seen, and what does in fact happen is that they create an account of something that they have not seen. But it is necessary to take into consideration that if a memory is implanted (false memory) by suggesting in a question that a problematic event happened, that event barely varies with the degree of pressure exercised, or when a positive or negative piece of information about the cause of the negative incident is given. In fact, although this is statistically not significant, the opposite seems to happen: If the level of pressure toward the child is bigger, the child has a higher tendency to tell the truth (it is difficult to manipulate a child) and if one tries to impose a negative image of this person, it does not entice the child to change his or her mind, but just the opposite, once again. Were these ideas applied to court cases, they would lead to the following situation: If a mother tried to instill a negative image of the father on the child and pressured the child (because they live together and there is an asymmetric relation of power), the child would not for those reasons change their mind. This means that a concocted account is independent of these two variables that were chosen by virtue of their origins in the ideas expressed by Gardner (1985, 1991, 1998).

Thus, the false memory hypothesized by Gardner (2004) is not manifested, nor does it aggravate, on account on the two referred manipulations. As Loftus, Miller, and Burns (1978) demonstrated, it is true that children (as well as adults) believe false memories under the suggestion of the interviewers. But, that implantation of a false memory does not aggravate, nor does it depend on an external manipulator—that Gardner identified normally as the custodial parent. Nevertheless, we consider that the most relevant information of the study is the verification that children tell the truth on observing an aggression in almost all the occasions (95 percent); therefore, there is no justification to claim that children lie.

This study has some limitations; perhaps the most notable is that participants were children who were not involved in judicial conflicts. The reason was that obtaining a large enough sample so as to be able to obtain statistically correct results was otherwise difficult, but other studies should indeed explore these issues with children in judicial conflicts. On the other hand, it must be considered that, due to the age of the children (in older ages, the weight of the child's statement is legally more determinant, and therefore we were not interested in taking them into account in the sample), it is difficult and even on some occasions impossible to use a wide collection of psychological trials; therefore, we limited ourselves to gathering their responses in a survey, without detecting other variables of personality that could be mediators of reporting what happened. And lastly, it is important to consider that an aggressive situation is created, but for ethical motives it is only verbal; several of the children subjected to a judicial process have witnessed major situations of violence, physical as well as verbal, but in an experiment, it is impossible to create such a scene. Undoubtedly future research should try and avoid these limitations.

We consider that this study verifies that one of the starting points of Gardner's theory—the fact that children are manipulable by a custodial parent—is not verifiable through experimentation, and that therefore Gardner's arguments should not be used upon considering the testimony of a child. Our data show that the most adequate and sensible assumption is that children tell the truth.

Chapter 7

Techniques for Evaluating the Veracity of a Testimony

In chapter 6, we established that children do not tend to lie. And yet, there are several specific techniques in psychology that are intended to verify such a fact. Let us focus on three of them—the most reliable most and used, especially the first: The SVA-CBCA system of analysis of verbal contents, reality monitoring, and cognitive interview.

Other systems refer to the responses of the subject that are due to psychophysiological indicators which cannot be consciously manipulated *a priori* by them. The polygraph, which is the most well-known, has been dismissed as a probationary technique in many countries due to a high margin of error of over 20 percent; recorded evoked potentials; the measurement of reaction time (RT) to problematic stimulus; the analysis of functional magnetic resonance imaging (FMRI), and the analysis of certain brain waves.

There are approaches which are also based on the notion that humans cannot control their autonomous nervous system, but with a focus on nonverbal correlates (blinking, eye contact, eye avoidance, head movements, self-manipulations . . .) and paraverbal (message duration, number of words, speech rate, tone of voice, latency of response . . .), on the grounds that they make it possible to differentiate the truthful story from the story that was made up with the purpose of deceiving. The analysis of facial expressions—and more specifically of micro expressions—also falls into the same category. Likewise, the voice stress analysis has been analyzed.

Certain instruments which entail unethical—and yet ineffective—procedures such as drug-assisted interviews (usually through the use of barbiturates), have also been used to evaluate the truthfulness of a statement.

Let us focus primarily on the analysis of the verbal content of the testimony of either the witness or victim, bearing in mind that we are not trying to ascertain if they are lying or not, but the difference between false and true messages.

There are three major models to analyze statements: The CBCA or Criteria-Based Content Analysis, by Steller and Koehnken (1989), is a tool to assess the credibility of the statements of victims of child sexual abuse; it is based on Anne Trankel's proposals and on what has been called the Undeutsch hypothesis; Reality Monitoring (RM), by Johnson and Raye (1981), differentiates whether memories are of internal or external origin; the cognitive interview is based on the Encoding specificity principle (Tulving and Thomson, 1973), which states that operations to retrieve information from memory will be more effective if the retrieval is done under conditions similar to those of the time the information was encoded, since each memory to be retrieved is associated with both external and internal stimuli that become key elements for its recovery. We will analyze these systems, but especially the first one, which is now consolidated as the most reliable technique to detect the truthfulness of the statements.

THE CRITERIA BASED CONTENT ANALYSIS (CBCA)

The CBCA became the central element of the Statement Validity Assessment (SVA), a protocol which was developed in the context of forensic psychology to estimate the truthfulness of the statements of children who allege to have been sexually abused.

The SVA comprises a semistructured interview, the analysis of the content (based on criteria applied to the transcript of the interview), and a validity test that assesses several circumstances (the linguistic and intellectual competence of the child, if the interview was conducted properly or not, whether the child has reason to make a false statement, and the existence of unquestionable and external evidence).

The Criteria-Based Content Analysis verifies the presence or absence of nineteen criteria, which are grouped into five categories. The more criteria that are fulfilled in the account of events, the higher the likelihood for these events to be true. A global assessment determines whether the story is credible, not credible, or indefinite. The Raskin and Esplin version is the most used (1991a, 1991b), followed by Steller and Koehnken's assessment criteria.

Are children easily influenced? Or, in other words, is it easy to convince them to lie? Research shows that the less the child remembers an event, the more specific the questions are, and the less the child's emotional involvement with the facts is, the more power suggestibility has. In situations of sexual abuse, suggestion may also affect the child, but not in the account of whether such events have occurred, but in how the facts are interpreted. The risks of suggestion exist only in preschool children, in which distorting effects as a result of biased questions are often found. There is evidence that older children show great resistance to suggestive questions, maintaining the main aspects of the facts when they referred to events in which they were involved.

Ceci and Bruck (1993) suggest four circumstances in which children may be more or less sensitive to suggestion:

- They are more prone to suggestion if the episode involves little stress, if the child is a mere observer of the action, if the questions are about minor details, or when they make reference to facts unrelated to the event.
- They are less prone to suggestion when the episode they are testifying about is quite stressful, if they have participated in the event, if they are questioned about key details, or when the questions specifically mention what happened.

How should children be interviewed? Obviously, the interview must be conducted by a suitable professional, who will consider the following characteristics:

- Avoid suggestive questions. Children should be allowed to narrate things as they come to their mind; interviewers may go on a topic only after children come up with it but should never bring about a topic of conversation related to abuses if the child does not mention it first.
- Overall adaptation of the interview: It must be created in an environment of psychological safety, whereby the child can trust the interviewer and conceive the interview as a game, enabling them to feel confident enough to relate the experience they have been through.
- Ascertain whether there are motivations for the child to give a false statement. In the case of children, the main, most common motivation to give false statement is fear. If they have been abused by their father, he often tells them that if they tell anyone about what happened, he will kill them, their mother, or someone else they love (usually the maternal grandparents). On other occasions, the motivation to give false statement is positive, since the parent might promise to give them fantastic presents if they do not talk. Although both motivations may be present, the former usually predominates—in which case, the child will be stuck; they will not be willing to talk, and they will show a dissociated behavior, as we will later discuss.
- Reasons to give statement. This aspect refers to whether it is the child who has an interest in giving statement or if they do so as a favor to one of their parents. For example, children may claim to be weary of seeing their father beating their mother (and sometimes them) and therefore want to declare, or that they want to give statement because their father is a good person, and they wish to defend him. The point is to determine

whether there is pressure on the child to file a complaint. It is of great importance to have a clear idea of what is called the context of revelation, which refers to the decisive element that made the child decide to tell what happened (it may be, for example, because they saw their father hitting their mother, or trying to choke her, or because he might have hurt her in a possible penetration, etc. In addition, if children reveal the information to someone in their everyday environment (the grandparents, for instance, or the teachers), the validity of such information is reinforced.

The proximity of the event in time is also a key element. In most cases, statements are much more credible when little time has passed between the event and the recovery of the memory. In children, the non-recall effect makes their statement much less credible.

With regard to lies, it is known that adults tend to lie more often than children, and that they are generally less reliable. Adults have more resources to disguise reality and adapt it to their needs and interests. Besides, it may sometimes seem that children's statements are contradictory because they use language differently, with a tendency to be rather literal. Children use language literally, in an idiosyncratic, more restrictive way than that of adults. They are more likely to deny traumatic experiences—or those they perceived as negative—than to make false statements about them. At around the time they reach the age of 3 or 4, children begin to differentiate truth from lies; they become aware of whether they are telling the truth, that lying is not right, and that they cannot maintain the lie for long.

The Statement Validity Analysis (SVA) is a tool that analyzes the validity of the testimony of abused children and assesses credibility.

The tool comprises three elements:

- A noninductive, nonsuggestive semistructured interview.
- An analysis of the child's narration on CBCA content criteria.
- An assessment of the validity criteria, external to the statement.

The goal of the interview is to obtain as much information as possible, without skewing the child's answers. Possible clarifying questions are asked at the end of the interview. Interviewer must have a clear idea of the three aspects to explore throughout the interview:

- The main hypothesis (the determination that the testimony is valid) and the alternatives (for instance, if there are alterations in the testimony, maybe for revenge, or the testimony is valid, but some fictitious elements have been added).

- To contrast what the children say with the additional information they have about the event.
- To assess if the information gathered is sufficiently detailed and whether or not there are contradictory statements.

Let us now analyze each of the 19 CBCA criteria, which are grouped according to the following classification:
Category 1: General characteristics.

- Criterion 1. Logical Structure: Determine whether the child's statement is logically consistent and homogeneous. It is necessary to verify whether contextual details can be combined as a whole, without discrepancies or inconsistencies, taking as a reference what is appropriate for the age of the child. It must also be checked that the details can be integrated with an organized and integrated coherence in which the contents of the statement are also consistent. Indeed, the age of the child must be considered when examining the consistency of the statement.
- Criterion 2. Unstructured Elaboration: Determine that there is no linearity in the narration. In a spontaneous statement, times overlap within the narration of events; when narrating the same events more than once, the order in which the child gives account of details varies—that is, it can be clearly perceived that there has been no preparation to give a completely coherent account of events.
- Criterion 3. Number of details: A statement containing several details is an indication of credibility because it is impossible for most witnesses to "furnish" a false statement with numerous details.

Category 2: Specific contents. At this stage of the statement analysis, specific parts of the statement are evaluated concerning the presence and the relevance of certain types of descriptions. Including these nuanced details when the statement is false would be beyond the cognitive ability of everyone.

- Criterion 4. Contextual Embedding: The narration of real events must have a temporal and a spatial context. The child should easily identify the reason for the possible aggressions and the moment when they occurred; contextual embedding provides credibility to the statement.
- Criterion 5. Description of Interactions: This requirement is more likely to be met when the account includes the vocabulary and language of those involved in the facts investigated, which are generally atypical for the age of the witness. The telling of the events should create the impression that, when giving the statement, the witness re-experiences the verbal context of the situation.

- Criterion 6. Reproduction of Conversation: A statement is considered to be more credible if the child "adlibs" as if they were that person, that is, the child does not talk about what they said or did, but interprets, impersonating the adults.
- Criterion 7. Unexpected Complications during the Incident. The scope of these complications may include either an unexpected interruption or some difficulty that interrupts the logical termination of the event. Sometimes this is manifested in the dates that the child mentions, in calculating the time as to when the aggressions began, in the calculations on their own ages, and, in general, in details that are related to time. Recognition of these difficulties adds validity to the credibility of the story.

Category 3: Peculiarities of the content. The analysis in this category focuses on specific details that can be found throughout the statement and increase the quality of its content. The rationale is based on the assumption—mentioned in the previous category—that someone who has made up a statement would not be able to include these details in the account, as this would be beyond their cognitive abilities.

- Criterion 8. Unusual Details: With regard to this criterion, it should be emphasized that a statement can be concrete and vivid by the account of unusual or unique details, including the appearance of unusual details that are not clearly realistic. Unusual details have a low probability of occurrence and are rather unlikely to appear on invented statements.
- Criterion 9. Peripheral Details: The inclusion of peripheral details enhances the credibility of the statement, as a false statement would never anticipate incorporating them.
- Criterion 10. Accurately Reported Details not Understood: This criterion is met when the child relates actions or provides details that they do not understand, but that can be understood by the interviewer. For example, the child does not understand why his or her father behaves as he does, but perfectly describes the scenes and everything that happened, and evaluates those scenes.
- Criterion 11. Related External Associations: A related external association occurs when the witness relates conversations that refer to other external events, so that each of the accounts given overlaps in at least two relationships. It is rather uncommon to find these associations in children's accounts of events.
- Criterion 12. Accounts of Subjective Mental State: This criterion refers to the child's description of feelings—such as fear or disgust—and cognitive states—such as thinking about escaping while the event occurred.

In other words, the child's account about the evaluation of emotions and their changes during the course of events gives credibility to the statement.

- Criterion 13. Attribution of Perpetrator's Mental State: The attribution of the mental state of the perpetrator or perpetrators is analyzed—hat is, the rationale is similar to that of the previous criterion but concerning the perpetrator of the possible aggressions. The mental states and motives that the narrator attributes to the alleged authors are signs of the credibility of a story, as well as the descriptions of affective reactions and physiological states of the authors of part of a criterion of reality.

Category 4: Contents Related to Motivation. This set of criteria refers to the child's motivation to make a statement—which provides an opportunity to assess the child's possible motivation to give false testimony, on the grounds that if someone deliberately offered false testimony, they would not include this content, because they would take away from their credibility.

- Criterion 14. Spontaneous Corrections: This criterion refers to instances when children spontaneously correct themselves during an interview, or they offer either new or clarifying details. These types of corrections enhance credibility, or at least allow to differentiate between a completely false account or one influenced by a third person; children are not afraid—and should not be—of correcting themselves and of going back and forth in time in their account of events . . . ; in other words, it is perfectly logical and coherent, to assume that they are not thinking of their own credibility, nor that it could be effected by adding or changing any element of their account.
- Criterion 15. Admitting Lack of Memory: This criterion stems from the notion that people who deliberately give false statements will always try to provide an answer to all questions rather than admitting a lack of memory of certain details. When children admit having forgotten certain parts of the events, this enhances credibility.
- Criterion 16. Raising Doubts about One's Own Testimony: This criterion is fulfilled when children raise doubts about the accuracy of their own testimony, because those who provide a false statement would normally not express reservations about it.
- Criterion 17. Self-Deprecation: This criterion implies that children incriminate themselves as a result of a self-critical attitude toward their own conduct in the events. This confession of inappropriate or erroneous conduct is not commonly present in a misleading statement that seeks to falsely incriminate someone.

- Criterion 18. Forgiving the Perpetrator: This criterion implies that credibility is enhanced if a statement tends to favor the defendant, or if the child witness does not make use of any possibility they may have to further incriminate the defendant.

Category 5: Specific Elements of the Offense. This category is intended to analyze the elements of the account that are not related to the general experience of what was spoken of in the statement, but are indeed related with the facts.

- Criterion 19. Details Characteristic of the Offense. This criterion is based on empirical criminological findings about what normally takes place, or the characteristics of possible crimes. More specifically, the truth can be recognized when the description of the facts deviates from popular false beliefs and is closer to what allegedly happened.

Once the nineteen CBCA are defined, the next step is the verification of the four validity criteria that were discussed above: psychological characteristics, interview characteristics, motivation to make false statements, and research-related aspects.

REALITY MONITORING

Johnson and Raye (1981) suggested that there might be qualitative differences between real and imagined memories; after analyzing how different memories originate, they established a differentiation between memories of internal or external origin. Memories of external origin are real and are generated by perceptual processes, whereas memories of internal origin are imagined and are the result of imagination or thought. This paradigm is built around the assumption that there is more sensory and contextual information in the events actually perceived than in those that are the product of imagination—which is guided mainly by cognitive information.

Johnson and Raye argue that memories may be comprised of four different attributes or types of information: contextual information (relating to space and time), sensory information (forms, colors, etc.), semantic information, and cognitive operations. They suggest that external memories (that is, those that are given rise by perceived or experienced events) will contain more contextual, sensitive, and semantic details than internally generated memories (imagined events). The latter, on the other hand, will contain more references to cognitive processes.

Based on perceptual processes, experience-based memories should contain more sensory, contextual, and affective information than non-experience-based memories. In contrast to CBCA, the RM approach not only contains truth criteria but also lie critera: Memories not based on experience must contain more indicators of cognitive operations such as thoughts and reasoning (Vrij, Mann, Kristen, and Fisher, 2007).

This rationale gave rise to the Judgment Memory Characteristics Questionnaire (JMCQ), a tool that comprises the following criteria:

- Clarity (distinctness, vividness rather than vagueness)
- Sensory information (such as sounds, tastes, or visual details)
- Spatial Information (places, locations)
- Temporary information (location of event over time, description of sequences of events)
- Affection (expression of emotions and sensory feelings during the event)
- Reconstruction of the account (plausibility of the reconstruction of the event after having been given information)
- Realism (plausibility, realism, and the general sense of the story)
- Cognitive Operations (descriptions of inferences made by others during the event)

THE COGNITIVE INTERVIEW

Verification of the reliability of a witness account according to the criteria of the cognitive interview is conducted through a process that involves four steps, which are the following:

- Mental Reinstatement (or restoration) of the Context. The individual is asked to try to reinstate, or re-create, as completely as possible, the context surrounding the event, including the internal emotional state.
- In-depth Reporting. Witnesses are encouraged to report everything they can remember, regardless of the level of subjective confidence they associate with the information.
- Recalling the Events in Several Orders. Witnesses are asked to recall the events in more than one sequential order, for example, backward, from the end to the beginning, or starting from the middle, etc.
- Reporting the Events from Different Perspectives. Witnesses are asked to report the events as if they were recalling them from someone else's perspective.

SOME CONCLUSIONS ON THE TECHNIQUES OF
EVALUATING THE VERACITY OF A TESTIMONY

Let us now summarize what we consider to be some of the key aspects to consider regarding the techniques to assess the credibility of testimony:

- Determining the credibility of a testimony is not the same as knowing whether an event has occurred or not. This is because people often deceive themselves and convince themselves to believe whatever they wish to believe, regardless of whether this is the truth or not. Thus, children may express that one of their parents treats them rather badly, even though any external observer might think the opposite. It is even more uncommon for anyone to falsely claim that they are being maltreated, especially if that implies physical or sexual abuse. Let us remember that, in general, our account of events differs from reality and are constructs that we shape from our experiences and perceptions. In psychology there is a distinction between feelings (what we perceive through our senses) and perceptions (what we believe is happening in reality). In addition, if a fact is stored in someone's memory, its retrieval will also imply following certain rules, which also alters the account of events.
- Furthermore, it must be considered that when we label a fact, we do so according to what we consider to be "normal." Thus, for instance, several married women would not consider it rape if their husband forces them to have sex, precisely because they are married. Similarly, physically punishing children is not considered maltreatment if those who do it are their parents or relatives. If we asked those who suffer the actions we are describing if they are suffering an aggression, they would say that they were not, even if any external observer might think otherwise.
- Today, despite those techniques having progressed, there is no procedure that allows us to determine with absolute precision whether a witness account is reliable or not. This chapter describes the most reliable techniques available today, but every technique shows a margin of error. In addition, the SVA-CBCA system only allows for the evaluation of reliability of statements about child sexual assault (not about other topics).
- As we have already mentioned, children generally tell the truth, whereas adults tend to lie much more often. It is a serious mistake to use diagnostic tools to detect deception or lying; the starting point should be that a witness child is not giving false testimony. Otherwise, we might be being unethical, not respecting the evaluated subjects, and having prejudices against them, a priori assuming they are liars. Legally speaking,

this is an aberration; one should never be against the presumption of innocence.

Let us now address the central theme of this book, institutional harassment through the use of the legal system.

Chapter 8

Legal Harassment

Using the Judicial System to Commit Violence

THE DIMENSIONS AND SCALE
OF LEGAL HARASSMENT

Harassment is a form of violence; two of the key terms that have been coined to refer to this concept—mobbing and bullying—are sometimes used as synonyms of psychological violence in the literature; nonetheless, they have slightly different meanings, and refer to two different contexts: mobbing is commonly used within the work environment and bullying at schools. Despite the use of different labels, this is a unique phenomenon which can be designated by the terms psychological harassment or psycho-terror. Both terms have emerged strongly within the literature on psychology, and one of the problems that has arisen is that some authors have attempted to interpret all violent or aggressive behavior as harassment; thus, it seems necessary to clarify the term (Bonafons, Jehel, Hirigoyen, and Coroller-Bequet, 2008).

Psychological violence can be defined as an abusive behavior, which takes the form of harassment, exercised by someone with a higher or lower status, a long-time colleague, relative, or client; it is characterized by malicious behavior, acts, words, gestures, or writings that threaten a person's dignity and mental health, degrading social relationships within the context in which it occurs. Psychological violence in the work environment makes keeping a job impossible for those who endure it; in schools, it impedes the progress of the students and sometimes causes them to leave the school. According to work psychologist Heinz Leymann, psychological violence is also characterized by the fact that coworkers, classmates, or the institutions themselves

121

intend to discriminate one or more workers or students. Leymann introduced the concept of "mobbing" as a severe form of harassment in the workplace or in other institutions (Leymann, 1990, 1996). One of the characteristics of mobbing is that it constitutes a psychological aggression that often involves a group of mobbers or a mob rather than a single aggressor. Thus, we use the term mobbing when, systematically, and over a long period of time (at least 6 months' duration), two or more people inflict extreme psychological violence over another person in the workplace; psychological terror in working life connotes the same concept and may be used as a synonym for mobbing. The term bullying usually designates a physical assault from a single person, especially one of a superior social or physical power; in school environments it might also refer to what is called the "bully" of the class, who acts alone and intimidates other students.

The term burnout—or burnout syndrome—also refers to phenomena in the occupational context, but from the perspective of those who suffer the harassment. In this case, the focus in on the consequences of severe stress on individuals. The term was coined by Maslach and is well known in the literature (Maslach, 1976; Maslach and Jackson, 1986). Unlike bullying or mobbing, the burnout syndrome may occur without an aggressor; the impact of the elements of the institution itself on the individual may cause the burnout syndrome (i.e., the structural characteristics of a job that entails working with terminally ill patients can strongly influence workers).

There is evidence that among other symptoms of stress, victims of harassment feel drained and mentally exhausted and that, as a result, they may become emotionally unbalanced, which leads to an emotional exhaustion syndrome known as burnout. Maslach and Jackson (1986) defined it as a syndrome of emotional exhaustion, depersonalization, and reduced personal accomplishment that can occur among individuals who work with people in some capacity. The syndrome is associated with an increased risk of sick leave, incapacity for work, job dissatisfaction, absenteeism, and an increasing intention to leave the workplace (see, for example, the study by Westerman et al., [2014], applied to nurses).

Considering the perspective from the justice system to date, few researchers have tackled the issue, yet on many occasions the citizens that make use of the justice system are victimized by the system itself, either as the plaintiff or as a defendant, although the effect of harassment should be more manifest in the defendant. Unfortunately, there are no studies about this, but it is indeed possible to analyze it through the association of different data that are shown across studies on the field.

In all societies there are groups at a disadvantage which are abused by both society itself and by the justice system. Athwal and Burnett's study (2014) is based on this assumption, but specifically applied to the issue of racism.

The study explains how members of certain collectives—mostly those related to the underground economy—are progressively "vanishing" as a result of low-level harassment, firstly from society as a whole, and secondly from the justice system, which either does not act or acts in a way that could also be defined as low-level intervention, leaving most crimes unpunished.

It has been demonstrated that the justice system stigmatizes both aggressors and victims. Stotzer's research (2014) analyzes 33 studies that focus on how the justice system treats its users. The study shows how transgressors suffer harassment, illegal detentions, assaults, and, in general, a notable lack of protection by the system; the agents of such aggression are the members themselves of the police and justice systems. And the same is true for victims who suffer harassment and discrimination by the system. The conclusion is clear: The police and justice system attack aggressors and victims.

Additionally, the mental health of victims is affected by the way in which the justice system treats them. This is demonstrated, for example, by two studies (Bell, Street, and Stafford (2014); these authors worked with 1,562 soldiers from the US Army Reserve who had suffered sexual abuse within their organization; the studies show how, when these people were treated by the justice system in an appropriate way, when their statement was taken in a proper and respectful manner, their mental health improved—in particular, their post-traumatic stress level; on the other hand, the mental health of those who were treated with a lack of respect by the justice system became worse. Smith (2012) carried out similar research, but applied to the prison system, and with similar results. Therefore, in general, we can state that when victims of crimes and aggressors are treated properly by the justice system, their mental health improves. Unfortunately, however, the opposite is also true.

One possible explanation of this discrimination from a legal point of view might be found in Silbey's concept of "legal conscience" (2005), which seeks to relate three elements: conscience, ideology, and hegemony. Silbey's approach clearly distinguishes between the theory and when the law is actually put into practice. It could be argued that law enforcement is often iatrogenic—that is, while it generally intends to defend victims, when it comes to specific cases, it often harms those directly involved. In her study, Silbey wonders how it is possible that people allow for the existence of a legal system that systematically iterates inequality, despite its promises of equal treatment.

Another phenomenon that manifests in the legal harassment of the citizen is the "Perverse Norm" created by Fernández-Dols (1993), which was defined as an explicit and unenforceable rule. The Perverse Norm is characterized as a norm that can only be met in ideal or exceptional terms (see also Oceja and Fernández-Dols, 1992). Thus, the police can punish those who fail to comply with a norm because they have violated the law, despite the fact that the whole of society violates it—not even knowing of its existence. For instance, sanctioning a restaurant or a pub is rather easy because there is always some regulation they are not complying with; therefore, if the police wants to sanction them, it is always possible. Perverse norms can be found in rather different contexts in everyday life. They are usually imposed on all groups of a social subsystem or at least on the groups with no authority, using the coercion of a hierarchically higher social system.

The issue becomes particularly relevant in the context of Family Law Court. Firstly, because loved ones, children, are jeopardized, and therefore the sensitivity of individuals is part of the equation. Secondly, because family judicial proceedings are not closed until children become of age. The situation has become more complex since Gardner (1999), a psychiatrist widely mentioned in this book, coined the term "Parental Alienation Syndrome" (PAS), specifying that often the custodial parent inculcates hate in their children toward the noncustodial parent, to prevent the latter's visitation rights. Unfortunately, parents who have been accused of sexual abuse often use these arguments, to the extent of stating that their children are capable of physically harming themselves to avoid those visits. Generally speaking, there are two trends of the reactions that the syndrome created by Gardner caused among scholars that can be broadly divided into those who defend the existence of PAS (for example, Vilalta, 2011) and those who criticize it on the grounds that there is no scientific verification to support its existence (for example, Clemente and Padilla-Racero, 2015b). In fact, the existence of the syndrome has not been scientifically verified—but what we would like to highlight at this point is that family legal processes are usually rather long, greatly damaging the parties involved in the process, especially the subject of these visits—the child—and the parent who must comply with a visitation schedule imposed by the justice system, handing their child over to the other parent, when they are aware that they are mistreating or sexually abusing the child (chapter 5 offers an extensive discussion of this issue). When faced with these situations, some children even commit suicide. On other occasions, the custodial parent, usually the mother, flees with her children as it is the only way out to avoid visitation arrangements that are effectively impossible to comply with, or when compliance may take a heavy toll on, or put the child at risk. During these processes, on the other hand, it is common that some lawyers, judges, and prosecutors disqualify, humiliate, and in general, harass one of the parties at the request of the other or by motu proprio.

As a result, some professionals found necessary the creation of a legal harassment scale or LHS (Clemente et al., 2019). When the scale was finally created, it was found that judicial harassment encompasses four factors:

- The first factor refers to how subjects suffer direct harassment, usually outside the Court Room, even within their family or work environment; this factor was referred to as "direct aggression."
- The second factor comprises issues involving harassment within the judicial process, more particularly in the Justice Chamber, ridiculing the victim in interrogations and/or declarations; this is what is called "procedural harassment."
- The third factor refers to a form of harassment by omission, that is, ignoring the victim, and despising them by omission; this is what is called "personal contempt."
- The fourth factor refers to the action of concealing the positive aspects of the victim while highlighting the negative ones, a concept that was designated by the term "manipulation of reality."

At this point, some readers might be wondering how it is possible that the justice system itself becomes a source of harassment. It seems thus important to clarify the role of the justice system as an institution of citizen protection, and that of the judge as the administering authority.

THE ROLE OF JUDGES AS CHIEF
AUTHORITIES OF A PUBLIC SERVICE

Until recently, it was thought that the role of judges should focus on the application of justice, regardless of how this must be done. The Bangalore Declaration meant a turning point in this matter, suggesting that together with the classic principles of how to apply justice, there is a need to maintain an ethical stance toward those who use the justice system. In a nutshell, the users of the justice system are officially acknowledged as such, and therefore are to be served with due respect (UN, 2007).

While the Bangalore Declaration begins by recognizing the classic role of the justice system (the administration of justice, which under no circumstances should be left aside), it adds two more points, paving the way to concern for the users of the system who are to be considered as individuals worthy of dignified treatment:

- It is essential that judges, both individually and collectively, respect and honor jurisdictional functions as a public commission, and strive to increase and maintain confidence in the judicial system.
- Each country's judiciary is responsible for promoting and maintaining high standards of judicial conduct.

This enables judges to ensure the proper treatment that must be applied to users of the system. Furthermore, the Bangalore principles of judicial conduct have led to the emergence of other similar precepts, such as those of the Ibero-American Code of Judicial Ethics (Código Iberoamericano de ética judicial, 2006).

Today, most countries where judicial independence exists have developed their own code of ethical conduct that is intended not only to preserve the classic principles of independence and good judicial conduct, but also to ensure adequate treatment for the citizens that are the users of the system.

Thus, in addition to demanding that judges be impartial, one must add, for example, that they be sympathetic and treat individuals properly. It is impartiality versus courtesy. Impartiality is the second great principle of judicial ethics contained in the Ibero-American Code of Judicial Ethics (more specifically, in articles 9 to 17). An independent judge is one that is not influenced by any political or economic power or by factors external to the process; judicial impartiality implies that judges are not influenced by any favoritism toward the parties or the object of the trial. And yet, impartiality should not become indifference to the parties, nor does equidistance have to be incompatible, for instance, with empathy with the victim. For the same reason, neutrality should not be contrary to the judge's commitment to establishing the truth. And by no means, neither impartiality nor neutrality may be used as a professional alibi to show discourteous treatment toward users of the justice system.

Andrés-Ibáñez (2013) suggests that judges commonly manifest a psychological and ethical difficulty in accepting that they often confuse impartiality and neutrality with discourtesy, to the extent that they even show discourtesy as a clear sign that they fight and defend impartiality and neutrality; in fact, by adopting that attitude, judges only manage to mistreat the users of the system, while also discrediting the administration of justice itself. It is as though the judge was situated above the circumstances at hand, acting on a "free pass" that saved him from all conditioning as a person in this regard. Along the same lines, Martínez-Calcerrada (1970, p. 208) asserts that "the judge is only and always a judge." The classic interpretation of this role furthers the judge from being conceived as a human being, and thus subject to the laws of science, such as psychology. The notion of showing consideration toward plaintiffs and defendants as users of the system was shut down through that concept of what being a judge entails.

Ost (1993) shows how ideas about the functions to be performed by the judge have evolved over time; in his study, he draws on figures from Greco-Roman mythology to illustrate three types of judges and three corresponding models of law: Judge Jupiter, Judge Hercules, and Judge Hermes.

- Jupiter is the judge that represents the code, the Kelsen Pyramid of Law (see Clemente, 2010), which exercises jurisdiction in a legal monism system, monopolized by a single legal source, the law. The adoption of this model implies that particular solutions are derived from general rules, which in turn stem from even more general principles.
- This model comes into crisis with the development of the welfare state, which attributes several "labors" (tasks) to the judge, as with Hercules, who was punished by Hera's curse to perform enormous feats—to open the Strait of Gibraltar, among others—to expiate the infanticide that she himself forced him to commit. Thus, Judge Hercules is urged to perform multiple tasks. Judicial decisions become relevant vis-à-vis the law. Hercules is the judge of the American legal realism (Clemente, 2010), with a role that becomes prominent because it entails being involved in the control of the constitutionality of laws and a mission to implement fundamental rights.
- The Hercules model is followed by the Hermes model, which characterizes postmodern law, and it is built on the principles of exchange and mediation, the two competences that, according to mythology, were attributed to Hermes—the messenger of the gods, the god of commerce, communication, and intermediation. It is a "liquid law," akin to quicksilver. As Ost (1993) suggests, it might not be a coincidence that alchemists of the Middle Ages coined the term mercury, which is Latin for Hermes, to name such a special metal that is naturally presented in liquid form. A liquid law that correlates to the—also liquid—society in which we live.

In short, Hermes is the god of the relationship, and relationships between individuals is precisely the new object of law, of the norms that the judge interprets and applies; thus, a science such as psychology, and within it, social psychology, become a fundamental source of the principles of law (Clemente, 2010).

Some authors have developed certain theories about judicial behavior. For instance, Posner (2008) identifies nine of them in an attempt to understand the most important personal motivations that influence the work of judges:

- Attitudinal: The decisions that judges take may be explained in terms of their personal values, beliefs, ideologies, and political preferences.
- Strategic: Judges act in light of the reactions of other judges, legislators, and public opinion.
- Sociological: A combination of attitudinal and strategic motivations which focuses on the theory of groups; on the basis of social psychology, the theory of rational choice is the main form of analysis.

- Psychological: Entails an analysis of the strategies that judges use to manage uncertainty, mostly based on preconceptions.
- Economic: Conceives the judge as a utilitarian maximizer, with a rational self-interest. It has a utilitarian function.
- Organizational: Judges and their employer (the government) have conflicting interests; thus, the employer will try to create an organizational structure that minimizes this divergence, and the judge will try to resist, to remain independent.
- Pragmatic: Entails an ability to ground a court decision on the effects it will have. It is also a utilitarian approach.
- Phenomenological: It is a global conception of the mind of the judges, based on their conscience.
- Legalist: The decisions of judges are determined by law.

Systematizing all these motivations, Posner suggests his own theory of the judge's conduct and creates a mathematical model that accounts for it. However, he makes no reference to the judge's role as a watchdog of the processes of citizen protection.

If we take as a starting point the principles of judicial ethics contained in the Ibero-American Code of Judicial Ethics, approved by the XIII Ibero-American Judicial Summit, we can see that some of these principles, such as independence or impartiality, in most cases situate the judge as the incumbent Power of State. And yet, there are other principles, such as diligence or courtesy, which portray the judge as a professional integrated into a public service (Ibero-American Judicial Summit, 2006). Canales (1995, p. 63) understands that the division of powers today requires "not dissociation, but synthesis between normative and factual spheres, between legality and effectiveness."

The principles of independence and impartiality have a clear constitutional significance and are the object of reflections within the fields of philosophy of law or political philosophy. In contrast, diligence or courtesy are reflected in codes of ethics, in citizen's bills of rights, or in recommendations from international institutions which, by definition, are not binding. They have a strong impact on the media, especially when a flaw in the system becomes apparent.

The Bangalore Principles (UN, 2007) on judicial conduct represent a further development and are complementary to the United Nations Basic Principles on the Independence of the Judiciary, ratified by the General Assembly in its resolutions 40/32 and 40/46. They seek to establish standards for the ethical conduct of judges and are intended to serve as a guide to judges and to provide the judiciary with judicial conduct regulatory framework. They also aim to help members of the executive and legislative, lawyers, and the general public, better understand and support the judiciary. These principles presuppose that judges are responsible for their conduct toward the institutions established to maintain judicial standards and that these institutions are independent and impartial.

The values referred to in the Bangalore Principles are six: independence, impartiality, integrity, correctness, equality, and competence and diligence. Let us make some relevant comments on the subject (UN, 2007).

The value of equality indicates that during the performance of their judicial obligations, a judge will not express predisposition or prejudice to any person or group for irrelevant reasons. That is, they should refrain from making denigrating comments. A judge must endeavor to ensure that their conduct is such that any reasonable observer has justified confidence in their impartiality. They must avoid comments, expressions, gestures, or conducts that might be interpreted as signs of insensitivity or disrespect.

Judicial observations are to be made with care and courtesy. A judge should not make improper and insulting observations about litigants, lawyers, parties, or witnesses. There have been occasions when, upon administering a guilty verdict, the judge launched a number of insulting observations to the accused. Judges' observations should always be moderate, and they must show self-control and courtesy.

Judges will fulfill their judicial obligations with proper consideration for all individuals involved in the proceedings: Parties, witnesses, lawyers, court personnel and other judges, without differentiation for any irrelevant reason and without affecting the proper performance of their obligations.

All this implies that individuals who appear before a court must be treated with dignity. Judges are the ones that set the tone and create the atmosphere for a fair trial in their court. Unequal or differentiated treatment of individuals in court—whether it actually happens, or is perceived—is not acceptable. All persons before the court—lawyers, litigants, or witnesses—have the right to be treated in a way that respects their human dignity and their fundamental human rights. The judge must ensure that, in court, all persons are protected from any form of prejudice.

Similarly, the value of competence and diligence specifies that judges will maintain order and decorum in all proceedings in which they participate, and that they will be patient, dignified, and courteous to litigants, juries, witnesses, lawyers, and other people they deal with from within their official capacity. They will also require similar conduct from legal representatives, court personnel, and other persons subject to their influence, direction, or control. Judges have a duty to maintain order and decorum within the court. The Bangalore Principles understand by "order" the degree of regularity and civility necessary to ensure that the court's activities are conducted in accordance with the rules governing trials. "Decorum" means the atmosphere of diligent attention and effort that enables participants and the public to realize that the matter before the court is receiving serious and fair consideration.

The judges' conduct is critical to maintaining their impartiality because that is what others perceive. Improper conduct may undermine the judicial process by giving an impression of favoritism or indifference. Disrespectful conduct toward a litigant violates the litigant's right to be heard and compromises the dignity and decorum of the courtroom. Lack of courtesy also affects the satisfaction of litigants in handling the case, creating a negative impression of the courts in general.

Both in the court and in the courtrooms, judges must always act courteously and respect the dignity of all individuals that play a part in this context. They must also demand similar courtesy from those who come to court and from court personnel and other individuals subject to the direction or authority of the judge. Judges must be beyond personal animosities and must not have favoritism with respect to attorneys who come to court. Unjustified reprimand to lawyers, offensive remarks about litigants or witnesses, cruel jokes, sarcasm, or an intemperate conduct undermine the court's order and decorum. When judges intervene, care must be taken that impartiality and the perception of impartiality are not adversely affected by the form of the intervention.

In today's postmodern society, the notion prevails that the job of a judge resembles that of Hermes. Yet the problem is that, on many occasions, judges do not have the capacity to determine that the assessments of those who advise them are indeed correct—or scientific, in the case of professionals of a specific branch of knowledge. In particular, this book is concerned with litigation between parents in family law cases. These cases are often problematic until children grow up and become economically independent or until they have the capacity to report for themselves because they are older.

When one or both parents file a complaint against the other, the next sensible step should be that the judge and/or the prosecutor analyze whether such complaints are substantiated. However, as it has already been mentioned, both judges and professionals in the judicial system advisory teams often believe in the existence of a false syndrome—what has been termed the Parental Alien Syndrome (PAS).

The application of a doctrine such as the PAS, with no scientific basis, obviously constitutes unfair action, since awarding custody to a parent in a prejudiced and subjective manner is, in fact, an injustice. The situation is further aggravated by the fact that according to Gardner's doctrine, children lie, because they are manipulated by the custodial parent, who advises them to do so (being normal for them to claim that they are even sexually abused by the noncustodial parent, usually the father). Thus, according to Gardner, children will invent all kinds of excuses so as not to have contact with the noncustodial parent. Unfortunately, in most judicial proceedings, the evidence that children hardly ever lie (Clemente et al., 2015b) is not being considered; as a result, cases of possible maltreatment of the noncustodial parent (including sexual abuse) are not investigated, because the account of the child is seen as a consequence of the PAS. Thus, the PAS hinders the investigation of possible cases of child abuse.

The PAS has attracted widespread criticism; besides, in view of Gardner's own manifestations in support of pederasty, and of the fact that the concept that he devised is clearly discriminatory toward women (not to mention that it goes against science, and children), his continuers have changed to calling it parental alienation, the term that is most commonly used today.

Gardner himself created the "threat therapy," which is also discussed in this book, a program aimed at separating allegedly alienated children from their mothers, in order to "deprogram" the children of the manipulation allegedly carried out by them. An example of this is the Reay program (2015).

In an effort to defend the previous concept created by Gardner, some authors have published a few studies that collect information "a posteriori," interviewing adults who come from families in which the parents' cohabitation was broken (Baker and Verrocchio, 2015; Bernet, Baker and Verrocchio, 2015; Verrocchio, Marchetti, and Fulcheri, 2015); data from such studies seem to suggest that every parent is a manipulator, and that every child raised in a broken family has suffered parental alienation. Such a claim seems difficult to believe, even more so when it is based on self-reporting data from adults and individuals who lived in other times. The same authors criticize those who do not defend Gardner's position, claiming in their papers that the publication of research that does not confirm the notion of mothers' manipulation should be banned. (See Bernet, Verrocchio, and Korosi's [2015] study, which includes a gross and rude criticism of Clemente and Padilla-Racero [2015a] confirms this; see also Clemente and Padilla-Racero's reply [2015b]). And yet, almost all the claims derived from the previous PAS postulates are fallacies (Warshak, 2015a, 2015b).

Science is sometimes driven by trends, and society by clichés. Shared custody has become the option that contemporary society considers to be more just when both parents are to be in contact with their children, and some male associations have emerged requiring that shared custody be applied in all cases; yet those who support it tend to forget that shared custody is sometimes a perversion of equality; there are abusers that conceal themselves behind the claim that fathers must have access to their children in the same way as the mothers; while this is a fact that no one must or can deny, what these abusers want is not to have contact with their children but to harass both the children and their mothers (Clemente, 2013b); this is indeed a perversion of the notion of equality.

Rather than trying to solve problems through the justice system, it would be more sensible to try to prevent children from being involved in the conflict (Pedzich, 2014; Trampotova and Lacinova, 2015). Both children and the custodial parent are sometimes subjected to "light" forms of this harassment such as, for instance, addressing the children with a name that is not theirs, even if that bothers them (Warshak, 2015a, 2015b). According to Pignotti (2014), child manipulation should be conceived as a case of domestic violence.

If a judge believes in the arguments that stem from the PAS, or if they simply receive reports from their technical team stating that such a false syndrome is thoroughly accepted, they will tend to treat the complainant inappropriately, as they will think of them as manipulators and will thus consider the complaint to be false. To make matters worse, they will not investigate whether the noncustodial parent is abusing the children, but will reverse the burden of the evidence, requiring the complainant to prove that they are not manipulating the facts—which, unfortunately, would be sometimes rather difficult or even impossible to empirically prove. Thus, the complainant becomes a defendant, which is often inappropriately treated by the judge, and the judge may even suggest to award custody to the parent that was originally reported, who is sometimes an aggressor or even a sexual abuser. Eventually, the PAS doctrine seriously jeopardizes the child and the justice system.

HOW DOES THE JUSTICE SYSTEM DEAL WITH THE PARTIES IN FAMILY LAW CASES?

In order to be able to verify how complainants and defendants are treated within family law courts, our research team selected all courts—of a city in northwestern Spain—that handled complaints of child abuse which had been filed by the custodial parent, accusing the noncustodial parent. Overall, the conduct of twenty-eight judges, twenty-eight prosecutors, plaintiffs, defendants, lawyers of the plaintiffs, and lawyers of the defendants—a total of 168 individuals—was analyzed. Although it was a small sample, the procedure was notably complex. We created a scale of observation ad hoc, as a tool to collect the interventions that can be made in the justice chamber and that could identify the issuer and the recipient of each. These are some of the results:

- Data concerning the conduct of judges toward complainants shows that the most frequent activity that the former perform in relation to the latter is the organization of the proceedings—which is indeed one of their tasks. The second, most common category that was analyzed was that judges are attentive to the plaintiffs, although they also express disagreement with the plaintiffs' opinions in equal proportion. Both may be said to be proper conducts because disagreement does not entail disrespect. While other categories were hardly used, it is worrying that in 14 percent of the cases, judges expressed their personal opinions to the plaintiff, and that in 10 percent of the cases they showed insulting or disdainful conducts. Another cause for concern is that judges' interventions that focused on socio-affective elements (emotions and issues related to feelings) predominated, compared with categories that emphasize the analysis of the prosecuted facts.

- With regard to the way judges act concerning the defendant, the main category used by judges is to organize the proceedings, as in the previous case—because this activity is intrinsic to their role. Similarly, the second most used category is to be attentive to the defendant. However, the third most widely used category (occurring in 25 percent of trials) is to show antagonism (being ironic or sarcastic), followed by expressing disagreement to the defendant. This means that, in trials, judges regularly treat defendants in ways that are inadequate, if not rather inadequate. Only in 10.7 percent of the trials, judges asked the defendant to provide a description of the facts; in the same proportion, they only requested general or nonspecific descriptions, and gave personal advice. Thus, judges can be said to fulfill their function of coordinating and organizing the proceedings, and they pay attention to the accused. And yet, at the same time, in 25 percent of the cases, they show antagonism to the defendant. Moreover, they barely focus on the facts of the case, paying much more attention to the socio-affective and negative elements, thus undermining the defendant.
- As regards the conduct of judges toward the plaintiff's lawyer, the category most used is to show antagonism (35.7 percent), followed by categories that show both signs of attention and antagonism.
- The way judges act with the defendant's lawyer is also rather similar to how they do with the plaintiff's, although somewhat less abrupt (they score lower in negative socio-affective categories); they show antagonism in 32.1 percent of the cases, attention in 14.3 percent of the cases, and express disagreement in 10.7 percent of the cases.
- The role of prosecutors is rather different from that of judges. Thus, the most widely used category for prosecutors with plaintiffs is to attend them with good manners; what might not be so positive is that the second most used category is to request rather general explanations. The category of insulting, discrediting, or undermining is used in few cases, but unfortunately it is also used.
- With respect to the defendant, the prosecutor shows a quite similar conduct to that manifested with the plaintiff, but there seems to be an

increase in the level of aggressiveness and disrepute (showing attention in 17.9 percent of the cases, and insulting, discrediting or undermining in 14.3 percent of the cases). In other words, their conduct is more hurtful and disrespectful. In addition, they tend to ask for nonspecific, general descriptions (14.3 percent) and to express personal opinions (14.3 percent).

Lastly, it was analyzed how the lawyers of both parties treated the users of the system, both the plaintiff and the defendant.

- When addressing defendants, the plaintiff's lawyers mostly expressed personal ideas, insulted, discredited, and undermined them; gave personal advice; and, to a lesser extent, showed antagonism. In general, the plaintiff 's lawyer is the most destructive person with the defendant.
- The defendant's lawyers, when addressing plaintiffs, used antagonism (in over 80 percent of cases), followed by expressing personal opinions and showing other inappropriate ways of acting. In other words, it may also be stated that they are rather destructive with them.

CONCLUSIONS REGARDING THE TREATMENT OF USERS OF THE JUDICIAL SYSTEM

The results confirm that there are indeed differences of treatment in oral hearings. More specifically, it is noted that the fundamental task carried out by judges is the organization of the process, which they do to help plaintiffs and defendants, who are clueless on the subject, with greater emphasis on plaintiffs. When dealing with complaints from custodial parents, family law judges use worse—even humiliating—treatment with plaintiffs, that is, usually the mothers who claim that their children are being abused by their fathers.

There is evidence that, during the trials, the socio-affective elements predominate much more than those related to the issue that is litigated. In addition, the whole process is essentially about socio-affective elements, and usually these affective aspects are either negative or rather negative, in clear opposition to what the Bangalore Principles dictate. Judges are the ones who humiliate, scorn, and ridicule both the plaintiff and the defendant in a higher degree. In addition, the defendant receives a much more degrading treatment than the plaintiff by all individuals involved in the process.

If we focus on the treatment given only to those who are not experts in the proceedings, plaintiff and defendant, the lawyers on each side are the ones who treat the opposite parties the worse, with insults, humiliation, and discrediting.

Another aspect that is worth mentioning is that both judges and prosecutors barely focus on the subject being judged, and therefore on the facts themselves, because when they address an issue, they tend to express and argue personal opinions, which should not happen. On the other hand, when they ask the plaintiff or the defendant questions about the matter of the case, such questions are often rather ambiguous and general, of the type "tell me . . . ," which does not allow specific information to be obtained in order to clarify the reason behind the facts.

However, the major cause for concern is that there are interventions—of judges, prosecutors, and lawyers alike—which are humiliating for users of the system, thus accounting for a system that, in itself, despises users.

As other jurisdictions of law, family law must combine impartiality with courtesy, assuming that, in times when what is called "liquid law" is imposed, it is necessary to become—as Ost suggests (1993)—a judge of the little things too, as Judge Hermes.

To this date, judges have been regarded as those responsible for issuing verdicts as fair as possible, but little attention has been given on their task of organizing the process of holding oral hearings and of respectfully and appropriately treating the users of the system. Failure to consider this issue may lead to serious injustices for the user, and even to maltreating them, especially in family law, due to the belief in the ideas of the PAS.

Once the existence of legal harassment is pinpointed, it seems evident that work must be done on the creation of protocols that prevent individuals from being harassed judicially, either by imposing a code of ethics in the procedure that lawyers follow to question the opposing party, in the way in which the other judicial operators address—and in how they act with—parties to the dispute, or in the conduct of judges and prosecutors. The search for the truth of the facts and the delivery of justice must not be in conflict with treating individuals with respect.

Following his father Zeus' orders, Hermes organized the Paris trial. He found an exiled pastor, gave him an apple, and told him how to proceed by choosing between Hera, Athena, and Aphrodite. The outcome of such decision was the war in Troy. It seems advisable to care for small details and to promote good treatment and respect to users of the courts dealing with family issues; let us dismiss the preconceived ideas that derive from unscientific theories.

THE EFFECTS OF PARTICIPATING IN JUDICIAL PROCEEDINGS ON THE MENTAL HEALTH OF THE PARTIES INVOLVED IN A LAWSUIT

The mere possibility of having to go to court, for those who have rarely or never had to, creates a rather problematic situation. It is common for people in this situation to show physiological symptoms such as redness of the face (and in general, of the skin), high levels of anxiety, gastrointestinal disorders, and so on. This is evidence that the physical and the psychological parts of the notion of health cannot be separated and must be conceived holistically. More notably, those who are constantly involved in judicial proceedings, especially if they are a defendant or if they are at risk of losing something or someone dear to them (e.g., a child), are constantly exposed to the possibility of developing health problems. In general, these are effects of stress, which are indeed harmful at that moment, but they are particularly harmful if the effects are prolonged over time. Let us try to imagine the level of stress that individuals—usually mothers—may endure, when they know that what is at stake is the possibility of their children visiting someone they know will rape them; furthermore, the need of having to permanently visit the courts will continue until the child reaches legal age; that is, in some cases, there might be 15 years of judicial struggle ahead of them, to defend their children. The health of both parents and of the children will be seriously affected.

How much time is taken off one's life expectancy after being judicially harassed for years? This may be calculated through an extensively used index of health which measures the years of life that are potentially lost. That figure is reached by, out of the persons who die, calculating the statistical average of the years that they should have lived in other circumstances.

It is, therefore, an indicator of premature death. These are the years individuals do not live because they die at an earlier age than the life expectancy for their social environment. The methodology proposed by Romeder and McWhinnie (1978) has been used to calculate deaths that occurred before the age of 70 as premature, not including deaths under the age of 1 year, since these are considered to be caused by other reasons. Thus, according to this index, women that are exposed to this stressful situation for more than 10 years, lose a total of 10 years of life (Clemente, 2013b).

There are several studies that account for the effects of long-term stress in detail. For practical purposes, we may establish an arbitrary separation between those which are more concerned with psychology and those which focus on physiology. The former encompass the following types: adjustment disorders (of the anxious, depressive, or mixed type), anxiety disorders (panic disorder, acute stress disorder, and post-traumatic stress disorder), mood disorders (mainly major depressive disorder), somatic symptom disorders (somatization, hypochondria disorder, pain), substance use disorders (abuse, dependence, and other mental disorders caused by the consumption of substances), sleep disorders, sexual disorders, and eating disorders. The latter include psychophysiological disorders—that is, those that occur because stress alters our body, such as cardiovascular diseases (coronary disease, hypertension, infarction, arrhythmias . . .), digestive disorders (irritable bowel syndrome, stomach ulcer), respiratory disorders (asthma), skin disorders (psoriasis, acne, eczema), tension headaches, back pain, arthritis, chronic pain, fertility disorders, some diseases related to the immune system (cancer, rheumatoid arthritis, etc.). Therefore, it seems that the ongoing judicial struggle described above seriously affects health.

At this point, one may wonder how being a user of the legal system can affect health in general and especially mental health. Most research focuses only on the mental health of the victims, but not on the fact that they are involved in a judicial process. The term secondary victimization has been coined to refer to the victims' point of view. This concept has been analyzed, for instance, by Gutiérrez de Piñeres-Botero, Coronel, and Andrés-Pérez (2009). Thus, it has been analyzed how, eventually, victims of a crime become victims of the legal system, experiencing suffering which is caused by the system itself. A characteristic of this phenomenon is that it affects not only the victim but also families, friends, community, persons in charge of their assistance and care, and even the aggressor (Palacio, 2001).

On the other hand, the theory of role has been used as an explanatory key from the aggressor's point of view, mainly within the framework of the symbolic interactionism approach, which states that, when someone commits a criminal action, the legal system labels them as offender or aggressor, making it much more likely for them to be condemned in the future, even if they do not commit more crimes (see, for example, Shim and Shin, 2016; Theimann, 2016).

Indeed, in family law cases, it is difficult to pinpoint the distinction between the plaintiff and the defendant, the accuser and the accused. The complaints are chained to each other, and who the aggressor is and who is attacked is no longer clearly identified.

Undoubtedly, the suffering to which a person is subjected to by the mere use of the justice system is secondary victimization. This can be defined as the suffering that a person experiences as a result of the negative psychological, social, legal, and economic consequences—both the victim of a crime and the aggressor (if such distinction can be possibly drawn)—that derive from the use of the legal system. This is an effect the users of the system face, immense frustration caused upon experiencing institutional reality as compared to their legitimate expectations. Besides, the real victims—that is, those who had to report a situation that required them to defend their children, and that, in turn, requested the defense of the system—suffer from a general misunderstanding of their psychological and physical suffering caused by the criminal act, which leads them to feel desolate and insecure. This feeling causes those victims to lose confidence in the community, in the professionals, and in the institutions, the very places where they should be able to turn for support (Kreuter, 2006; Landrove, 1998). Sometimes, secondary victimization has more negative repercussions than primary victimization (Berril and Herek, 1992; Beristain, 2001; García-Pablos, 1988; Landrove, 1998; UN, 1999; Wemmers, 2005).

Albertin (2006) suggests that secondary victimization derives from relations between victims and social institutions (social services, health care, the media, legal services, etc.), which sometimes offer poor or inadequate care that does not meet their needs (Beristain, 2001). Secondary victimization—or revictimization—also encompasses poor therapeutic or medical psychological intervention provided by unscrupulous professionals that are poorly trained to assist victims (Rozanski, 2013).

The sole fact of resorting to the justice system as a victim is stressful, since it involves reviving the emotions that were generated during the criminal acts; furthermore, the aids that victims usually need to preserve their mental health (social support, understanding, a sense of control and power over their life, being listened to, being respected, keeping their privacy, etc.) are often opposed to the requirements of the judicial process (victims must answer questions that are made publicly, demonstrate the credibility of their testimony, follow the rules and procedures, and recall their experience which will be stood up against that of the aggressor, etc.). This has been analyzed by authors such as Campbell (2005) or Lewis (2003). Again, what has not been studied is the stress that the legal system certainly causes on the aggressor.

As Garcia-Pablos (1988) suggests, victims often suffer from a severe psychological impact that adds to the physical or material damage resulting from the crime. The crime they experienced is relived and perpetuated in the victim's mind. Impotence in the face of evil and the fear of it recurring produce acute neurotic processes, prolonged feelings of anguish, anxiety, depression, and so on. The dejection sometimes generates psychological reactions which stem from the need to explain the traumatic event that was suffered, and gives rise to feelings of guilt, such as the attribution of self-responsibility or self-blame. Society itself, on the other hand, stigmatizes victims. Far from responding with solidarity and justice, society labels victims, responding with empty compassion, if not with distrust and suspicion. Thus, victimization generates social isolation and marginalization which will henceforth increase the risk of victimization, making those who suffered the effects of the crime more vulnerable. In the short term, victimization modifies the lifestyles and habits of the victims, negatively affecting their daily and domestic life, their interpersonal relationships, their professional and social activity, and so on.

Is there a possible solution? Researchers have found two forms of justice that can help reduce the impact of secondary victimization: interactional justice and procedural justice (Latham, 2006; Vardi and Weitz, 2004).

Interactional justice refers to the dignified and respectful treatment individuals who are users of the justice system must receive, and to the quality of interpersonal treatment received during the application of procedures (Omar, 2006; Vardi and Weitz, 2004). It comprises two types—informational and interpersonal justice:

- Informational justice refers to the use of appropriate information to explain each stage of judicial proceedings; the more individuals receive adequate information about the process, the better they feel they are being treated, with fairness, impartiality, and equity. It therefore refers to truthfulness and justification.
- Interpersonal justice refers to the impartial treatment received during the proceedings, as well as to the respect with which the parties should be treated; it implies concern and sensitivity for others—and thus empathy, manners, and respect.

In addition to interactional justice, scholars have also described the concept of procedural justice, which refers to the fact that formal procedures are present and used in the organization (Latham, 2006; Vardi and Weitz, 2004).

The Citizen Participatory Trial System was created in Korea in 2008. This system is based on the idea that made possible the creation of the Committee for Citizen Participation in the Judicial System, integrating citizens, as members of the jury, into the delivery of justice in cases of female victims of sexual abuse. The procedure is intended to avoid secondary victimization by, for instance, choosing juries composed only of women. Some authors have proposed a number of measures to promote the effectiveness of this system, also with the goal of improving the mental health of victims. Thus, for example, Kim (2015) proposes three measures to improve the system, and the third refers to ways to avoid the anxiety created in victims (1) when they know that their identity will be revealed in trials and (2) as a result of the distress that involves reliving the aggression that they suffered in a trial. In fact, the idea is to create a system that is closer to criminal mediation. One of the programs aimed at preventing secondary victimization is the "Sexual Assault Nurse Examiner" or SANE. The professionals who participated in the program said that the likelihood for the criminal justice system to victimize individuals is rather high, followed by the medical system and the legal system in general. According to those that are professionally involved in the justice system, it is the police who contribute most to generating anxiety in the victims, especially because they ask questions without any sort of sensitivity, which creates a sense of guilt. On the other hand, the way in which the legal system acts calls into question the credibility of the victims, which causes them high dissatisfaction.

Aranda-López, Montes-Berges, Castillo-Mayén and Higueras (2014), as well as Patterson (2011), have published empirical studies on the phenomenon of secondary victimization and sexual assault. Aranda-Lopez's study also expanded the research to gender-based violence. They showed that when women have a more negative perception of the judicial system, they feel secondary victimization more intensely. On the other hand, those women who feel less need for the justice and police system to help them not to suffer future abuses show more satisfaction with the justice system. There is also a homeostatic phenomenon, that women with more extensive support from their family show a greater satisfaction with the police system.

In their study, Calton and Cattaneo (2014) concluded that when victims perceive judicial processes as fair, that helps them better their mental health, and they may wish to use the justice system again in the event of problems. Two of the variables that were significantly modified in terms of the perception of fair judicial treatment were the perception of quality of life (which increased) and the level of depression (which decreased). The findings in these studies cannot be generalized to victims of sexual offenses, as previously demonstrated by Laxminarayan (2012). The effects that have been analyzed are the result of the crime of sexual assault.

Since research has focused almost exclusively on victims, and in particular on secondary victimization, the study carried out by this research team aims to provide information on the psychological effects of being in contact with the justice system, whether it be the aggressor or the victim.

After analyzing the results, it can be stated that being reported implies a clear differentiation from those who are not. Specifically, individuals who are reported show a pessimistic outlook for the future and low strategies to defend their health, as well as less empathy. Those that file the complaint are also at risk of suffering health problems, since they have a more negative view of their life, and in general, greater psychosomatic symptoms. In other words, both the defendant and the plaintiff have health problems. Furthermore, if we compare them in view of the judicial procedures that are still open, the group with the greatest exposure to judicial proceedings also presents a more deteriorated health, although in rather specific variables. Thus, it is demonstrated that the fact of being in contact with the justice system causes a deterioration in the mental health of the users, whether they are plaintiffs or defendants. Besides, the greater the contact with the justice system (the greater number of open cases), the further the health deteriorates. There is also evidence that the reported individual has greater variations in their psychosocial health; while plaintiffs show a small number of effects, these are qualitatively more problematic.

Thus, the research by Gutiérrez de Piñeres-Botero, Coronel, and Andrés-Pérez (2009), Palacio (2001), Shim and Shin (2016), and Theimann (2016), which separately analyzed the victim (in our case, the plaintiff) and the aggressor (in our case the defendant), reached the right conclusion: The justice system affects the mental health of its users.

Chapter 9

Dark Personality and Moral Disengagement in the Context of Couple Relationships

The question we might have to ask ourselves now is, Is an individual of sound mental health capable of using their children to take revenge on their former couple, or is that always a sign of an underlying mental health disorder? Most people would agree with the latter option; let us not forget, however, that individuals are a product of the socialization they receive—or, in other words, of the education, the "environment" they are surrounded by. On the other hand, that option targets the individual and is comforting for society, as it places the responsibility for denigrating actions on individuals with a mental health disorder, not on society as a whole. Therefore, before exploring the issue of the dark personality (which is inherent to the self, and comes from within), another question remains: How do we define normal and abnormal behavior? In psychology, we define normality by means of statistics: What is normal is what most people do. Nevertheless, the scales we use to measure different degrees of normality rely on cultural elements which evolve with the societies in which they are used. Thus, someone considered to be an introvert in Latin America may be labeled as an extrovert in North America or in Europe, as the trait of interpersonal openness is culture-bound. Similarly, if we were to assess children's behavior toward their parents today (for instance, the degree of obedience) according to the criteria of how children behaved 30 years ago, practically all of them would be diagnosed with antisocial behavior (which is the term that designates psychopaths if they are children); in other words, it was unthinkable in those days to consider child disobedience as normal, whereas today it seems almost normal for children to disobey and ignore their parents. When a person's behavior deviates from the normality established by each society over time, we consider that this person is suffering from a mental illness. Taking these considerations into account, let us now address the notion of dark personality and its different types.

The term dark personality was coined to designate a set of socially aversive traits, typical of those whose behavior goes against the established morality and who sometimes even find pleasure in attacking others. Dark personality is not only a problem for some individuals, but also for society, since those who have these traits jeopardize social coexistence. Initially, it was thought that the three characteristics that comprise the dark personality were Machiavellianism, subclinical narcissism, and subclinical psychopathy, and these types were studied under the term Dark Triad of personality. Sadism was subsequently added to this set of personality traits, hence the label Dark Tetrad. However, the most appropriate term seems to be dark personality, as it is now widely accepted that more variables can be added to the list.

Let us begin by exploring Machiavellianism, the first of the traits that the dark personality comprises.

MACHIAVELLIANISM

Machiavellianism entered as a field of study within the thematic agenda of social psychology, one of the branches of psychology, thanks to a study by Christie and Geiss (1970), who created the first scale that could measure this construct. The dimensions that Christie and Geis's scale comprises parallel the traits that define the personality of the main character in Nicolo Machiavelli's *The Prince*, written in 1513 and published in 1531: opportunism and pragmatism; distrust of the human species, and adherence to the maxim that the end justifies the means. In fact, authors such as Pastor (1982) have pointed out that Machiavelli himself, who worked as a diplomat, stood out for the lack of affection and sentimental involvement he showed in his interpersonal relationships and for an absence of ethical and ideological commitment. When he wrote *The Prince,* he was in prison, accused and condemned for conspiring against the Medici, a powerful and influential, prominent Italian family of the Renaissance, which includes four popes (Leo X, Clement VII, Pius IV, and Leo XI).

In his works, Niccoló di Bernardo dei Machiavelli—or more commonly known as Machiavelli—introduced the concept of *virtù*, a set of traits associated with creative intelligence and emotional detachment that were intended as a reference for political leaders and heads of state. As Pastor (1982) puts it, "*Virtù* is not synonymous with morality but with intelligence and practical strategy capable of counteracting the imponderable game of destiny" (p. 29). Pastor also mentions three main psychological traits of the Machiavellian personality:

1. Lack of affection and feelings of the subject in their interpersonal relationships (manipulative, distant, dominant character, etc.); apparently, Machiavelli's personality was also of this type.
2. Lack of an ethical-moral feeling and guilt in the subject's conduct (Machiavelli did not question his own pragmatism; on the contrary, he magnified the importance of achieving objectives and did not hesitate to establish a *modus operandi* for it (Dingler-Duhon and Brown, 1987; Pandey and Rastogi, 1979); The saying "the end justifies the means" originated and became popular with Machiavellianism.
3. Ideological flexibility or lack of dogmatism. Machiavelli did not adhere to any political, religious, or philosophical ideal; he followed his own ideas without being guided by laws or doctrines established by others. This is what is popularly known as being a turncoat.

From a psychological point of view, people characterized as Machiavellian present a high motivation for success, achievement, and social influence, accompanied by a remarkable carelessness for the ethical qualification of their actions (Pastor, 1982, p. 41). Thus, what matters for Machiavellian individuals is the effectiveness of the tactics they employ, and not their ethical attainment. According to Bragues (2008), Machiavelli challenges the norms of traditional morality.

Furthermore, Pastor sets forth that although he himself uses the term personality when defining Machiavellian subjects (Machiavellian personality, sagacious personality, even upholding that these characterizing traits of these subjects constitute what he calls the "cool syndrome"), Machiavellianism is in fact an attitude; and indeed, if there is something that characterizes this type of person, it is their ability to chameleonically alter themselves; they do not concern themselves with values or precepts as expressed in Kantianism, but their adaptability is total. From this perspective, Jaensch would have defined their personality as being similar to that of the Jewish, a type S personality, qualifying them as anti-authoritarian. Pastor (1982) emphasizes this positioning of his cool syndrome or Machiavellian personality as something variable and subject to environmental circumstances. Having a Machiavellian personality depends on two elements; on the one hand, the personality of a Machiavellian individual should be such that they find no problems in breaking any previously established agreement, or in avoiding involvement in any kind of moral precepts (those that practically all of us acquire when we socialize, which enable individuals to live together); on the other hand, there must be a social and group environment that allows Machiavellians to develop their traits. Unfortunately, those who are victims of a Machiavellian person suffer enormously and describe their situation as harassment, but those who find their actions to be beneficial for a specific social group they belong to, admire and worship them, valuing, in particular, their sagacity in interpersonal relationships.

Pastor summarizes these ideas as follows (Pastor, 1982, p. 59): "Machiavellianism is an acquired attitude, a seasoned way of being and living, toughened over time, not temporary; furthermore, to manage that conduct one requires an especially adept social demeanor."

Machiavellian people are often raised in families in which ethics and morals have no value. Not unexpectedly, several authors have stated that the family is the most violent group in which human coexistence develops; as an anecdote, sardonically, a sociobiologist, Durrell (1956) wrote the book *My Family and Other Animals*. The families in which the Machiavellian subjects are socialized typically show a lack of structuring of social relations, a lack of assignment of specific roles to each member (ambiguity and conflict of roles), and a lack of punishment for those who fail to comply with the rules. In short, a child that is born and raised in an environment in which, for example, opposing the decisions of their parents is acceptable will indeed develop a way of interacting with others that implies not respecting anyone, if that is what helps them achieve their objectives. However, in the face of structured, highly normalized, rigid situations, Machiavellians seem unable to apply their tactics. They take advantage of the vagueness of rules to impose their tactics. Authors such as Gunnthorsdottir, McCabe, and Smith (2002), Sakalaki, Richardson, and Thepaut (2007), among others, have shown that Machiavellian people are prone to take advantage of some opportunities to increase their own benefit, rather than cooperating, trusting others, or focusing on common benefit. In fact, common benefit does not make sense for the typical Machiavellian, only their personal benefit, and in several cases, they become leaders of a group only to achieve their goals, but what they achieve is only beneficial for them, not for the group.

One of the main ideas in Machiavelli's treatise is that a ruler who feels empathy would neglect his personal interests (Pastor, 1982). Christie and Geis (1970) point out that Machiavellians are emotionally disengaged and easily detach themselves from their determining characteristics in their actions; in contrast, the non-Machiavellian people become "distracted" by the feelings that interpersonal relations bring out in them; as a result, their way of acting is less effective than that of Machiavellians. Therefore, one of the characteristics of the Machiavellians' cool syndrome is their greater capacity for attentional control, so the "less Machiavellian" person will be better able to sympathize with others, and their feelings will distract them from their main purposes—that is, they will become inattentive, while Machiavellians are much more efficient in making use of the means to achieve their ends.

Durkin (1970) describes Machiavellians as unable to show their feelings toward others, unable to treat everyone as worthy beings, and non-Machiavellians as humble and empathetic persons. In short, non-Machiavellian persons will be mostly affected by moral values such as loyalty, affection, justice, kindness, and so on, which act as a deterrence to achieve the objective they pursue. However, Machiavellians focus on the end, the objective, and make use of all the necessary means omitting all moral value; they will not feel empathy or displeasure upon implementing what enables them to achieve their goal, regardless of the opinion of others and of ethical values.

Christie and Geis (1970) noted that Machiavellians lie better than non-Machiavellians when the benefits outweigh the risks: "The perception of the person who accuses them does not distract them; even having to blatantly lie does not disturb their mental processes" (Pastor, 1982, p. 94). Christie and Geis, as well as Pastor, also highlight that Machiavellians have notable skills: "Machiavellianism is a cooperative factor that contributes to improving acuity, sagacity, and perceptual accuracy in matters of interest" (Pastor, 1982 p. 94). Thus, Machiavellian persons are not more intelligent than the rest, but they have a cold-blooded control over their feelings, which leads them to achieve better results.

For their victims, it might seem easy to detect Machiavellians' traits, but Machiavellian individuals usually obtain normal scores in other personality variables; they "enjoy a notable healthy personality and are rather unlikely to suffer from psychotic symptoms" (Pastor, 1982, p. 100).

Although Christie and Geiss (1970)—as well as Guterman (1970)—consider Machiavellianism as a sociopolitical attitude (as authoritarianism, dogmatism, or hard personality), they prefer to use the term "Machiavellian personality." This might be the reason that, for some time, Machiavellianism has been analyzed as part of what is known as the Dark Triad of Personality, together with subclinical narcissism, psychopathy, or sadism—which indicates that, in fact, these individuals have no serious personality disorder (Paulhus and Williams, 2002).

The existence of Machiavellian individuals—or, should we say, the fact that others allow them to develop their strategies—is a danger to society as a whole. According to Rodríguez, Padilla, and Fornaguera (2010, p. 110), "Prosocial behavior trends negatively correlate with Machiavellian behavior trends." Altruism and Machiavellianism are two antithetical concepts; altruism unites people to allow peaceful coexistence, while Machiavellianism separates them and fosters attitudes which allow some to take advantage of others.

SUBCLINICAL NARCISSISM

The term narcissistic personality disorder was introduced by Kohut in 1968. Subclinical narcissism (which does not involve a serious personality disorder and can be observed in socially integrated people) was suggested in a study by Raskin and Hall (1979; see also Raskin, 1980).

Before Paulus's studies, the most widely used test to measure narcissism in the general population was the Narcissistic Personality Inventory, which assesses different degrees of narcissism as a personality trait—although, as Raskin and Hall (1979) remark people with narcissistic personality disorder score higher in this inventory.

As it is the case with the other dark personality traits, there are certain, distinct features that define narcissism. These individuals are prone to exaggerate their own achievements, and as they often blame others for their failures, they do not accept their own faults. Raskin and Shaw studied the frequency in which narcissists make use of first person personal pronouns in conversations and concluded that they have a propensity to talk about topics that are related to their personal lives.

Narcissists tend to have a positive—and yet, rather unrealistic—view of themselves. They have a need for attention and admiration, often treating others with disdain and reacting stubbornly and irritably—sometimes aggressively—to pertinent criticism (Wolfsberger, 2015).

As Wolfsberger points out, "Narcissists believe themselves to be superior, but their weakness is that they are no one without the admiration of others. Narcissists are arrogant and overbearing and think of themselves as unique and special. This grandiose concept of their personality and life leads them to think that they cannot relate to anyone, that they should only look for people of their same category; others mean very little to them in most cases."

Although it might seem otherwise, narcissists are aware of their flaws, and some even know that they exaggerate their capabilities far beyond reality; this could be the reason why they need to be constantly admired. In their eagerness to excel, they go to great lengths to magnify their achievements and become tremendously competitive. They strive to give the impression of being the only ones who succeed in life (the others are not anywhere near their standards); in their attempt to stand out by comparison, they always underscore the negative aspects of those around them. They also consider their experiences to be of more value than others' and feel compelled to set the example for those around them—not because they are willing to give any advice, but because they need to be the center of attention. As a result, their social relationships deteriorate gradually, and they find themselves in constant demand of new acquaintances to admire them.

Narcissists do not care about others, so they rarely listen to them. Their craving for admiration leads them to believe that everything in their life is exceptional; they live no ordinary experiences; they have outstanding, wonderful lives abounding in triumphs and notoriety. Envy is a pervasive element in their personal and social relationships—what they feel for other's achievements and what they think others feel when they succeed.

Narcissists have no real friends, since they have no qualms about taking advantage of them, and they do not value fidelity whatsoever. They might be said to be the worst friends, because their lack of receptivity makes them unable to help others.

Another identifying trait of narcissists is that they construct a parallel reality that they inhabit most of the time. The misconceptions they entertain about their abilities bring them to a world of fantasies and power over others. In the hope of achieving success at all costs, they only focus on deceiving themselves and others.

Narcissistic people can only accomplish their goals by means of an overstretched imagination. They often lie and always blame others, because for them, failure only happens in the outside world. They also hide their emotions, especially their vulnerability. The reason is that they feel the need to hide their flaws at all costs, and they turn their insecurity into an artificial fortress so that no one can harm them. They will do everything that is necessary to hide their vulnerability, such as speaking excessively, reconducting conversations, undermining others, pointing out their flaws, and so on; everything is acceptable, as long as they do not appear weak.

Whether to shopping, alcohol, other drugs, sport, sex, or play, addictions are quite common so as to compensate for the feelings of envy or frustration that they suffer and cannot recognize. Such addictions interfere with their personal, professional and social life, and arise as a result of their compulsion to feel euphoria permanently and to cushion discomfort, because narcissists cannot allow pain to enter their life, and they are unable to cope with gloomy feelings or sadness. The main character in the film *The Wolf of Wall Street* illustrates this behavior.

Narcissists master the actions that enable them to take both people and situations to their terrain. They are always lurking, ready to reconduct those who try to say or do something they do not like or that does not allow them to express their grandiosity and power in the presence of others.

Let us say that opposing a narcissist is rather dangerous. If their partner breaks the relationship with them, and not otherwise, they will feel that they are being judged, and if their narcissism ceases to be subclinical, they may end up killing their former partner or their children.

SUBCLINICAL PSYCHOPATHY

In the field of subclinical psychopathy, the first study that presented psychopathy from a clinical perspective is Cleckley's "The Mask of Sanity"; although the book was published in the 1940s, Cleckley's complete work only appeared in 1976, in the last edition of the book. Cleckley (1976) postulates that psychopathy is a constellation of affective, interpersonal, and behavioral traits characterized by an absence of nervousness, lack of sincerity, inability to love, absence of remorse or guilt, and a general lack of affective reactions (Halty and Prieto, 2011).

Cleckley found 17 diagnostic criteria for psychopathy, all of which were measurable in the normal, nonpathological population: superficial charm; remarkable intelligence; absence of hallucinations and other signs of irrational thinking; absence of nervousness and/or psychoneurotic manifestations; untrustworthiness; falsehood or lack of sincerity; inability to experience remorse or shame; antisocial behavior without apparent justification; lack of judgment and difficulties in learning from experience; pathological self-centeredness and the inability to love; poor affective reactions; specific loss of intuition; insensitivity in ordinary interpersonal relationships; exaggerated and unpleasant behavior after alcohol intake; sometimes constant but rarely consumed suicide threats; impersonal, frivolous, and unstable sexual life; and inability to follow any life plan (Pozueco, Romero, and Casas, 2011).

Lack of empathy and inability to show repentance are among the main characteristics shared by people with subclinical psychopathy. Psychopaths are dominant in interpersonal relationships and rarely show scruples. This allows them to have a great manipulative capacity, and in the long term they are perceived by others as undesirable (Rauthmann, 2012).

Later, in the 1980s, Cleckley created the Psychopathy Checklist, and began to differentiate pathological psychopathy from subclinical psychopathy (or primary versus secondary psychopathy). Primary psychopathy (or factor I) encompasses personality traits such as grandiosity, cruelty, lack of empathy, lack of guilt and remorse, emotional coldness, and the ability to manipulate others. Secondary psychopathy (or factor II) refers more to an antisocial behavior style that is described as a chronically unstable pattern of behavior, impulsivity, and criminal versatility (Halty and Prieto, 2011).

SADISM

The Dark Triad of Personality became the Dark Tetrad when sadism, the last component of the dark personality as we understand it today, was introduced.

There are still some authors such as Chabrol, Van Leeuwen, Rodgers, and Séjourné (2009) who suggest adding the disposition toward antisocial behavior as a fifth element; a sixth element, the disposition to lying, might be also be added. Individuals who are sadists in their daily lives experience joy and satisfaction when they observe the suffering of others or when they can contribute to it (Wolfsberger, 2015). One of the traits that sadism shares with the other elements of the dark personality—and more particularly with psychopathy—is insensitivity and lack of empathy (Međedović and Petrović, 2015). Furthermore, a high score in Machiavellianism and psychopathy is positively related to the existence of daily sadism (Meere and Egan, 2017).

There are still few studies on sadism; Dinić, Bulut-Allred, Petrović, and Wertag (2020) were the first authors to explore it, not in clinical or forensic contexts, but in the general population. These are the tools that have emerged to date to measure this variable:

- Sadistic Impulse Scale (SSIS), by O'Meara, Davies, and Hammond (2011). The results indicate a positive correlation between sadism measured on this scale and interpersonal domination in social relations, as well as a negative relationship between empathy and parental care and affection (Dinić, Bulut-Allred, Petrović, and Wertag, 2020; Pineda, Piqueras, Galán, and Martínez-Martínez, 2021).
- Varieties of Sadistic Tendencies (VAST), by Paulhus and Jones (2015). This scale assesses the predisposition to sadistic behavior and distinguishes between direct sadism (feeling pleasure by physically or verbally hurting others) and indirect sadism (feeling pleasure by watching others be hurt). It comprises three subscales: direct verbal sadism, direct physical sadism, and indirect or vicarious sadism.
- Assessment of Sadistic Personality (ASP), by Plouffe, Saklofske, and Smith (2016). This scale demonstrates if the relationship with the other three components of the dark personality scores positive, and a negative relationship with kindness, honesty/humility, and emotional intelligence.

THE RELATIONSHIP BETWEEN DARK TRAITS

As mentioned, dark traits generally refer to subclinical personality traits that relate to dubious behaviors in ethical, moral, or social terms. High levels of dark traits are associated with selfishness or unjust decisions (Moshagen, Hilbig, and Zettler, 2018). Dark traits are also connected with other personality variables such as impulsivity, sensation-seeking, short-term tactics, and risky behaviors (Crysel, Crosier, and Webster, 2013).

Paulhus and Williams (2002) coined the term "Dark Triad" to include three distinctive personality traits related to harmful behavior toward others: Machiavellianism, narcissism, and psychopathy; they later added sadism as a fourth element. Having a Machiavellian personality implies being manipulative, cold, and cunning. Narcissism is a subclinical version of a personality disorder that encompasses certain aspects associated with feelings of superiority, dominance, exaggerated importance of the self, megalomania, the need to be admired by others, a belief in having more rights than others, and a lack of empathy. Psychopathy also has a subclinic variant, related to high impulsivity and a never-ending search for sensations, insensitivity, and a low level of empathy and anxiety. Sadism can be defined as the development of behaviors that inflict physical or mental suffering on others, which makes sadists experience sexual arousal and satisfaction; in most cases, it implies exercising cruelty over others, and such cruelty produces pleasure to those who inflict it.

These traits share some characteristics; the most notable is that those who show them carry out actions that are harmful to others to accentuate their personal grandeur; they appear apathetic and can even attack others if necessary. According to Jones and Paulhus (2014), while psychopaths act impulsively, abandon their friends and family, and ignore their reputation, Machiavellians make plans, build alliances, and try to maintain a good reputation. Narcissists are also characterized by being manipulative, but their arrogance hides a sense of insecurity. Narcissism also differs from Machiavellianism in that the former is not deliberate and implies a certain level of self-deception. Narcissists tend to be optimistic, overconfident, and believe in their exaggerations even when those are obviously false. The driving force of narcissists is to increase their egos, while the Machiavellians have instrumental motivations. In turn, Machiavellians in most cases have long-term objectives, while the goals of a psychopath are usually immediate.

Some authors (Moshagen, Hilbig, and Zettler, 2018) argue that dark personality traits overlap significantly, on the grounds that they are characterized by insensitivity and the manipulation of others; they suggest the existence of a common core—a tendency toward dubious behavior in ethical, moral, or social terms—which they call the dark factor of personality. Thus, according to this approach, the dark traits of personality would be specific manifestations of a general tendency to maximize personal benefits, ignoring possible harm to others.

In order to be able to carry out an assault against anybody, those who score high on the dark personality scale, just as it would be for anybody, need to devise convincing reasons to reassure themselves that what they are doing is, in effect, the right thing to do. In other words, one needs to create beliefs that serve as justifications. When those who score high in dark factor tests explain their actions or evaluate their actions they do not negatively consider the consequences for others, but rather positively value the results obtained for themselves. Dark traits or dark personality are not only the four cited; there could be several others, although it is unclear whether they are new factors or are included in those cited. Even though we are commenting about the high correlation among them, it is not of great interest to further explore them. In any case, such factors as selfishness (pursuing advantages or pleasure for oneself at the expense of others), the sense of justice (the belief that one deserves more than others), self-interest (pursuing socially valued benefits), or malevolence (a tendency to harm others even if you damage yourself) could be included in that denomination.

Other authors also include moral disengagement—finding justifications for certain behaviors toward others in specific contexts—as a typical characteristic of a dark personality. And yet, as explained above, moral disengagement may also be considered not an element of the dark personality but a justification of evil.

MORAL DISENGAGEMENT

According to Bandura (1990, 1999), when people develop moral identities, they adopt norms about what is right or wrong that guide or restrict their behaviors. Through a process of self-regulation, we behold our behaviors and assess them in relation to our moral principles, the circumstances, and the consequences of our actions. We do things that enhance our sense of integrity and refrain from violating our moral principles to avoid perceiving a negative image of ourselves. Bandura, Barbaranelli, Caprara, and Pastorelli (1996) argue that people self-regulate their behaviors when they estimate that they are violating, or will violate, their own internal rules or standards. Failure to comply with personal standards of behavior creates a state of aversion for the individual that triggers control processes to prevent that violation. However, these control processes must be active in order to operate, but self-regulation is sometimes put on hold owing to the triggering of a process of disassociating internal controls. Individuals can avoid this aversive state when they commit a harmful act by reinterpreting their actions, removing themselves from being agents of harmful acts, minimizing or ignoring negative consequences, or blaming the recipients of their behavior. This concept refers to a psychological scheme whereby moral authorizations can be disconnected from those behaviors that would be harmful, making harmful acts acceptable and allowing immoral and antisocial behavior (Caprara, Tisak, Alessandri, Fontaine, Fida, and Paciello, 2013).

The first set of characteristics, which focuses on reinterpreting harmful behavior in positive terms, encompasses moral justification, euphemistic labelling, and advantageous comparison:

- Moral justification involves explaining harmful behavior as morally positive and as personally and socially acceptable.
- Euphemistic labelling involves using sophisticated language or explicitly positive expressions to describe a reprehensible behavior and present it as benign.
- Advantageous comparison involves comparing a reprehensible behavior with a much more serious transgression, and in so doing, the action committed seems irrelevant or even positive in comparison.

Other mechanisms involve distorting the actions that are going to be carried out or that were carried out, through the displacement or diffusion of responsibility:

- Displacement of responsibility implies attributing the responsibility for the harmful act to the situation or to others, to minimize personal responsibility, while also avoiding self-condemnation.
- Diffusion of responsibility involves admitting only an irrelevant part of one's responsibility in a harmful action or attributing it to a collective decision. It is common that any negative action committed by one group is attributed mainly to others through this mechanism.

The third group of mechanisms involves ignoring or distorting the consequences of the action, focusing on its positive effects (personal benefits, for example), thus minimizing the negative effects on victims.

Finally, there are mechanisms of disengagement from the victim or the recipient of a harmful behavior.

- One of these mechanisms is dehumanization. When we perceive someone as an individual human being like us, it is difficult not to empathize with them, and hurting them would make us feel uncomfortable. Dehumanization consists of stigmatizing the victims and attributing negative traits to them that make them worthy of negative behaviors, preventing us from perceiving them as people with the same feelings, desires, and concerns that we have.
- Another mechanism that focuses on victims is the attribution of guilt. Aggressors often hold their victims accountable for the damage they suffer; as a result, this damage is interpreted as retaliation caused by their conduct, never the aggressor's.

Moral disengagement mechanisms do not make the individual automatically insensitive and cruel. As self-censorship caused by minor transgressions lessens, the individual becomes more inclined to tolerate harmful behaviors, eventually feeling no discomfort (Bandura, 1990, 1999). Individuals use these mechanisms as neutralization techniques—that is, rationalizations through which certain actions, despite being against their own moral principles, are deemed appropriate in certain situations. This allows those individuals to feel committed to their moral principles while taking on behavior that violates their standards. The motivation to carry out actions against one's moral principles would arise from the discrepancy between the personal toll of violating their principles and that of losing the potential benefit that the action might carry. At least in situations that involve minor acts of social deviation, it is common that individuals distort the moral implications of the behaviors they wish to perform and act against their principles (Bersoff, 1999). Moral disengagement focuses on avoiding internal sanctions associated with the violation of moral principles. In the case of other dark traits, beliefs related to justifications for harmful behaviors are more general (cynicism, maximizing profits at the expense of others, sense of superiority, etc.), and individuals who hold these beliefs do not deny that their behavior is harmful, but they can justify it on the basis of the personal results that they obtain. People avoid internal sanctions by using disengagement strategies in pursuit of their own interest but need to rationalize their immoral behavior and cannot ignore their moral principles when they clash with their desired outcomes. The discrepancy between the behaviors and the principles that they violate give rise to an aversive state which motivates individuals to distort their perceptions until they devise a rationalization that allows them to reconcile their principles with the behaviors that violate them.

Individuals who show high levels of moral disengagement tend to be irritable, more prone to revenge, to physical and verbal violence, and to conflict. Notwithstanding, they feel less foreseeable guilt due to their detrimental behavior. Morally disengaged individuals are also antisocial and less able to resist peer pressure to carry out potentially harmful activities (Paciello, Fida, Tramontano, Lupinetti, and Caprara, 2008). Moral disengagement is directly connected to aggressive and violent behavior (Espejo-Siles, Zych, Farrington, and Llorent, 2020). There is a positive relationship between moral disengagement and aggression, mainly in men (Rubio-Garay, Carrasco-Ortiz, and García-Rodríguez, 2019). Moral disengagement allows individuals to carry out harmful behavior without placing self-blame or feeling harmful emotions (Caprara, Tisak, Alessandri, Fontaine, Fida, and Paciello, 2013).

Recent studies show that there are differences in gender and moral disengagement, being higher in men than in women (Paciello, Fida, Tramontano, Lupinetti, and Caprara, 2008). Age also appears to be a factor that conditions moral disengagement, which is more common in childhood, adolescence, and youth. Young people who have dark personality traits are more likely to have morally disengaging attitudes.

People who score high in traits of the Dark Tetrad also tend to show high levels of moral disengagement, which allows them to justify their actions under the pretext that they are against their moral standards (Erzi, 2020). The feature of the tetrad that is closest to moral disengagement is Machiavellianism, as it allows individuals to justify their acts of deception and manipulation. Lack of empathy is a trait of the Dark Tetrad that is also present in moral disengagement, since moral disengagement is motivated by feelings of selfishness. It would be difficult for an empathic person to justify or ignore the negative consequences of their acts on others, and this would prevent moral disengagement (Clemente, Espinosa, and Padilla, 2019).

As mentioned before, moral disengagement is related to antisocial behaviors, which may be enhanced when combined with dark personality traits. For psychopaths, the need to resort to moral disengagement is not so urgent because they do not always perceive their immoral behaviors as being wrong. Both psychopathy and Machiavellianism are related to moral disengagement and antisocial behavior, due to the similarity between these two personality traits. Narcissism, on the other hand, relates differently to moral disengagement. antisocial behavior can be related to feelings of guilt or shame because being antisocial entails an inherent threat of losing other's approval, thus increasing the need for moral disconnection. Therefore, while Machiavellianism and psychopathy are related to antisocial behavior, narcissism is not (Sijtsema, Garofalo, Jansen, and Klimstra, 2019).

THE DARK TETRAD OF PERSONALITY AND INTIMATE AND/OR PARTNER RELATIONSHIPS

Those who exhibit traits of the Dark Tetrad see their social relationships affected—in particular, their intimate and partner relationships. Their sexual relations are often deteriorated due to factors such as promiscuity, jealousy, violence toward the couple, and so on.

Lack of empathy, which is one of the common traits of the tetrad, leads to a lack of involvement in sex-affective relationships. Furthermore, the dark personality is directly related to having more than one sexual partner, living an unrestricted sociosexuality, and having a clear preference for short-term relationships (Jonason, Li, Webster, and Schmitt, 2009).

In addition, those who exhibit these traits tend to attract people that are already in a couple and try to form a new one with them, while at the same time, their partners are attracted by others. As a result, this disposition that both parties have toward forming new couples elevates the variety and hence the number of couples they may have, favoring short-term relationships (Jonason, Li, and Buss, 2010).

Men seem to prefer short-term relationships more often than women. Men also score higher in dark personality traits more often than women. Men who score high on dark personality tests are more likely to establish short-term relationships (Jonason, Li, Webster, and Schmitt, 2009). This is associated with infidelity, since establishing short relationships promotes the search for relations with others outside the couple to satisfy one's own desires (Jia, Ing, and Lee, 2016).

Dark personality individuals find it easier to establish short-term relationships because they generally hold low expectations of their future partners. Even when those expectations are initially high, they are willing to lower them to have more pairing options (Jonason, Valentine, Li, and Harbeson, 2011). On the other hand, women who score high on narcissism and Machiavellianism maintain their expectations toward their future partner and are more likely to focus on the qualities of the partner which sometimes leads to infidelity (Brewer, Erickson, Whitaker, and Lyons, 2020).

Jonason, Luevano, and Adams (2012) pinpoint four different short-term relationships: one-night relations; "booty-calls" (where one contacts the person they are having a short-term relationship with to have sex); "friends with benefits" (friends who have sex but do not define their relationship as romantic); and serious romantic relationships. The first three cases involve a sexual encounter with someone who is not a stable partner.

Narcissists are slightly predisposed toward more open sexuality in general, such as "booty-calls" or "friends with benefits." Machiavellians are reluctant to engage in serious relationships and prefer one-night relationships and "booty-calls." Psychopaths show a preference for "booty-calls" because, in this type of relationship, the other person is basically "used" to have sex—as in one-night relations and with "friends with benefits" (Jonason, Luevano, and Adams, 2012; Koladich and Atkinson, 2016). Studies suggest that narcissistic men give importance to the social status of the couple to begin a serious relationship, while women do not (Jonason, Valentine, Li, and Harbeson, 2011).

Other factors that are crucial when it comes to pairing and establishing sexual preferences are emotional intelligence, jealousy, and the different style of attachment of each person. Thus, having dark personality traits can influence the dynamics of romantic couples through anxious and evocative attachment, accommodation, and the control of the couple (Apostolou, Paphiti, Neza, Damianou, and Georgiadou, 2019; Brewer, Bennet, Davidson, Ireen, Phipps, Stewart-Wilkes, and Wilson, 2018).

A study conducted by Chin et al., (2017) associated the Dark Triad of personality with the three dimensions of romantic jealousy, which are behavioral, cognitive, and emotional jealousy. Their initial conclusions were that all traits of the triad are associated with cognitive and behavioral jealousy, but only narcissists are involved in emotional jealousy. Cognitive jealousy is less related to Machiavellianism and narcissism. Psychopathy is the trait of the triad that most closely relates to behavioral jealousy, followed by narcissism and Machiavellianism. The study also related emotional jealousy to a high degree of self-esteem and sense of authority, which is more associated with narcissism and with emotional and behavioral jealousy (Chin, Atkinson, Raheb, Harris, and Vernon, 2017).

Male psychopaths are more unfaithful than female, while in Machiavellianism there are no differences between genders. Narcissists are not systematically unfaithful, but they might be it if they find it worth their while (Jia, Ing, and Lee, 2016). A sense of revenge often arises as a result of unfaithfulness. Machiavellians are more likely to leave the couple, while psychopaths are not (Jones and Weiser, 2014). Similarly, women who score high on dark personality are not only more likely to be unfaithful, but they also believe they are more vulnerable to their partner's unfaithfulness (Brewer, Hunt, James, and Abell, 2015). Unfaithfulness might be said to be one of the ways in which people who have a dark personality can maintain a long-term relationship (Jones and Weiser, 2014).

Individuals who have dark personality traits tend to be violent in their interpersonal relationships, and couple relationships are one of the main areas where they can show that violence, which is usually psychological in nature. Given the characteristics and personality behaviors of each of these disorders, it is common for this type of violence to be made invisible within couples. Marshall (1999) mentions that certain indicators such as threats, criticism, insults, and humiliation contribute to making it more obvious; others, however, such as manipulation of information or disregard for the other person's emotions, are more subtle.

According to different studies, it is more common for Machiavellians and psychopaths to exercise psychological abuse than for narcissists. Psychopaths also make more use of intimidation and domination, and they are prone to denigrating their partner (Carton and Egan, 2017). Besides, those who score high in psychopathy tend to look for people with low levels of kindness, facilitating the creation of a volatile environment that might help them calm their impulsivity. Since dark personality traits are associated with aggressive behaviors, it is common for people who have them to accept those traits in their partners as well (Jonason, Valentine, Li, and Harbeson, 2011).

Exerting control over the couple is an important aspect of that form of psychological violence; individuals with primary psychopathy are more likely to exercise that control over the couple, and along with Machiavellians, they show a need to master and control the behavior of the couple. Narcissism, on the other hand, is not associated with the exercise of control over the couple (Brewer, Bennet, Davidson, Ireen, Phipps, Stewart-Wilkes, and Wilson, 2018).

REVENGE

Let us once again emphasize how an individual who has a dark personality may react when interacting with others, and what actions they might take against others, especially their partner, former partner, or children. Perhaps the most dangerous personality when it comes to interpreting reality is the narcissist, as they may understand any action from their partner or former partner as a radical attack on them.

Revenge is one of the main causes of crime (including cases of abuse or sexting), and it also serves as an explanation for most homicides (Kopsaj, 2016). Revenge is a phenomenon that is present in practically all societies. In some cases, acts of revenge extend for long periods, even years after the fact that triggered it occurred. Revenge comes in many guises, depending on whether it is sought out by a unique individual or by a group (Pereira and Van Prooijen, 2018). On an individual level, it is generally more intense. Group revenge requires the existence of entitativity—that is, a unique thought that is created to unite the group.

Jackson, Choi, and Gelfand (2019) suggest a definition of revenge, which they consider an assault and therefore a behavioral response from an individual or group. It is based on the perception of an injustice suffered by the individual or group—which, in turn, becomes an aggressor—and is directed against the person the aggressor identifies as the root of the damage stemming from the injustice they previously have perceived. Thus, while revenge is behavioral, it is essential that the person seeking revenge be perceived to have been damaged and that the damage they believe to have suffered is not involuntary (Gray and Wegner, 2007; Young, Scholz, and Saxe, 2011). This might explain why revenge and anger are often closely related (Lerner and Tiedens, 2006) and also why anger is a good predictor of revenge (Tripp and Bies, 2010). The relationship between anger and revenge with the variables of dark personality has been widely studied, and it is particularly notable in narcissism (Exline et al., 2004; Twenge and Campbell, 2003).

Revenge also serves as an alternative mechanism to the judicial system. As some studies suggest, justice does not "subjectively" satisfy the alleged victim or those who consider themselves victims (Jackson, Choi, and Gelfand, 2019). In fact, a court ruling may often give occasion for revenge, as both sides may feel that the judicial decision did not solve the problem or that the one who believes to be the injured party is not properly compensated.

The situation becomes even more complex in cases of conflict between parents, whereby issues are to be resolved by family law courts. Not only it is rather difficult for the justice system to solve a problem of parent-child relations, but in some cases, the system itself will worsen the existing relations (Clemente et al., 2015; Clemente and Padilla-Racero 2018a, 2018b). One of the characteristics of revenge is that it can be carried out despite the judicial actions and has nothing to do with that system. This may also occur because the future aggressor considers that the damage caused must be repaired directly, regardless of the judicial actions. Revenge is harmful; its goal is to inflict pain on others, and it is accompanied by bitterness, a concept that is excluded from criminal codes but not from personal decisions.

The idea of revenge, and especially when it focuses on harming others, is opposed to forgiveness, a more religious than psychological concept which has been particularly explored by positive psychology (Adam-Karduz and Saricam, 2018; Garzón-Azañón and Barahona-Esteban, 2018). Although—after analyzing previous studies by Kaminer, Stein, Mbanga, and Zungu (2000)—Casullo (2005) has created a scale (CAPER) to measure forgiveness, the concept has not been thoroughly defined or studied from a psychological point of view.

Forgiveness is a process that involves decreasing the motivation to retaliate, as well as the negative emotions that are felt toward the person that is considered the aggressor. Forgiveness implies that negative emotions become positive emotions such as compassion or benevolence. Adam-Karduz and Saricam (2018) demonstrated that positive thinking, forgiveness, and happiness are interrelated concepts, which are negatively correlated with revenge.

The functionality of revenge and what is gained by whoever takes revenge has been the subject of much debate (McCullough, Kurzban, and Tabak, 2012). There is still no evidence that revenge generates any personal benefit (Jackson, Choi, and Gelfand, 2019; Carlsmith and Darley, 2008). With regard to family courts, some authors claim that the use of the justice system itself may be a way of assaulting the other parent (Clemente, Padilla-Racero, and Espinosa, 2019a, 2019b); in their view, there is an individual aggression through the system itself, which becomes an accomplice of the aggression. Such aggression usually comes from individuals who score high on the dark personality traits, but the main predictor is a high score on variables involving narcissism and moral disassociation (Clemente, Espinosa, and Padilla-Racero, 2019). The reasons these individuals might have for revenge often originate from the fact that their former couple was the one who separated (Padilla-Racero and Clemente, 2018a, 2018b), and they seek indirect revenge through the children they have in common. The analysis of the situation from the point of view of forensic psychology is of particular interest, since parents who score high on the scale of judicial manipulation created by Clemente,

Padilla-Racero, and Espinosa (2019b) are prone to manipulating their children, sometimes occasionally physically and sexually assaulting them, and even causing their death, as a form of revenge on the other parent.

In fact, revenge tends to be more harmful if the allegedly injured party is close to the person perceived as an aggressor, especially if this person was their partner (Chester and DeWall, 2016; Thau, Aquino, and Poortvliet, 2007). Furthermore, when revenge is carried out by emotionally close people, in addition to judicial harassment (Clemente, Padilla-Racero, and Espinosa, 2019b, 2019c), they use all kinds of elements at their disposal such as gossip, offensive comments to acquaintances of the partner, coercive actions such as persecutions, and the like (Elshout, Nelissen, and Van Beest, 2016; Yoshimura and Boon, 2014). The aggressors make use of what is called "virtuous violence" (Fiske and Rai, 2014) as a form of moral disengagement, in such a way that they perceive that the only way left for them is to take revenge. In addition, they seek—and make sure they obtain—the support of those around them, in order for their revenge to become a social and moral obligation, even supported by social values. On the other hand, it has been argued that the justice system of societies in which there is a greater culture of honor tend be more tolerant toward male practices of assaulting females (Aquino, Tripp, and Bies, 2006; Dietz, Ostrom, and Stern, 2004; Grosjean, 2014). The process of revenge has a limit, which is usually reached when the person that is the object of the revenge is more powerful and resourceful than the one seeking revenge. However, the opposite is often the case—that is, the one that seeks revenge (and therefore believes that they have been wronged) is usually the one who has the most power to attack the other (Aquino, Tripp, and Bies, 2006).

CONCLUSIONS

Reality is obstinate. A single example may suffice to illustrate the ideas we have explored in this chapter; it happened in Spain, and it is known as the "José Bretón case," named after the name of the father, or the "Ruth and José case," the name of his children. When they disappeared, Ruth was 6 years old and Joseph 2 years old. Both were killed by José Bretón, who also burned their bodies, leaving hardly any remains to identify the corpses.

In September 2011, Ruth Ortiz informed her husband, José Bretón Gómez—with whom she had two children, Ruth and José—of her intention to divorce him. Joseph Bretón then conceived the idea of killing his children as revenge against his wife. He knew it was the best way to bury the mother in life, as it meant taking away from her what she loved most. After picking up his children for the weekend the day before, on October 8, 2011, the crime was committed.

To develop his plan, José Bretón decided that the safest place to kill his children was his parents' country house. He asked his psychiatrist for more of the tranquilizers he was taking, with the intention of, once the time came, to be able to numb and kill his children easily. He also collected some firewood and bought some fuel in order to make the corpses of his children disappear. Meanwhile, he was devising an alibi to justify the disappearance of the children, arguing that he had lost them in a playground.

After fetching his children, he gave them an unspecified number of tranquilizers to provoke their total numbness or death. Once they arrived at the country house, he prepared a sort of funeral pyre, in which he placed the bodies of his children and started a large bonfire which quickly came to full force thanks to the use of firewood and fuel, reaching temperatures of up to 1200 °C, which caused an effect similar to a crematorium oven. Such high temperatures caused the soft parts of the children's bodies to disappear quickly, leaving only a few bones as remains. José Bretón stood next to the bonfire feeding it with fuel (accelerant) to keep the high temperature that allowed the total calcination and disappearance of the corpses of his children.

That night, he went to the police to file a complaint about the alleged disappearance of his children, leading to the inception of judicial proceedings, despite the fact that he obviously knew that there had been no such disappearance, because he himself had killed them.

José Bretón was sentenced to 40 years in prison for double murder. Aggravating circumstances in the sentencing were the familial relationship, premeditation, and the ruthless nature of his actions in the execution of the facts.

The news story ends here, without specifying that José Breton achieved his goal, revenge on his former wife for having separated from him and divorced. Bretón interpreted his wife's decision as an unacceptable attack, which triggered an irreversible process of revenge. We do not have a psychological evaluation of José Bretón; therefore, we do not know how he might have scored on a dark personality test, but his plan was meticulous (not typical of psychopaths), void of empathy with his victims, including his children (this characteristic is typical of all types of dark personality); there is no evidence whatsoever as to whether he felt pleasure through the aggression (in fact the way of killing his children was not such that he could take pleasure with their suffering); thus, everything seems to indicate that his profile is closer to that of a narcissist, someone who, when felt questioned and ridiculed, is capable of becoming a killer. It is possible that what triggered his perception of being under attack is that he, as a male, could not tolerate that his wife decided to end the relationship; he, as a male, could end the relationship with his wife, but the other way around meant that his role as a male was called into question; this is what we call a "culture of honor," one in which men cannot be called into question by women. José's plan for revenge achieved such an accomplished attack on his ex-wife that he "buried her alive." The fact that he had to kill his children was the least of his worries; after all, he might have thought, "the end justifies the means."

Our belief is that this example illustrates how the notions explained at the beginning of this chapter are not mere theory, and that scoring high on the dark personality tests is not a trivial matter. We have no information about the explanations that José Bretón gave—and probably still gives—to himself in order to justify what he did, but those of us who interview imprisoned, convicted persons know perfectly well that all of them claim to have done nothing wrong (see Gomez, Ortega-Ruiz, Clemente, and Casas, 2021, which analyzes the information collected from 92 men convicted of attempted homicide or the homicide of their partners).

Chapter 10

Revenge on the Other Parent

We referred to revenge at the end of chapter 9, specifying how it is an explicative factor in the majority of criminal action and therefore also used when a conflict unravels between parents. We have also seen the connection between revenge and dark personality.

THE SCALE OF JUDICIAL MANIPULATION

One of the current problems in society today is the growing number of couples that separate, which leads to many children growing up under the protection of only one parent. If the couple that separates has children, and they have a troubled relationship, it becomes difficult to leave the children out of the parents' fight; even worse, the children become a weapon to attack one of the parents, under manipulation and provoking damage.

From a legal standpoint, the topic is of great relevance (it concerns the protection of children); and yet, from the psychological standpoint, it is no less important, since the variable of manipulation is introduced in the father-daughter relationship. Thus, from a psychological point of view, it should be determined if the parents offer their children affect and sincerity and do everything possible to educate them with positive values, or on the contrary, if they are willing to use their children to attack the other parent, often out of revenge of the other if he or she is the one that separated. Unfortunately, as we can see in the papers almost every day, that act of vengeance sometimes results in the death of the child, as the attacker sees it as the worst possible attack against their couple. Obviously, as we have already mentioned, that implies that one of the members of the couple feels love for the child, and the other does not; if one of them does not feel that love, they may jeopardize the life of the child.

In the previous chapter, we also explained how people who manifest larger levels of Machiavellianism, psychopathy, narcissism, and/or sadism (that is, the variables of the dark personality) are more capable of tricking and lying before a court about the maltreatment inflicted on the other member of the couple toward them or toward their own children. Although it has not been possible to demonstrate it, it could be reasoned that if an individual accepts an "unfair" court behavior, this might suggest the existence of a dark personality, which could be a limiting factor in encouraging contact between them and their children.

THE USE OF COURT MANIPULATION AS REVENGE

Some studies have demonstrated that parents who are willing to lie in a court process with the object of going against the other parent, even manipulating their children, are Machiavellian, narcissist, and have a subclinic psychopathic personality. For this reason, this research team created a scale in which the parent is asked if they would be willing to cheat and lie before justice to achieve a goal, when that goal is revenge on another parent who wanted to end the relationship. The first part of the scale refers fundamentally to providing false information about the other parent; the second part focuses on the manipulation of the children. That scale, which has been called the Judicial Manipulation Scale, signifies a major contribution to the scientific advancement in the psychological-forensic field of analysis. Consequently, it might be of great help for the justice system when determining what parent should have the custody of the children and how the visitation rights should be established for the other parent.

As it was also the case with other basic premises of Gardner's PAS (Clemente and Padilla-Racero, 2015a, 2015b), the results of this study confirm that the possible manipulative behaviors of the parents during and after the family rupture depend on the specific personality variables of each person, and not, as Gardner defends, on a disease or syndrome that mothers have and pass on to their children. These results coincide with other studies which specify that the ranking of an individual on the Dark Triad scale does not depend on the gender but on each specific variable (Jonason and Davis, 2018; Jonason, Oshio, Shimotsukasa, Mieda, Csatho, and Sitnikova, 2018; Tran, Bertl, Kossmeier, Pietschnig, Stieger, and Voracek, 2018). This line of investigation generates results that refute Gardner's unscientific ideas (1985, 1991, 1998, 1999) and those of his followers (Bernet, Boch-Galhau, Baker, and Morrison, 2010; Bernet, Baker, and Verrocchio, 2015; Clawar and Rivlin, 2013; Gardner, Sauber, and Lorandos, 2006; Gottlieb, 2012; Lorandos, Bernet, and Sauber, 2013; Warshak, 2015a, 2015b). The results offer a way of working based on empirical evidence, considering the consequences that the children and their parents endure from being constantly subdued to judicial imperatives that accept the unscientific PAS in court hearings. That acceptance in the courts—as well as the validation and dissemination of the PAS— is what fosters (Kleinman and Kaplan, 2016; Nichols, 2014; O'Donohue, Benuto, and Bennett, 2016; Padilla-Racero and Clemente, 2018a; 2018b; Shaw, 2016) the physical or psychological abuse that is infringed on the other parent.

An important contributing aspect of this study is that it opens the possibility to scientifically determine who is manipulating the court, and, therefore, to scientifically assist justice. The scale was called judicial manipulation because Machiavellianism is the most analyzed and recognized variable of the Dark Triad.

THE ACTS OF REVENGE THAT PEOPLE ARE WILLING TO TAKE

The question is: Is the general population capable of taking legal action against their former couple? If the answer were yes, to which extent would they manifest it? To answer that question, our team selected a number of facts that, according to the professionals (psychologists and social workers) who work for the justice system, usually emerge in cases in which there is a problematic relationship between parents. Let us to point out that fathers and mothers who were divorced—but who had not gone through a conflicting separation—were also asked; though they had never taken the actions that were going to be set out before them, they were being asked to state whether they would be willing to take such actions. This is a brief summary of the results, starting with ranking the actions that the subjects would accept to engage in, from most likely to least likely.

Firstly, it is worth noting that revenge against the other parent after a separation is not common, but manifests in a statistically (and socially) important degree. Although most of the parents dismiss revenge, the percentage taking revenge once they believe they have been attacked is, in some cases, around 5 percent. That is, 1 in every 20 persons would not oppose taking revenge against their former couple; although if that implies sexual aggression toward the children, that percentage is much less, being somewhat below 1 percent (it is a rather low figure, but socially it is high, and it implies the necessity to protect the children when they are living in that circumstance).

The results of our studies indicated how the behavior with a larger degree of agreeability ("solicit custody of the daughter only for not having paid the alimony") is accepted by 5.2 percent of the subjects, while the less acceptable behavior (e.g., "sexually assault your daughter by putting things in her vagina or anus, in such a way that it bleeds, but in the case of the vagina that it is not deep enough for it to break the hymen, and later say that she did it herself") was accepted only by 0.8 percent who were willing to take action. That indicates that the use of the children is not accepted by the majority, but it is alarming that 5 percent of the parents are willing to use their children to take revenge on the other parent, and even worse, that close to 1 percent of the fathers are willing to sexually abuse their children, provoking serious harm.

As each one of the actions is representative of facts that do in fact take place with conflicting ex-couples, we believe it is important to mention all of them, as meaningful examples of the interactions. However, we should clarify that we understand that being in conflict does not mean that both parents are at fault and responsible for generating problems. Commonly, the situation heeds to the norm that one of the members of the couple is the aggressor, and the other is the attacked. Besides, as we mentioned before, aggressors do not care for their children (or much less), and those who are under attack are the ones who actually love their children.

As we said, the first action that the interviewed subjects were willing to take was to request sole custody of the child just because the other parent had stopped paying alimony, with 5.2 percent of the parents willing to follow through with that process. The second action was to explain to the child that you are living a terrible situation, and that your former couple—who is to blame—had decided unilaterally to break up the relationship, and that is the reason that provoked the entire problem, with 3.6 percent. The third action was, in the case that your child refused to go with you on the visits, request the court for the police to escort your child to you, taking them from their home (of your former couple) against their will, 2.6 percent. Another act with a similar proportion of points was convincing your common friends to no longer have any contact with your ex-couple. With a score of 2.3 percent, the action of convincing the child that the alimony was being spent whimsically by the custodial parent, and not on the child's well-being, food or education. Vilifying your ex-couple for everyone to know about how their decision devastated you, this happens in 2.1 percent of the cases. Refusing to pay any amount beyond alimony, any expense on health or the education of the child, is 2 percent. Convincing children that they have a different name and they need to use it in your former couple's house only to annoy them, is represented by 2 percent. Generating damaging false rumors about your former couple occur in 1.8 percent of the cases. Other hypothetical cases were: "As you know that your former couple is bothered by the fact that your daughter does not study or do her homework"; "Request the sole custody, which means that the child would live with you and your parents, even if you were not keen on the idea, but you would do so out of spite and to separate your ex-couple from your child"; "Continuously report to the courts that your child is refusing to see you and blame your ex-couple, who is manipulating, and ask the court to punish (your ex-couple and your child) them accordingly"; "Use all of the resources at your disposal to take revenge on your ex-couple"; "Speak with the parents of your ex-couple and try to win them over so that they think of their child as a bad person"; "Wait all the necessary time, even years, to take revenge on your ex-couple"; "Stop paying money to your ex for the alimony of your child, even though you are obligated by a judge, with the risk of being fined or even arrested"; "Take advantage of any moment to speak poorly of your ex-couple to your child"; "Call your ex on the telephone with a withheld private number at any hour of the night to bother them"; "Report to the authorities at every possible opportunity that your ex-couple treats your child poorly, does not feed them or care for them properly, etcetera, even if you know that is a lie"; "Threaten your ex with taking revenge and using your child to do so"; "Contrive the story and report it to the court, that your child shows markings as if he or she has been hit, accusing your ex-couple to get them into trouble"; "Request the courts to admit your child into a center for minors to separate him or her from your ex-couple"; "Destroy the change of clothes of your child when it is your turn to have them for the weekend, so that your ex-couple will be afraid of what you could do to the child, and later say that it was your child who ripped the clothes, and that you cannot do anything about it"; "Hit your daughter lightly so that she has bruises and signs of hitting, and later say that the child is very restless and is always falling, so that it cannot be demonstrated that it was you"; "As you know that it bothers your ex-pair if your child is not clean, after a weekend, return them very dirty without having had a bath any day"; "As you know that it bothers your ex-pair if your child does not eat properly, give them only candies to eat"; "Contact the neighbors of your ex-couple to tell them your version and criticize her"; "Paint messages on the walls of the house of your ex-couple and of your child with insults towards your ex-couple"; "In the case that you have assaulted your child, say that they did it themselves, and provoke that they hurt themselves"; "Go to the school of your child and speak poorly of your ex-couple to the teachers and to those who work at the center"; "Whenever possible, damage their things, for example, streaking the car, puncturing the tires or staining the clothes that are hanging or to what you have access when they open the door for you to pick up your daughter"; "Stalk your ex-couple when you can, following them with your car so that they feel threatened"; "Sexually assault your child putting things in their anus or vagina without it being deep so that the hymen remains intact, and later say that the child did that herself"; "If your son becomes ill or suffers an accident, do not take them to the doctor in order to bother your ex-couple"; "Ask your current couple to help bother your previous couple, mother or father of your children"; "Ask other people to lie before the courts to harm your ex-couple"; and "Do not doubt in using your child whenever necessary to harm your ex-couple."

Let us highlight that, after analyzing the results of the survey, there were no major differences found between men and women in any of the variables of revenge. But upon verifying who, in effect, use these strategies (actions that were set forth), they were normally men, and women were the victims. This reveals how the techniques of self-reporting present a significant bias.

DETERMINING THE COMPONENTS OF REVENGE

Afterward we sought to ascertain if revenge is a unique variable or has various components. We applied a technique called Factor Analysis, and the results showed three existing factors:

- Revenge through the children and third parties: The actions that this form of revenge entails refer to the commission of sexual abuse on the children, as well as convincing people from the inner circle of the aggressor, above all his family, of the wickedness of the victim—as a form of assault.
- Revenge through economic manipulation: This includes all the attempts of not paying the alimony corresponding to the child. This implies the use of economic harassment to the other parent, even the constant use of the justice system to incite vast expenses for the legal defense of the attacked person, above all, by having to pay lawyers.
- Revenge by cutting off communication: This refers to extreme behavior that implies cutting of any type of negotiation with the ex-couple, including threats, cutting off communication with common friends, or using all the necessary resources and time to take revenge on the ex-couple.

It is worth noting that in men, the ideology of the role in the relationship is between the dark personality and revenge, but not so in women. Thus, the model shows differences between sexes when conceiving revenge. Men who are machista and who have a dark personality are the ones who take revenge.

To a great measure, the behavior of revenge involves children. In fact, statistically the use of children is common within the behaviors of revenge.

Expect narcissism, every component of the dark personality is related with revenge. In fact, authors such as Egan, Hughes, and Palmer (2015) have argued that narcissism is the "less dark" factor within the dark triad, and that its correlation with other indicators of negative behavior is not as high as that of Machiavellianism or psychopathy.

The results verify that there are people who perverse the manner in which "justice" is administered, using the system as a weapon of attack against those they wish to harm; this idea led Clemente, Padilla-Racero, Espinosa,

Reig-Botella, and Gandoy-Crego (2019) to create a scale to measure judicial harassment (see chapter 8 of this book). Previous research on psychology and family law have suggested how sometimes, one parent would cause either psychological or physical harm to the children in order to attack the other parent. This other parent, observing this maneuver, would feel obligated to file a report which entails the need to prove aggressions that are usually impossible to prove, as they occurred behind closed doors. This, in turn, works against the parent that filed the report, who is then charged by the parent who assaulted the child (Clemente, Padilla-Racero, Gandoy, Reig-Botella, and Gonzalez-Rodriguez, 2015; Padilla-Racero and Clemente, 2018). This study has offered data that until now has been unknown, such as the percentage of persons capable of using procedures for revenge against the other parent.

Undoubtedly, the use of one's own children to take revenge, to the extent of sexually abusing them, is clearly related to the dark personality and to the driving forces of moral disengagement, which are part of the Dark Personality Factor (Clemente, Espinosa, and Padilla-Racero, 2019). Those who use their children to take revenge must reify them in an attempt to dehumanize them and the couple, placing the need to take revenge—after having been humiliated—above them. Clemente, Padilla-Racero, and Espinosa (2019b, 2019c) already established that the origin of such thought is usually the fact that the offense suffered by that person is that the couple decided to separate. Besides, if it was a woman who decided to stop the relationship, that was an affront against his manhood, as he regards himself as the one who has the capacity of taking such decision, while that is not even an option for the woman. This phenomenon is usually called "virtuous violence" (Fiske and Rai, 2014), a concept that coincides with what shows the disheartening fact that the more patriarchal a society is, the more women are attacked within the frame of the intimate relationship, but especially after the separation, which is understood by the male as an act of offense.

Another important issue is that the separation of the couple is one of the most significant areas in which revenge occurs, as Chester and DeWall (2016) established. Revenge is more far-reaching if the person who feels injured is close to the alleged aggressor—and, above all, if it is their couple (Aquino, Tripp, and Bies, 2006; Dietz, Ostrom, and Stern, 2004; Grosjean, 2014). Unfortunately, statistical data about the deaths of mothers and children at the hands of the father support this explanation.

Harassment and revenge usually go hand in hand. Those who take revenge use the children, manipulate those around them, and harass their ex-couples financially. Financial harassment is usually a clear example of how to use the justice system, as the wealthier parent can pay judicial processes that are long and costly, while the parent with less economic resources struggles to defend themselves (Clemente, Padilla-Racero, Espinosa, Reig-Botella, and Gandoy-Crego, 2019).

ASSESSMENT AS A TECHNIQUE TO AVOID
REVENGE THROUGH THE USE OF CHILDREN

One way to avoid parents who have no qualms about using their children is through psychological tests that determine if the parents are prone to this. In the following lines, we shall refer to the existing tests or instruments, putting our focus on two specific scales, the MMS and CPS.

Some years ago, Emery, Otto, and O'Donohue (2005) pointed out issues with the forensic analysis tests that were applied to custody cases of children:

- They are usually inadequate for scientific reasons.
- The statements of some guru-like experts—when they mention the PAS, for example—are totally banal and invalid upon subjection to scientific criteria.
- The forensic expert usually measures variables—for example, measures of intelligence, personality, psychopathology, or academic performance—that are irrelevant when it comes to taking judicial decisions.
- There is little scientific data that would actually be relevant for the judicial process (when the testimony of a child should be taken into account, for example).

Sometimes science is governed by trends, and society by clichés. Today, shared custody seems to be the way in which society esteems things to be fair for both parents, as they both share the contact with the children. There are even some men's associations that demand shared custody in every case; but society forgets that sometimes this implies a perversion of equality; hidden behind the complaint that fathers should have equal access to the children in the same way that the mothers do (nobody should nor can deny this matter), are abusers who do not want contact with their children but do want to harass their children and the mothers (Clemente, 2013b); it is a perversion of the concept of equality. Before trying to solve the problems through the justice system, it would be more sensible to try to avoid the involvement of the children throughout the conflict (Pedzich, 2014; Trampotova and Lacinova, 2015). This harassment of both the child and the custodial parent sometimes seems "moderate," like changing the name of the children when addressing them if that is something that causes anguish (Warshak, 2015a, 2015b). According to Pignotti (2014), the manipulation of children should be considered domestic violence.

Children can also be Machiavellian. Besides, this trait is further developed as a result of being attacked by at least one of the parents. As suggested by Allroggen, Back, and Plener (2016), the desire of power and social domination play a key role in the development of social aggression, all present in Machiavellianism. Geng et al. (2016) studied the relation between Machiavellism in adolescents and the fact that they externalize their problems. These authors show that Machiavellianism is positively associated with hyperactivity, the emotional symptoms, the behavior problems, and problems of a relationship between equals. Curiously, contrary to what had been found in other studies, these authors found a higher proportion of Machiavellianism in girls than in boys. More specifically, Lang and Birkas (2015) established that for girls, maternal alienation becomes the only significant predictor of Machiavellianism, while for boys it is the low intensity and quality of verbal communication.

Are there more adequate procedures to determine the suitability of the custody or the preferences of the parents? Let us explore two of them, the MMS and the CPS scales, created by this research team.

THE MMS SCALE

In line with these approaches, we believe it would be interesting to create a procedure that measures the level of Machiavellianism in each one of the parents, and in so doing foster the abandonment of terminology that lacks scientific proof and that has clear ideological connotations, such as the PAS, or more recently, parental alienation. We consider the concept of Machiavellianism to be more appropriate to identify the parent (custodial or noncustodial) who attacks by using the children. The characteristics of the parents who behave in such a way are found in the Dark Triad, and specifically in the variable of Machiavellianism. The goal is to create an instrument that enables the identification of Machiavellianism in the parents, while also identifying the possible consequences concerning the manipulation of the children. That is the reasoning behind the Machiavellian Manipulation Scale (MMS), created by Clemente and Diaz (2020).

This scale integrates the five following factors:

1. Positivity. The items that saturate in this factor verify the correct treatment of the parents toward each other, including verbal, or nonverbal, and even if compliments are used. Additionally, if both parents positively value the way of being of their children (their attitudes and personality), their capacity and aptitudes, and if they speak of them with

positive emotions, expressing care. It is a factor that expresses a positive way of educating and loving the children.

2. Negativity. This comprises the most negative aspects used by the parents (contempt, insults directed to the other parent), together with the fact of emotionally expressing disdain toward the children and if there is disdain toward their way of being. However, with respect to the criticism of the capacity of the children, only the father's scores count in this factor, not the mother's.

3. Discrepancy between parents. This refers to the lack of agreement between the parents. A discrepancy is not a threat against the other (as it has already been mentioned in the second factor).

4. Looking down upon the children. Making a point of laughing at the children in their interventions, making jokes in bad taste about them. Added to this is that the mothers think that their children do not have capacities.

5. Avoiding confrontation with the other parent. Ways of calming the environment, laughing at negative matters that may refer to problematic issues with the children. This is a mechanism for the parents not to blame the children for the problems.

Factors 1 and 5 imply positive aspects of the interaction, and 2, 3, and 4 negative aspects. Evidently, the parents who score less in the positive aspects and more in the negative aspects are less prone to have the custody of their children.

This proposal of a scale complies with the objectives of creating trustworthy diagnostic procedures within forensic psychology, taking up the challenge that was set forth by Emery, Otto, and O'Donohue (2005), and that has been pointed out recently by Clemente and Padilla-Racero (2015a, 2015b), which breaks away from the ten fallacies that Warshak (2015a, 2015b) referred to.

CPS SCALE

Another of the scales developed by this research team is the CPS, the Children's Preference Scale (Clemente, Diaz, and Espinosa, 2020).

Determining how the children perceive their parents is important for three reasons:

- Because it tackles a key issue within family psychology, that of being able to determine what the interactions among members of the family are like, studying their evolution; within this perspective, there is more emphasis on the concept of attachment.

- From a social point of view, it is important to be able to determine the evolution of the children who have suffered the consequences of abuse within the family, and especially if they have been victims of sexual abuse.
- Determining the child's preference for a parent is important as forensic analysis within psychology in order to recommend a suitable parent to have the custody of the children and a way to establish the contact with the noncustodial parent.

Perhaps the main problem concerning the theoretical framework of theories about the importance of taking into account the preference of the child is the lack of definition of the concept of attachment. Perhaps the lack of an operative definition comes from having considered it to be so obvious and hence unnecessary to define, that researchers starting using it without much thought. Kurdek is one of the authors who studied this concept, indeed broadening it (for example, including pets). This inclusion was considered out of proportion by some researchers, out of whom Kobak (2009) is included, who insists on the necessity of defining the concept. Furthermore, attachment varies depending on specific variables such as age, sex, et cetera (Furman and Buhrmester, 1992). These authors act on the assumption that the parents are the most influential agents of socialization affecting the children and that the consequent attachment is owing to them. As children approximate the age of adolescence, other agents come into effect, specifically, friendships and couples, that may exercise even a larger influence than the parents. This attachment is generated because parents and children do activities together, as demonstrated by Sukys, Lisinskiene, and Tilindiene (2015), who verified that when parents play sports with their children, the attachment is higher.

If attachment takes place mainly with the parents, the concept of marital adjustment becomes more relevant. Kurdek (1998) emphasized the importance of adjustment between the parents for the development of the children. This author especially focused on the relationship between the lack of marital adjustment and depression, as much in the parents as in the children. For that, the study by Fincham, Beach, Harold, and Osborne (1997) was used as a base. This issue has generated controversy, which was tackled by Beach, Davey, and Fincham (1999) and answered by Kurdek himself (1999).

Within this line, we should highlight the study by McGue, Elkins, Walden, and Iacono (2005), who explored the warmth of the relationships between the children and their parents. Their research took a large sample (1,330 children of 11 years of age, twins), and three years later they managed that 1,176 of them followed through.

The brothers and sisters are another source of socialization, and there is also little research in this area. In general, the relationships within siblings have been described as love-hate, as both feelings usually coexist, and with large emotional intensity. Whiteman, Solmeyer, and McHale (2015) studied how the siblings combined both aspects, the positivity and the negativity.

The need to study children's preference and verify the evolution of abused children through the treatments that were sought out to overcome the after-effects of maltreatment, as well as the necessity of having instruments of forensic analysis available, both stem from the necessity to create procedures capable of measuring the preferences of children for their parents—that is, to verify attachment—that we believe would be higher or lower, depending on the existing marital adjustment.

In the following points we shall analyze a brief list of samples that allow us to determine the quality of the parent-child relationship, before commenting on the test that is offered as an alternative, the CPS.

- One of the classic tests and the few that exist to measure children's perception of the parents is the PPI (Parent Perception Inventory) suggested by Hazzard and Christensen (1983). Since that test was created, several researchers have highlighted its value, adding information that completes the initial study of the creators of the PPI (for example, Glaser, Horne, and Myers, 1995). All studies coincide in that the test allows to differentiate the unstructured families from the structured ones and how meaningful correlations with other elements are obtained, for example, with behavioral indicators. The idea of Hazzard and Christensen when creating their scale was to have a tool that allowed for the detection of changes when dealing with children from unstructured families. In fact, Hazzard, Kleemeier, Pohl, and Webb (1988) created a treatment program for sexually abused children to recover. From the dissemination of that program, there have been several works that report of the application of it in diverse populations of abused children—for example, Randolph and Gold's study (1994).
- The second best known and employed scale is that of Kurdek and Berg (1987), called CBAPS (Children's Beliefs about Parental Divorce Scale). It is composed of six factors: peer ridicule and avoidance; paternal blame; fear of abandonment; maternal blame; hope of reunification; and self-blame. However, some of the reliability indices are low, and that is a disadvantage when choosing this instrument.
- Another of the tools that has been used is based on the typology of Baumrind (2010, 2012). It was deemed useful to foretell the aggressiveness of children. It includes the following factors: rejection, corporal punishment, warmth, responsiveness, and support. These dimensions are used, for example, in the studies by Hernandez-Guzman,

Gonzalez-Montesinos, Bermudez-Ornelas, Freyre, and Alcazar-Olan (2013).

- The "Children's Perception of Interparental Conflict Scale" is also used Schaefer (1965b). This tool measures the children's perception of how they are being brought up (raising styles) and the paternal and maternal relationships. This is based on a tridimensional model that identified three pairs of orthogonal factors called: acceptance versus rejection; psychological autonomy versus psychological control (parental control through the domination of induction of guilt and anxiety); and firm control versus lax control (parental control through the imposition of rules and establishing limits versus the lack thereof). Studies such as those published by Schludermanna and Schludermanna (1970) demonstrate the validity of this scale.
- Another of the alternatives is the "Child's Report of Parent Behavior Inventory" (Schaefer, 1965a). Samper, Cortés, Mestre, Nácher, and Tur (2006) adapted this scale to the Spanish population.
- Less well-known is the tool EMBU (Egna Minnen Barndoms Uppfostran; My memories of upbringing). This tool was adapted for the Turkish population (Dirik, Yorulmaz, and Karanci, 2015).
- On other occasions, instead of using measurements that refer directly to the parental preferences, measures of related variables were used. This is the case, for example, of the tests related to memory. That is how Hedges, Drysdale, Drysdale, and Levick (2015) analyzed the factorial structure of "Children's Memory Questionnaire-Revised (CMQ-R)."
- One last possibility of analysis is the use of general instruments, normally derived from pediatrics. This is the case of HRQOL (Health-Related Quality of Life), which allows to detect the quality of life of children and therefore, to determine if they have problems derived from a deteriorating family situation. It is a multidimensional instrument that includes measures of self-reporting in physical health as well as in mental health. One of the last works carried out with this instrument is that of Kobau, Seligman, Peterson, Diener, Zack, Chapman, and Thompson (2011). The problem with HRQOL is that its application is excessively time consuming. One possibility for obtaining a quicker analysis is that offered by Varni, Seid, and Rode (1999). These authors created an alternative, the PedsQL (Pediatric Quality of Life Inventory). The truth is that due to the samples used for the statistical adaptation, as well as for its orientation toward physical problems (it was tested mainly on children with cancer), it does not seem that this last instrument is suitable to measure the preference for parents in the cases of custody or maltreatment.

All of the explained tools are based on the perceptions and beliefs of the children. After gathering and analyzing the beliefs of the children about their parents, and conditioned by the attachment with each parent, a suitable level is established, and not of family relation. These beliefs have been analyzed, for example, by Ramirez, Botella, and Carrobles (1999), using for that the scale of Kurdek and Berg (1987). Thus, these tools have allowed to reveal the relationship between being an overprotective mother (maternal overcontrol) and the provocation of depression in children, as the study by Sichko, Borelli, Rasmussen, and Smiley (2016) demonstrates; as a matter of fact, Mota, Matos, Pinheiro, Costa, and Oliveira (2015) developed two tests, the "Social Phobia and Anxiety Inventory for Children-11 (SPAIC-11)" and the "Social Phobia and Anxiety Inventory for Children's Parents-11 (SPAICP-11)," that the authors created as a shorter version of the instrument "Social Phobia and Anxiety Inventory—Child and Parent Versions," and they measure social phobia and anxiety. Therefore, a verifiable tendency exists to relate any type of mental dysfunction with child preferences. A good example of that is Melo and Mota's study (2014) that related the Children's Perception of Interparental Conflict Scale and a questionary of symptoms.

This revision reveals that the main tools used to identify the child preferences toward each parent shows a series of problems:

- The theoretical base is weak, as it is based on an ambiguous concept, such as attachment.
- Evidence exists that the more activities that are done with each of the parents, the higher the attachment, and consequently, a higher preference toward that parent, making it more adequate to create an instrument that is based on the children specifying the behavior that each one of the parents has with them, and not so much on their beliefs or opinions.
- It would be convenient to create an instrument to be as brief as possible, complying with the adequate psychometric requirements, naturally.

The CPS scale aims to overcome these problems and is based on analyzing the behavior of the parents versus their beliefs. It is brief and of quick application. Therefore, it can be useful to determine the suitability of each parent within a custody battle.

With regard to the traditional scales, the PPI (Parent Perception Inventory) created by Hazzard and Christensen (1983) and the CBAPS (Children's Beliefs about Parental Divorce Scale), created by Kurdek and Berg (1987), the CPS scale implies an important alternative to consider. The proposal, as it is based on behaviors, does not reflect factors such as those pointed out by the previously quoted authors. Thus, concepts such as "paternal or maternal blame," "fear of abandonment," "self-blame," etc., are not considered. We believe this to be an advantage, as it deals with rather difficult concepts to conceptualize and that are often not based on scientifically tested theories. We have even considered some concepts that exist in some scales, such as "rejection" to which Baumrind (2010, 2012) refers and that has been studied by Hernandez-Guzman, Gonzalez-Montesinos, Bermudez-Ornelas, Freyre, and Alcazar-Olan (2013); it is better to verify them in their effects and not on opinions. But it is not always the case: Some factors that were pointed out by these last authors correspond with those of the CPS scale, especially if we refer to behavioral elements, such as the case of "support."

The elements highlighted by Schaefer (1965b) for the Children's Perception of Interparental Conflict Scale are the ones that coincide the most with the CPS scale. In the first place, because the factors always revolve around two main points: acceptance versus refusal, autonomy versus psychological control, and firm control versus lax. In fact, the factor that the CPS scale puts forward of predisposition to help and positive control, as well as negative control and excessive worrying, gathers the factors of acceptance and control set out by Schaefer.

The literature on the topic has left out the importance of school for the children, and the necessary help from the parents to solve the academic problems that may emerge. The proposal verifies this fact and includes it in the scale. Something similar happens with the lack of communication, be it in this case the previous authors have indeed created factors that reflect the existence of this variable, although not in a specific manner.

We believe that this scale is useful as a way of achieving the best possible relationship between the children and their parents. This is especially important in the cases of granting sole custody to one parent and to be able to determine if shared custody is suitable.

Chapter 11

Institutional Violence
or Legal Violence?

The objective of this book is to address how a new type of harassment came to exist; we have called it institutional harassment, and we have focused on a specific type of institution, the legal system. More specifically, we have approached the subject as to how certain people use the legal system to attack other persons. This use given to the system by some people to harass others is made possible by two facts:

- The first factor is that professionals who are integrated in the justice system show self-evident machista stereotypes and mind-sets, which make them prone to treat women as though they were malicious and liars and children as if they were easily manipulable by their mothers. Consequently, the justice system easily assumed a theory such as Gardner's PAS. It was inspired by and is practically a copy of the theoretical current to which this author subscribed, psychoanalysis. Psychoanalysis has been and is the most machista and unscientific doctrines that has existed and exists within psychology, through many psychologists and psychiatrists, although today it is considered a philosophical, cultural, and artistic current. This theory is easily believable by many professionals in the legal sector as they share similar mentalities to those of the rest of the population, and because everybody tends to look for ways of thinking that corroborate their own. Precisely for that matter theories such as the PAS will continue to be used—although, as we previously commented, given the rejection of society toward machismo, some other names have been used to masquerade it (simply, "parental alienation"). Nonetheless, we hope that this book contributes to some people understanding reality in a different light, especially concerning the reasons behind the behavior of the justice system with the children and their mothers, which, on many occasions, has given the custody of the children to the sexual abusers.

- The second factor is that the justice system has allowed its use to harass someone, breaking with the maxim that justice is blind and that it is the same for everybody (it is supposed that justice should be equal among equals and unequal with the unequal)—that is, the guiding concept in itself is broken. Upon that taking place within justice, a phenomenon is produced, similar to what occurs in other contexts, called institutional violence. Therefore, if violence and harassment are permitted by the legal system (that becomes a tool for some people to attack others), it becomes institutional violence.

WHAT IS INSTITUTIONAL VIOLENCE?

Institutional violence is what those who represent the state institutions may exercise in an abusive way upon taking action from within their position. This indeed includes judges, district attorneys, psychologists, social workers, and all the administrative employees who may have influence throughout the process. In the case of judges, institutional violence includes the partisan or malicious interpretation of the laws, regulations, and protocols, and even the oversights that allow one party to be favored over the other. On occasions those actions benefit one of the parts (as is the case of males versus females), and on others the system itself benefits (for example, agreeing with an official organization before a person who is acting in their own name). That violence is of all kinds: physical (allowing an aggressor to not be condemned), sexual (putting a child into the hands of a sexual aggressor), mental (considering some insults as not important enough), symbolic (starting from the idea and expressing that women are liars and manipulators), economic (allowing for the process to be never-ending in such a way that one of the parties cannot take on the economic burden), and so forth. Therefore, institutional violence is characterized by the use of the power of the state to cause harm, thus reinforcing the established mechanisms of domination.

Institutional violence is manifested in several environments; here we are focused on the justice system, which is the case at matter. However, police abuse is the issue that has been the object of more studies of this type, creating the concept of the existence of police who are "trigger happy." There are too many examples, especially in the United States, of this type of violence, exercised more so on the black population, which brings us to specify another large area in which institutional violence is exercised, the discriminatory treatment toward other races (that is, in racism). But there are more: the favoring of the interests of the large economic groups, the criminalization of social protests, and the like.

Women, as we have verified throughout this book, represent the population that suffer the highest level of legal harassment; the problem has been referred to as legal androcentrism—that is, the law understands what the characteristics of machista violence are. Thus, the idea remains that a lesion, either physical or mental, against a woman within the couple, is simply a lesion, and that in any case it could be made worse by the parental bond, being a constant idea in legal discourse. And that conception implies that if the aggressor is condemned, that sentence will be minimum. To consider the androcentrism of criminal concepts is conducive toward understanding how the phenomenon of institutional violence is constructed in the cases of gender violence. The forms of machista violence within the couple are not lesions, nor do they have to do with what is known in the criminal area as lesions, but rather, they are gender violence, machista violence, or violence against women.

The recognition of that specificity indicates that the legal system is getting prepared to understand and deal with that specificity, accepting two elements that should characterize any legal understanding of gender violence: first, that violence is a manifestation of a social discrimination, of a social structure that is unequal and oppressive, in this case against women; second, that the legal interventions, especially those that come from the criminal area, may include and do include practices of institutional violence toward the victims—that is, that the legal intervention should be done starting from the consideration that the state itself is an actor that can produce and reproduce violence against persons, and it does so specifically against women.

Over the last few years, the feminist movements have echoed institutional violence. This implies a total change in mentality because people are used to an aggressor being a unique, physical person, not an institution or an organization. To think that the state itself harms the citizens (and in this book we have commented how the mental health of those persons who resort to the justice system, either by filing a report or by having been reported, manifest a deterioration in their mental health). Institutional violence allows individual responsibilities to become diluted in such a way that individuals who exercise it do not perceive themselves, nor are they perceived by society, as the ones responsible. Curtin and Litke (1999) sustain that institutional violence acts in contexts of systemic violence, that is, in a diffused manner, and that is why it is centered more on racism or sexism. Institutional violence is less visible, it is what has been silenced the most, the least punished of all. This way of manifesting institutional violence, in a diffused way, makes it easy for the public powers (the state) to recognize what is exercised by the army or police as violence, however, it is not so easy in the case of gender violence being generated and continued, for example. Gender violence is more subtle, among other things because it does not produce so much physical harm, but mostly because it is symbolic. The case of gender violence is a good example of how the state commits a crime by omission of due diligence, or by questioning the victim's story, or not giving validity to children's accounts of events.

The fact of recognizing another type of violence, the institutional, leads us to go over the existing diverse types. There have been two authors, Garver and Friedenberg (1968), who, decades ago, set forth that necessity and created a typology based on two dimensions, which implies referring to four types of violence. The two articulated main points of distinction are: the personal dimension versus institutional, and the open versus the hidden or silent. To what concerns institutional violence, that means to say that it can be open or hidden. The former has its best example in wars or those clear manifestations against some human rights, such as the universal access to health care. The latter finds a clear example in poverty, but we may add, with respect to that subject, the negative prejudice and stereotypes that have acted and are reproduced by the institutions and laws.

Garver and Friedenberg's classification is not perfect, because among other matters it recognizes that there are types of violence that can present themselves in both formats, and specifically it brings gender violence to the fore as an example of this bidimensionality. And yet, it recognizes and gives visibility to the fact that in society, it is easier to center the attention on the maltreaters than on the state. It is easy for the state to find the guilty party in someone over whom the actor has no legal authority, and therefore must not recognize his or her own guilt.

One of the reasons why the two dimensions of classification of Garver and Friedenberg are not independent is because, even though institutional violence may be manifested and does in fact manifest in an open way, the consolidation of inequality may only occur in a hidden way, using two large mechanisms for that purpose: education and means of communication. Educating the new generations in the continuance of violence (logically concealed) and offering unilateral visions of reality through the press, it is possible to present the persons who are victims of institutional violence as the individuals who are responsible of the problems they undergo, even so far as them being the guilty parties (this is the phenomenon known as victim blaming). Therefore, the resistance against institutional violence is presented as unjust.

One could be led to believe that there are no laws to defend persons against institutional violence. But that would not be true, the problem being that the aforementioned legislation usually slides past unnoticed within the legal domain and is scarcely ever applied when concerning judges. In any case, for objectivity, we believe it is important to cite some legislation in reference to that, beginning with that of the United Nations:

- In 1993, the declaration of the elimination of violence against women in the General Assembly of the United Nations, already contemplated "physical, sexual and psychological violence perpetrated or tolerated by the State." Article 4 gathers more than seventeen duties with which to comply by, on behalf of the States, to protect from violence against women.
- In a similar way it is expressed in the Convention of Belém do Pará, of 1996, when it defines institutional violence as that perpetrated or tolerated by the state or its actors, where it takes place.
- With respect to the necessity of making the states responsible of the institutional dimension of violence against women, and the obligation of compensating them, the Council of Europe Convention about preventing and combating violence against women and domestic violence (2011). Known as the Istanbul Convention, in its article 5 it states the obligations of the state, and it gives this responsibility to the "authorities, civil servants, agents, and other actors on behalf of the state institutions."
- Following with the European Union, the Directive 2012/29/UE established minimum standards on the rights, support, and protection of victims of crime and, in its article 57, makes a reference to the processes of secondary victimization that the victims of gender violence suffer in the area of Justice.

HOW DOES THE PRESENCE OF INSTITUTIONAL VIOLENCE AND LEGAL HARASSMENT MANIFEST?

There is much proof as to how persons are aware that the system maltreats them, and on several occasions, the battle is not worth the while, and the most advisable option is to renounce what they would consider to be just. In the specific case of legal processes of cases with maltreatment toward women, the number of women who abandon the process is rather high, and they clearly express that they do not believe in the institutions, cease from filing complaints, and therefore let the maltreater benefit from the state. The statistics demonstrate that in general there is little trust in the justice system and that this is more often the case with women.

The organization Save the Children (2012) cites a series of characteristics illustrating clear indicators that the system itself is geared toward acting against the protection of the children and of the persons who report possible sexual abuse, the mothers. The list elaborated by that organization has been re-elaborated by us, and is set out in the following points:

- In every case, the complaint was filed with the authorities after the existence of medical or psychological reports warning specifically of possible sexual abuse. The majority of the medical exams are done in the emergency units of hospitals, upon the boys and girls returning from the visits with their fathers.
- In every case analyzed, the mothers are witnesses of the physical manifestations of possible abuse and receive verbal information from their children that they are being assaulted, something that the children only communicate to them and perhaps a professional.
- The children are normally very young, and the verbalization of the aggressions does not usually take place with other people, as do the nonverbal signs of being nervous that are indeed shown, as well as many other symptoms that characterize a dissociative behavior.
- As a reference, this is of key importance when dealing with children of a young age, who have only verbalized the sexual abuse with a professional or their mother.
- There was no study, upon analyzing the mothers who filed a complaint, where the mothers have psychiatric precedents, nor had they filed previous reports, nor were they accused as authors of any crime. Despite this, it is common that throughout the judicial process (criminal as much as civil), the judges order multiple psychological exams on the mothers.
- This profusion of exams and tests practiced on the mothers is in contrast with the scarce tests and analysis practiced on the one who had originally been reported.
- The psychological reports carried out by the judicial administration continue to reflect the use of PAS argumentation, perhaps concretely or perhaps with more generic references of the manipulation of the child on behalf of the mother.
- From the first report filed on, and especially if the mother continues to file a report after the first stay, the suspicion of maternal manipulation of the children is installed.
- As a response, there is a tendency among the judges to protect the relationship between the father (the supposed abuser) and the boy or girl.
- In all these cases the supposed victims (the children) are taken, at least once, to a health center, normally after the visit with the fathers, due to the lesions of which they complain and that are discovered by the mothers. In all cases there is more than one medical report confirming physical evidence of indicators of sexual abuse (anal fissures, vulvovaginitis, sleep and eating disorders, behavior with an elevated sexuality in boys or girls who are very small, anxiety, submissiveness, aggression, fear of the father).

- When the experts express in their reports the impossibility to extract the child's account, the judges and district attorneys do not question the techniques used and do not usually approve if new tests are used, even if on many occasions the official expert advice is lacking or even wrong, and these tests are usually used by professionals who are not experts in obtaining information from children.
- When dealing with children, it is normal to use the technique of a structured interview (versus an open interview), the only one which is adequate for children. On several occasions, they use closed questions in interviews with children.
- Several of the interviews with children resemble authentic interrogations.
- On some occasions there are joint interviews with the child and the aggressor.
- The results of the applied psychological tests are omitted from the reports of the court administration itself. This fact prevents other experts from being able to assess those results and verify if the conclusions of the official reports are correct or not. Legally this generates defenselessness of the victims and invalidates those reports.
- The experts usually conclude in their reports that the child's statement is not true and that it is influenced by the mother, and they are indifferent to the child evincing rejection or closeness toward the supposed aggressor.
- It is worrisome, before any complaint of possible abuse to a child, when it is produced with a couple who has not divorced, as much as it is if they have divorced, everything is attributed to the disputes within the couple, omitting an investigation toward the maltreatment.
- Unfortunately, the complaints about possible aggressions are usually filed, some of the typical reasonings being the influence of maternal induction; the lack of credibility; the age of the children; the existence of psychological reports that dismiss sexual abuse; the context of the family conflict; the existence of contradictory versions; the generic assertion of not appreciating indications of any criminal commission; and so on.

CHILDREN, THE BIG VICTIMS

Legal psychology takes care of the children in various aspects. It concerns itself with the children who remain in defenselessness (children with social difficulties or protection, such as those who are abandoned and without family); it also helps the children who commit a crime (minors in social conflict or in reform) and the children who face the separation of their parents; legal psychology also concerns itself with the parents. Here we are going to focus on those children that suffer the problems derived from the relationships of their parents.

When a child is found in a home in which the relationships of the parents are problematic, or having to share two homes with different characteristics, or before an aggression of any type by one of the parents, that child presents a behavior that expresses that situation and a deteriorated mental health. This is called behavior problems or disorder. The manifestation of that behavior problem is different according to the age of the child. Some of them are described in the following points:

- Small children show behavior problems when they are not able to adequately control what is called the circadian cycles, that is, what regulates our bodily activity. The most well-known is sleep, so we therefore are referring to children who do not sleep well at night and consequentially sleep during the day, deregularizing rest (and that of the parents or parent with whom they live). And together with the "twenty-four hour" cycles (that is why they are called circadian) come others, so that these children often do not control their sphincter, manifesting enuresis, encopresis, trichotillomania (pulling of one's hair), and the like. That is, these children show problems that differentiate them from other children and affect their health. Normally these problems have a psychological origin, in a way that the child challenges the parents by not wanting to go to bed when it is time (and if the parents allow it, the children will abuse the night timetable and therefore sleep during the day) or not want to make an effort to control their sphincter because it is more comfortable to use a diaper; or they simply wish to call the attention of their parents (revealing that they do not receive the necessary care, and they should look for strategies to do so, even at the cost of, for example, pulling out their hair until they are bald). These are examples that reveal how our body and our mind interrelate, if in effect the causes of the problems are situated either biologically or psychologically, the aforementioned being of a psychological origin. Children become unbearable and constantly hit their parents (above all, the one who is not the aggressor, because they think that that parent should protect them but does not).
- If the children are a little older, they tend to have serious academic problems, which brings them to concomitantly believe that they do not have the capacity to study, leading them to even more family problems. From this point of view, the children, if they do not present a pathology that prevents having enough cognitive capacity, usually manifest one of three possible problematics that are due to the situation that they are living and not to a biological problem: a deficit in their capacity of attention, a problem of hyperactivity, a combination of both. Many doctors,

upon not taking into consideration the family problem of the children, prescribe medication, a matter that does not help if the problem is social. The psychologists, educational psychologists, and pedagogues may greatly help by creating life guidelines and ways of facing problems.

- In children who are even older, already in preadolescence or adolescence, the minors become rebels against society and struggle to obey the rules that most young people accept. It is true that minors, at this age, usually present antisocial behavior to a large degree. They smoke, drink, and consume drugs, but in this case the consumption is worse.

Ultimately, children suffer problems related to parenting. It has always been argued that the ones to "blame" are the parents, omitting that one of them is the alleged aggressor (and therefore the person who created the problem) and the other is the person who is fighting to defend the child (and that normally is also a victim). But the fact that another guilty party exists is omitted: the system that does not protect the children, that does not take measures to protect either their physical or mental health.

PRE-CONSTITUTED EVIDENCE: FROM A WAY OF DEFENDING A CHILD WITH DIFFICULTIES TO BEING AN OBSTACLE FOR INVESTIGATING ABUSE

In some countries there is what is called "pre-constituted evidence," which consists in avoiding a child being exposed to declaring on situations such as sexual aggression that may cause them harm upon recalling. Normally, when a judge orders that pre-constituted evidence be taken, the child has already declared at least once before the police, another before the court psychologist, and most likely before the judge him- or herself—that is, the child has repeated the facts a considerable number of times, and the objective has already been unfulfilled.

The pre-constituted evidence normally takes place in the justice room, with the presence of a judge, a district attorney, a lawyer from the other party, the child, and a psychologist from the court administration, whose role varies according to the designs of the judge, as the judge may determine if the child is to be in the other room with that psychologist or in the same room. Logically, the most adequate situation for the children is to be in another room with that psychologist, and for the psychologist to listen to the questions that should be asked through some sort of wireless device. However, it is more common that the child is in the same courtroom, and the role of the psychologist consists in reformulating the questions that the legal agents specify so as to make them more adequate in their language and the child may understand them. This second option implies an authentic maltreatment to the child, and a way to avoid that the children may express themselves, as they feel threatened and incapable of commenting on such a delicate topic in those conditions.

One of the major limitations that the pre-constituted evidence presents is that it does not allow for a psychologist who had not participated until then in the procedure to verify the hypothesis of the existence or not of possible maltreatment, as there is no possibility of interviewing the child again. The pre-constituted evidence omits the idea that when a psychologist interviews a child (the same as if it was with an adult), the questions are not standard but are a reflection of the hypothesis that is being built in his or her head to be able to detect the truth and defend that child, and they are expressed in an active process, as the answers of the child determine the way to proceed. That is, the pre-constituted evidence goes against the fundamental principle of any interview, that the questions are framed to try to verify the hypothesis of the interviewer.

Another of the limitations of this procedure is that the questions are formulated by persons who are agents of the law and are clueless in psychology and ignore how to formulate these questions as well as how to interpret the answers of the children. Specifically, they do not know how to interpret the nonverbal communication in the three aspects: kinesics, paralinguistics, and proxemic. It is as if a clueless person is facilitating the results of a blood test, instead of giving an interpretation of the results. How should silence be interpreted as an answer? How is it possible to know if dissociative symptoms are manifested? No comment.

But the largest of the problems is the physical context, which has to do with one of the nonverbal communication variables, proxemic. Imagine how a child may respond when there are at least 10 meters of distance, a high ceiling, and classic furniture between who is asking him or her the questions. The environment itself in which the declaration is taken inhibits the response of the child.

We consider that it is a mistake to subject children to multiple and continuous analysis, but for legal validity, three evaluations are inevitable: the one completed by the legal system itself through its professionals, that of a psychologist of one of the parts, and that of the psychologist of the other part; in some cases the last two are nonexistent if each part wishes to renounce. The police declarations should be eliminated, as well as those taken previously by the judges, and therefore should all be done by a professional psychologist.

THE FAMILY MEETING POINT: FROM THE WAY OF GETTING THE ADEQUATE CONTACT OF THE CHILD WITH THE PARENTS, TO COERCING THE CHILD TO HAVE CONTACT WITH THE AGGRESSOR

Lastly, we would like to briefly mention the family meeting point. The family meeting point is a service that is a neutral space to guarantee the visiting rights of the children so that they may have a relationship with their parents and family during the processes and situations of divorce or other supposed family separations.

Therefore, it is intended to guarantee the right of the children to have a relationship with the noncustodial parent, as well as the rest of the biological family, supposedly in a temporary and exceptional manner, and only until the moment in which the circumstances that brought on the necessity of this service are normalized.

Through the creation of these centers it is intended, among other objectives:

- To favor the compliance of the basic right of the children to maintain a relationship with both parents after the separation, establishing bonds to ensure good mental, affective, and emotional development.
- To prepare the parents so that they may have autonomy and may afterward, have a relationship with their children without depending on this service.
- To guarantee the compliance of the visitation arrangements agreed upon in the process of or during the divorce.
- To facilitate the meeting of the children with the parent who does not have the custody and with the extended family of that parent.
- To allow the children to have a relationship and express their feelings and necessities in a supposed climate of equality and freedom without fearing that it is against the express wish of their parents.
- To facilitate the orientation to improve the parenting relationships and the parental education of the noncustodial parent.
- To obtain information about the attitudes of the parents concerning the defense, in the case of necessity, for the good of the children.

The decision that the meeting point should be used, as well as the compliance of the visitation arrangements through this service, is taken by the judge, and various possibilities exist:

- Handing over and picking up the children, to avoid the contact of the parents in conflict.

- Picking up and handing over on a permanent basis at the meeting point, that is, the noncustodial parent may enjoy the visit with the children at the meeting point, if they do not have a home in that city as that parent lives elsewhere, if the living arrangements do not comply with the standards for the stay of a child, or other similar circumstances.
- That, on occasions, the visits between the noncustodial parent and the children, tutelary or supervised by professionals (for example, if the visit is between the child and an alleged sexual aggressor).

But in reality, what is a meeting point? It is no more or less than a resource that the judges use to oblige the children to see one of the parents, normally the father, when those children refuse to have contact with him. Unfortunately, many judges put the wish of the father to continue seeing his children ahead of the child's refusal to see him. Therefore, it becomes a legal and institutional affront against that child. In our understanding it is perfectly respectable that if a child has been raped by the father, or the father has killed the mother, that child would not like to see him at all. As we explained before, that is not the case for many judges.

CONCLUSION

We believe that it has been demonstrated that legal harassment exists and that it is a form of institutional violence. Sometimes it is the legal system that exercises violence in an active manner, and on other occasions it passively allows itself to be used as an affront against one of the parties of the process, normally the children and their mothers. We believe that this situation should be avoided, and the public powers themselves should ensure that they do not act in that fashion. External controls of the legal administration should be created to observe the process. And we should raise awareness in society concerning that violence so that it may be fought and will cease to take place. We hope that in some way this publication helps the defense of the children and their parents who find themselves, directly or indirectly, being harassed by the legal system.

References

Adam-Karduz, F. F., & Saricam, H. (2018). The relationships between positivity, forgiveness, happiness, and revenge. *Revista Romaneasca pentru Educatie Multidimensionala*, 10, 1–22. doi.org/10.18662/rrem/68.

Al Ghazi, L. (2016). Parental alienation as a risk factor for delinquency. In M. Tomita (Ed.), *Probation as a field of study and research: From person to society* (pp. 13–17). Universul Juridic Publishing House.

Albertin, P. (2006). Psicología de la victimización criminal [Psychology of criminal victimization]. In M. Soria & D. Saiz (Eds.), *Psicología criminal* [Criminal psychology] (pp. 245–276). Pearson.

Allroggen, M., Back, M. D., & Plener, P. L. (2016). Power to the children? Machiavellianism in children and adolescents. *Zeitschrift fur Kinder-Und Jugendpsychiatrie und Psychotherapie*, 44(1), 21–29. dx.doi.org/10.1024/1422-4917/a000395.

Alonso-Quecuty, M. L. (1995). Psicología y testimonio [Psychology and testimony]. In M. Clemente (Ed.), *Fundamentos de la psicología jurídica* [Principles of legal psychology] (pp. 171–184). Pirámide.

American Academy of Pediatrics. (1999). Guidelines for the evaluation of sexual abuse of children. Subject review. *Pediatrics*, 3, 186–90.

American Psychiatric Association. (2014). *DSM-5. Manual diagnóstico y estadístico de los trastornos mentales* [DSM-5. Diagnostic and Statistical Manual of Mental Disorders]. Editorial Médica Panamericana.

Anderson, E. (2008). "I used to think women were weak": Orthodox masculinity, gender segregation, and sport. *Sociological Forum*, 23(2), 257–280. doi.org/10.1111/j.1573-7861.2008.00058.x.

Andrés-Ibáñez, P. (2013). *Cultura constitucional de la jurisdicción* [Constitutional culture of the jurisdiction]. Siglo del Hombre Editores.

Apostolou, M., Paphiti, C., Neza, E., Damianou, M., & Georgiadou, P. (2019). Mating performance: Exploring emotional intelligence, dark triad, jealousy and attachment effects. *Journal of Relationships Research*, 10, e1.

Aquino, K., Tripp, T. M., & Bies, R. J. (2006). Getting even or moving on? Power, procedural justice, and types of offense as predictors of revenge, forgiveness, reconciliation, and avoidance in organizations. *Journal of Applied Psychology*, 91(3), 653–668. doi.org/10.1037/0021-9010.91.3.653.

Aranda-López, M., Montes-Berges, B., Castillo-Mayén, M. R., & Higueras, M. (2014). Percepción de la segunda victimización en violencia de género [Perception of secondary victimization in gender violence]. *Escritos de Psicología*, 7(2), 11–18. doi.org/10.5231/psy.writ.2014.1502.

Athwal, H., & Burnett, J. (2014). Investigated or ignored? An analysis of race-related deaths since the Macpherson Report. *Race & Class*, 56(1), 22–42. doi.org/10.1177/0306396814531694.

Austin, W. G., Bow, J. N., Knoll, A., & Ellens, R. (2016). Relocation issues in child custody evaluations: A survey of professionals. *Family Court Review*, 54(3), 477–486. doi.org/10.1111/fcre.12224.

Azizli, N., Atkinson, B. E., Baughman, H. M., Chin, K., Vernon, P. A., Harris, E., & Veselka, L. (2016). Lies and crimes: Dark triad, misconduct, and high-stakes deception. *Personality and Individual Differences*, 89, 34–39. doi.org/10.1016/j.paid.2015.09.034.

Baker, A. J. L., Asayan, M., & LaCheen-Baker, A. (2016). Best interest of the child and parental alienation: A survey of state statutes. *Journal of Forensic Sciences*, 61. doi.org/10.1111/1556-4029.13100.

Baker, A. J. L., & Verrocchio, M. C. (2015). Parental bonding and parental alienation as correlates of psychological maltreatment in adults in intact and non-intact families. *Journal of Child and Family Studies*, 24(10), 3047–3057. doi.org/10.1007/s10826-014-0108-0.

Bandura, A. (1990). Selective activation and disengagement of moral control. *Journal of Social Issues*, 46(1), 27–46.

Bandura, A. (1999). Moral disengagement in the perpetration of inhumanities. *Personality and Social Psychology Review*, 3(3), 193–209.

Bandura, A., Barbaranelli, C., Caprara, G. V., & Pastorelli, C. (1996). Mechanisms of moral disengagement in the exercise of moral agency. *Journal of Personality and Social Psychology*, 71(2), 364–374. doi.org/10.1037/0022-3514.71.2.364.

Bantekas, I. (2016). Discrimination against fathers in Greek child custody proceedings: Failing the child's best interests. *International Journal of Children Rights*, 24(2), 330–357. doi.org/10.1163/15718182-02402008.

Barnard, C. I. (1938). *The functions of the executive*. Harvard University Press.

Bauman, Z. (1989). *Modernity and the Holocaust*. Cornell University Press.

Baumrind, D. (2010). Effects of preschool parents' power-assertive patterns and practices on adolescent development. *Parenting: Science and Practice*, 10(3), 157–201. doi.org/10.1080/15295190903290790.

Baumrind, D. (2012). Differentiating between confrontive and coercive kinds of parental power-assertive disciplinary practices. *Human Development*, 55 (2), 35–51. doi.org/10.1159/000337962.

Baumrind, D. (2015). When subjects become objects: The lies behind the Milgram legend. *Theory & Psychology*, 25, 690–696. doi.org/10.1177/0959354315592062.

Beach, S. R. H., Davey, A., & Fincham, F. D. (1999). The time has come to talk of many things: A commentary on Kurdek (1998) and the emerging field of marital processes in depression. *Journal of Family Psychology*, 13 (4), 663–668. doi. org/10.1037/0893-3200.13.4.663.

Bell, M. E., Street, A. E., & Stafford, J. (2014). Victims' psychosocial well-being after reporting sexual harassment in the military. *Journal of Trauma & Dissociation*, 15(2), 133–152. doi.org/10.1080/15299732.2014.867563.

Belsky, J. (1980). Child maltreatment: An ecological integration. *American Psychologist*, 35, 320–335.

Belsky, J. (1993). Etiology of child maltreatment: A developmental-ecological analysis. *Psychological Bulletin*, 114, 423–434.

Benatar, D. (2003). The second sexism. *Social Theory and Practice*, 29 (2), 177–210.

Benhabib, S. (1990). El otro generalizado y el otro concreto: Controversia Kolhberg-Gilligan y la teoría feminista [The generalized other and the other concrete: Dispute Kohlberg-Gilligan and feminist theory]. In S. Benhabib & D. Cornell (Eds.), *Teoría feminista y teoría crítica* [Feminist theory and critical theory]. Alfons el Magnànim.

Berger, C., & Caravita, S. C. S. (2016). Why do early adolescents bully? Exploring the influence of prestige norms on social and psychological motives to bully. *Journal of Adolescence*, 46, 45–56. doi.org/10.1016/j.adolescence.2015.10.020.

Beristain, A. (2001). Nuevo proceso penal desde las víctimas [New criminal process from the victims]. In A. Beristain (Ed.), *La administración de justicia en los albores del tercer milenio* [The administration of justice at the dawn of the third millennium] (pp. 17–33). Universidad de Buenos Aires.

Bernet, W., Baker, A. J. L., & Verrocchio, M. C. (2015). Symptom checklist-90-revised scores in adult children exposed to alienating behaviors: An Italian sample. *Journal of Forensic Sciences*, 60(2), 357–362. dx.doi.org/10.1111/1556-4029.12681.

Bernet, W., Boch-Galhau, W. V., Baker, A. J. L., & Morrison, S. (2010). Parental alienation, DSM-V, and ICD-11. *American Journal of Family Therapy*, 38(2), 76–187.

Bernet, W., Verrocchio, M. C., & Korosi, S. (2015). Yes, children are susceptible to manipulation: Commentary on article by Clemente and Padilla-Racero. *Children and Youth Services Review*, 56, 135–138. doi.org/10.1016/j.childyouth.2015.07.004.

Berrill, K. T., & Herek, G. M. (1992). Primary and secondary victimization in anti-gay hate crimes: Official response and public policy. In G. M. Herek & K. T. Berrill (Eds.), *Hate crimes: Confronting violence against lesbians and gay men* (pp. 289–305). Sage.

Bersoff, D. M. (1999). Why good people sometimes do bad things: Motivated reasoning and unethical behavior. *Personality and Social Psychology Bulletin*, 25(1), 28–39. doi.org/10.1177/0146167299025001003.

Bitzer, J. (2015). The pandemic of *Violence against Women*: The latest chapter in the history of misogyny. *European Journal of Contraception and Reproductive Health Care*, 20(1), 1–3. dx.doi.org/10.3109/13625187.2015.1005445.

Blass, T. (2004). *The man who shocked the world: The life and legacy of Stanley Milgram*. Basic Books.

Blush, G., & Ross, K. (2005). Sexual allegations in divorce: The SAID syndrome. *Family Court Review*, 25, 1–11. doi.org/10.1111/j.174-1617.1987.tb00155.x.

Bonafons, C., Jehel, L., Hirigoyen, M. F., & Coroller-Bequet, A. (2008). Clarifying the definition of bullying. *Encephale-Revue de Psychiatrie Clinique Biologique et Therapeutique*, 34(4), 419–426. doi.org/10.1016/j.encep.2007.06.007.

Boney-McCoy, S., & Finkelhor, D. (1996). Is youth victimization related to PTSD and depression after controlling for prior symptoms and family relationships? A longitudinal, prospective study. *Journal of Consulting and Clinical Psychology*, 64, 1406–1416.

Book, A., Visser, B. A., Blais, J., Hosker-Field, A., Methot-Jones, T., Gauthier, N. Y., Volk, A., Holden, R. R., & D'Agata, M. T. (2016). Unpacking more "evil": What is at the core of the dark tetrad? *Personality and Individual Differences*, 90, 269–272. doi.org/10.1016/j.paid.2015.11.009.

Bragues, G. (2008). The Machiavellian challenge to business ethics. *SSRN Electronic Journal*. doi.org/10.2139/ssrn.1093345.

Braithwaite, A. (2014). "Seriously, get out": Feminists on the forums and the war(craft) on women. *New Media & Society*, 16(5), 703–718. doi.org/10.1177/1461444813489503

Breiding, M. J., Smith, S. G., Basile, K. C., Walters, M. L., Chen, J., & Merrick, M. T. (2014). Prevalence and characteristics of sexual violence, stalking, and intimate partner violence victimization—National intimate partner and sexual violence survey, United States, 2011. *MMWR Surveillance Summaries*, 63(8), 1–18.

Brewer, G., & Bennett, Ch., Davidson, L., Ireen, A., Phipps, A. J., Stewart-Wilkes, D., & Wilson, B. (2018). Dark triad traits and romantic relationship attachment, accommodation, and control. *Personality and Individual Differences*, 120, 202–208. doi.org/10.1016/j.paid.2017.09.008.

Brewer, G., Erickson, E., Whitaker, L., & Lyons, M. (2020). Dark triad traits and perceived quality of alternative partners. *Personality and Individual Differences*, 154, 109633. doi.org/10.1016/j.paid.2019.109633.

Brewer, G., Hunt, D., James, G., & Abell, L. (2015). Dark triad traits, infidelity and romantic revenge. *Personality and Individual Differences*, 83, 122–127. doi.org/10.1016/j.paid.2015.04.007.

Burt, M. R. (1980). Cultural myths and supports for rape. *Journal of Personality and Social Psychology*, 38(2), 217–230.

Bustos, P., Rincón, P., & Aedo, J. (2009). Validación Preliminar de la Escala Infantil de Síntomas del Trastorno de Estrés Postraumático (Child PTSD Symptom Scale, CPSS) en Niños/as y Adolescentes Víctimas de Violencia Sexual [Preliminary Validation of the Child PTSD Symptom Scale (CPSS) in Children and Adolescents Victims of Sexual Violence]. *Psykhe*, 18(2), 113–126.

Calton, J., & Cattaneo, L. (2014). The effects of procedural and distributive justice on intimate partner violence victims' mental health and likelihood of future help-seeking. *The American Journal of Orthopsychiatry*, 84, 329–340. doi.org/10.1037/h0099841.

Campbell, K. B. (2005). Theorizing the authentic: Identity, engagement, and public space. *Administration & Society*, 36(6), 688–705. doi.org/10.1177/0095399704270582.

Canales, J. M. (1995). El servicio público de la justicia [The public service of justice]. *Política y Sociedad*, 20(3), 78–89.

Cantón, D., & Justicia, F. (2008). Afrontamiento del abuso sexual infantil y ajuste psicológico a largo plazo [Coping with childhood sexual abuse and long-term psychological adjustment]. *Psicothema*, 20(4), 509–515.

Cantón, J. (2003). El papel de las habilidades cognitivas en la declaración del niño [The role of cognitive skills in the child's statement]. In J. Cantón & M. R. Cortés (Eds.), *Guía para la evaluación del abuso sexual infantil* (2ª ed.) [Guide to the Evaluation of Child Sexual Abuse (2nd ed.)] (pp. 53–84). Pirámide.

Cantón, J., & Cortés, M. R. (2000). *Guía para la evaluación del abuso sexual infantil* [Guide to the Evaluation of Child Sexual Abuse]. Pirámide.

Cantón, J., & Cortés, M. R. (2003). La sugestibilidad de los niños [The suggestibility of children]. In J. Cantón & M. R. Cortés (Ed.), *Guía para la evaluación del abuso sexual infantil* (2ª ed.) [Guide to the Evaluation of Child Sexual Abuse (2nd ed.)] (pp. 85–122). Pirámide.

Cantón, J. & Cortés, M. (2008). *Guía para la evaluación del abuso sexual infantil* [Child Sexual Abuse Assessment Guide]. Pirámide.

Cantu, J. I., & Charak, R. (2020). Unique, additive, and interactive effects of types of intimate partner cybervictimization on depression in Hispanic emerging adults. *Journal of Interpersonal Violence*, UNSP 0886260520915552. doi.org/10.1177/0886260520915552.

Capaldi, D. M., Knoble, N. B., Shortt, J. W., & Kim, H. K. (2012). A systematic review of risk factors for intimate partner violence. *Partner Abuse*, 3(2), 231–280. doi.org/10.1891/1946-6560.3.2.231.

Caprara, G., Tisak, M., Alessandri, G., Fontaine, R., Fida, R., & Paciello, M. (2013). The contribution of moral disengagement in mediating individual tendencies toward aggression and violence. *Developmental Psychology*, 50. doi.org/10.1037/a0034488.

Carlsmith, K., & Darley, J. (2008). Psychological aspects of retributive justice. *Advances in Experimental Social Psychology*, 40, 193–236. doi.org/10.1016/S0065-2601(07)00004-4.

Carton, H., & Egan, V. (2017). The dark triad and intimate partner violence. *Personality and Individual Differences*, 105, 84–88. doi.org/10.1016/j.paid.2016.09.040.

Caspar, E. A., Christensen, J. F., Cleeremans, A., & Haggard, P. (2016). Coercion changes the sense of agency in the human brain. *Current Biology*, 26(5), 585–592. doi.org/10.1016/j.cub.2015.12.067.

Casullo, M. (2005). La capacidad para perdonar desde una perspectiva psicológica [The ability to forgive from a psychological perspective]. *Revista de Psicología de la PUCP*, 23(1), 39–64.

Ceci, S. J., & Bruck, M. (1993). Suggestibility of the child witness: A historical review and synthesis. *Psychological Bulletin*, 113, 403–439. doi.org/10.1037/0033-2909.113.3.403.

Ceci, S., & Bruck, M. (1995). *Jeopardy in the courtroom. A scientific analysis of children's testimony*. American Psychological Association.

Chabrol, H., Van Leeuwen, N., Rodgers, R., & Séjourné, N. (2009). Contributions of psychopathic, narcissistic, machiavellian, and sadistic personality traits to juvenile delinquency. *Personality and Individual Differences*, 47(7), 734–739. doi. org/10.1016/j.paid.2009.06.020.

Chester, D., & DeWall, C. (2016). Combating the sting of rejection with the pleasure of revenge: A new look at how emotion shapes aggression. *Journal of Personality and Social Psychology*, 112, 413–430. doi.org/10.1037/pspi0000080.

Chin, K., Atkinson, B. E., Raheb, H., Harris, E., & Vernon, P. A. (2017). The dark side of romantic jealousy. *Personality and Individual Differences*, 115, 23–29. doi. org/10.1016/j.paid.2016.10.003.

Christie, R., & Geis, F. L. (1970). *Studies in Machiavellianism*. Elsevier. doi. org/10.1016/C2013-0-10497-7.

Chui, C. W. S., & Dietz, J. (2014). Observing workplace incivility towards women: The roles of target reactions, actor motives, and actor-target relationships. *Sex Roles*, 71(1–2), 95–108. doi.org/10.1007/s11199-014-0367-7.

Cicchetti, D., & Rizley, R. (1981). Developmental perspectives on the etiology, inter-generational and transmission and sequelae of child maltreatment. *New Directions for Child Development*, 11, 31–55.

Citron, D. K. (2009). Law's expressive value in combating cyber gender harassment. *Michigan Law Review*, 108 (3), 373–415.

Clawar, S. S., & Rivlin, B. V. (2013). *Children held hostage, Second Edition: Identifying brainwashed children, presenting a case, and crafting solutions*. American Bar Association Press.

Cleckley, H. (1976 [1941]). *The mask of sanity: An attempt to reinterpret the so-called psychopathic personality*. Mosby.

Clemente, M. (1992). Psicología Social: Métodos y Técnicas de Investigación [Social Psychology: Methods and Techniques of Research]. Eudema.

Clemente, M. (2010). Introducción a la Psicología Social: Enfoques teóricos clásicos [Introduction to Social Psychology: Theorical classic orientations]. Universitas.

Clemente, M. (2011). La Psicología Jurídica ante el reto de la sociedad de la comunicación virtual [Legal Psychology facing the challenge of the virtual communication society]. Infancia, Juventud y Ley, 1, 27–33.

Clemente, M. (2013a). Evaluación psicológica forense del abuso sexual infantil [Forensic psychological evaluation of child sexual abuse]. In M. Lameiras & E. Orts, *Delitos sexuales contra los menores. Abordaje psicológico, jurídico y policial* [Sexual offenses against minors. Psychological, legal and police approach] (pp. 313–335). Tirant lo Blanch.

Clemente, M. (2013b). El Síndrome de Alienación Parental: Un atentado contra la ciencia, contra el estado de derecho, y contra los menores y sus progenitores [Parental Alienation Syndrome: An attack against science, against human rights and against children and their parents]. *Infancia, Juventud y Ley*, 4, 48–57.

Clemente, M. (2016). *Psicología para Juristas* [Psychology for Lawyers]. Síntesis.

Clemente, M., & Diaz, Z. E. (2018). Children with poor attachment to their parents: Explanatory variables as a function of their perception of their parents' behavior. *Children and Youth Services Review*, 87, 140–144. doi.org/10.1016/j. childyouth.2018.02.034.

Clemente, M., & Diaz, Z. E. (2020). Machiavellianism and the manipulation of children as a tactic in child custody disputes: The MMS Scale. *Journal of Forensic Psychology: Research and Practice. 21*(2), 171–193. https://doi.org/10.1080/24732850.2020.1847525.

Clemente, M., Diaz, Z. E., & Espinosa, P. (2020). Differential child perceptions of the parents' care and concerns as a custody measure: The Children's Preference Scale (CPS). *Child Indicators Research,* 14, 1089–1104. doi.org/10.1007/s12187-020-09785-x.

Clemente, M., & Padilla-Racero, D. (2015a). Are children susceptible to manipulation? The best interest of children and their testimony. *Children and Youth Services Review,* 51, 101–107.

Clemente, M., & Padilla-Racero, D. (2015b). Facts speak louder than words: Science versus the pseudoscience of PAS. *Children and Youth Services Review,* 56, 177–184. doi.org/10.1016/j.childyouth.2015.07.005.

Clemente, M., & Padilla-Racero, D. (2016). When courts accept what science rejects: Custody issues concerning the alleged "parental alienation síndrome." *Journal of Child Custody,* 13(2–3), 126–133. doi.org/dx.doi.org/10.1080/15379418.2016.1219245.

Clemente, M., & Padilla-Racero, D. (2020a). Influence of intrafamilial abuse in children's change of values towards their parents. *Zeitschrifte fur Familienforschung—Journal of Family Research,* pp. 1–18. doi.org/10.20377/jfr-157.

Clemente, M., & Padilla-Racero, D. (2020b). The effects of the justice system on the mental health. *Psychiatry, Psychology and Law* 27(5), 1–16. doi.org/10.1080/13218719.2020.175132.

Clemente, M., & Padilla-Racero, D. (2021). Obey the justice system or protect children? The moral dilemma posed by false parental alienation syndrome. *Children and Youth Services Review,* 120, 105728. doi.org/10.1016/j.childyouth.2020.105728.

Clemente, M., Padilla-Racero, D., & Espinosa, P. (2019a). Moral disengagement and willingness to behave unethically against ex-partner in a child custody dispute. *PlosOne,* 3. doi.org/10.1371/journal.pone.0213662.

Clemente, M., Padilla-Racero, D., & Espinosa, P. (2019b). Revenge among parents who have broken up their relationship through family law courts: Its dimensions and measurement proposal. *International Journal of Environmental Research and Public Health,* 16, 4950. doi.org/10.3390/ijerph16244950.

Clemente, M., Padilla-Racero, D., & Espinosa, P. (2020). The dark triad and the detection of parental judicial manipulators. Development of a judicial manipulation scale. *International Journal of Environmental Research and Public Health,* 17, 2843. doi.org/10.3390/ijerph17082843

Clemente, M., Padilla, R., Espinosa, P., Reig-Botella, A., & Gandoy-Crego, M. (2019). Institutional violence against users of the family law courts and the legal harassment scale. *Frontiers in Psychology,* 10, 1–8. doi.org/10.3389/fpsyg.2019.00001.

Clemente, M., Padilla-Racero, D., Gandoy, M., Reig-Botella, A., Gonzalez-Rodriguez, R. (2015). Judicial decision-making in family law proceedings. *American Journal of Family Therapy,* 43(4), 314–325. doi.org/10.1080/01926187.2015.1051895.

Cobo, R. (2005). El género en las ciencias sociales [Gender in the social sciences]. *Cuadernos de Trabajo Social*, 18, 249–258.

Cobo, R. (2008). Educar en la ciudadanía: Perspectivas feministas [Educating for citizenship: feminist perspectives]. Los Libros de la Catarata.

Coccaro, E. F., & Lee, R. J. (2020). Disordered aggression and violence in the United States. *The Journal of Clinical Psychiatry*, 81(2). doi.org/10.1080/10926771.2018 .1546246.

Código Iberoamericano de ética judicial [Ibero-American Judicial Summit] (2006). https://www.poderjudicial.es/cgpj/es/CIEJ/Codigo-Iberoamericano-de-Etica -Judicial/ Last Access: May 20, 2022

Conte, J. R. (2001). *Critical issues in child sexual abuse*. Sage.

Corral, P., Echeburúa, E., Sarasúa, B., & Zubizarreta, I. (1992). Estrés postraumático en excombatientes y en víctimas de agresiones sexuales: Nuevas perspectivas tera-péuticas [Post-traumatic stress in ex-combatants and victims of sexual assault: New therapeutic perspectives]. *Boletín de Psicología*, 35, 7–24.

Cortés, M. R., & Cantón, J. D. (1997). Consecuencias del abuso sexual infantil [Consequences of child sexual abuse]. In J. D. Cantón & M. R. Cortés, *Malos tra-tos y abuso sexual infantil* [Child abuse and maltreatment]. Siglo XXI.

Crittenden, P. (1993). An information processing perspective on the behavior of neglectful parents. *Criminal Justice and Behavior*, 20, 27–48.

Crysel, L. C., Crosier, B. S., & Webster, G. D. (2013). The dark triad and risk behavior. *Personality and Individual Differences*, 54(1), 35–40. doi.org/10.1016/j. paid.2012.07.029.

Cumbre Judicial Iberoamericana. (2006). www.cumbrejudicial.org/.

Curtin, D. W., & Litke, R. (Eds.). (1999). *Institutional violence*. Rodopi.

Dall'Ara, E., & Maass, A. (1999). Studying sexual harassment in the labora-tory: Are egalitarian women at higher risk? *Sex Roles*, 41(9–10), 681–704. doi. org/10.1023/A:1018816025988.

Darley, J. M. (1992). Social organization for the production of evil. *Psychological Inquiry*, 3, 199–218.

De Paúl, P. (2004). Evaluación de la credibilidad del testimonio en supuestos de abuso sexual a menores [Evaluation of the credibility of the testimony in cases of sexual abuse of minors]. In B. Vázquez Mezquita (Ed.), *Abuso sexual infantil. Evaluación de la credibilidad del testimonio* [Child sexual abuse. Assessment of the credibility of the testimony] (pp. 45–72). Centro Reina Sofía para el Estudio de la Violencia.

Del Río, C. (2005). *Guía de ética profesional en psicología clínica* [Guide to profes-sional ethics in clinical psychology]. Pirámide.

Díaz-Aguado, M. J., & Carvajal, I. (2011). Igualdad y prevención de la violencia de género en la adolescencia y la juventud [Equality and prevention of gender violence in adolescents and youth]. Ministerio de Sanidad, Igualdad y Servicios Sociales del Reino de España.

Diekman, A. (2005). What is the problem? Prejudice as an attitude-in-context. *On the Nature of Prejudice*, 50, 19–35.

Dietz, Th., Ostrom, E., & Stern, P. (2004). The struggle to govern the commons. *Science*, 302, 1907–1912. doi.org/10.1126/science.1091015.

Diges, M., (Ed.). (1997). *Los falsos recuerdos. Sugestión y memoria.* Paidós.

Dingler-Duhon, M., & Brown, B. B. (1987). Self-disclosure as an influence strategy: Effects of machiavellianism, androgyny, and sex. *Sex Roles,* 16(3–4), 109–123. doi.org/10.1007/BF00289643.

Dinić, B. M., Bulut-Allred, T., Petrović, B., & Wertag, A. (2020). A test of three sadism measures: Short Sadistic Impulse Scale, varieties of sadistic tendencies, and assessment of sadistic personality: Correction to Dinić, Bulut Allred, Petrović, and Wertag (2020). *Journal of Individual Differences,* 41(4), 228. doi. org/10.1027/1614-0001/a000323.

Dirik, G., Yorulmaz, O., & Karanci, A. N. (2015). Assessment of perceived parenting attitudes in childhood: Turkish form of the S-EMBU for Children. *Turk Psikiyatri Dergisi,* 26 (2), 123–130.

Dolinski, D., & Grzyb, T. (2016). One serious shock versus gradated series of shocks: Does "multiple feet-in-the-door" explain obedience in Milgram studies? *Basic and Applied Social Psychology,* 38(5), 276–283. doi.org/10.1080/01973533.2016.121 4836.

Durkin, D. (1970). A classroom-observation study of reading instruction in kindergarten instruction in kindergarten. *Early Childhood Research Quarterly,* 2(3), 275–300. doi.org/10.1016/0885-2006(87)90036-6.

Durrell, G. (1956). *My family and other animals.* Rupert Hart-Davis.

Dutton, M. A., & Goodman, L. A. (2005). Coercion in intimate partner violence: Toward a new conceptualization. *Sex Roles,* 52(11–12), 743–756. doi.org/10.1007/ s11199-005-4196-6.

Easteal, P., Holland, K., & Judd, K. (2015). Enduring themes and silences in media portrayals of *Violence against Women. Womens Studies International Forum,* 48, 103–113. doi.org/10.1016/j.wsif.2014.10.015.

Echeburúa, E., & Del Corral, P. (2006). Secuelas emocionales en víctimas de abuso sexual en la infancia [Emotional consequences in victims of sexual abuse in childhood]. *Cuadernos de Medicina Forense,* 12(43–44), 75–82.

Echeburúa, E., & Guerricaechevarría, C. (1998). *Abuso sexual en la infancia: Víctimas y agresores, un enfoque clínico* [Sexual abuse in childhood: Victims and aggressors, a clinical approach]. Arial.

Echeburúa, E., & Guerricaechevarría, C. (2000). *Abuso sexual en la infancia: Víctimas y agresores* [Sexual abuse in childhood: Victims and aggressors]. Ariel.

Echeburúa, E., & Guerricaechevarría, C. (2005). Concepto, factores de riesgo y efectos psicopatológicos del abuso sexual infantil [Concept, risk factors and psychopathological effects of child sexual abuse]. In J. Sanmartín (Ed.), *Violencia contra los niños 3 Ed.* [Violence against children 3 Ed] (pp. 86–112). Ariel.

Echeburúa, E., & Guerricaechevarría, C. (2006). Abuso sexual de menores [Sexual abuse of minors]. In E. Baca, E. Echeburúa, & J. M. Tamarit (Eds.), *Manual de victimología* [Handbook of victimology] (pp. 129–148). Tirant lo Blanch.

Echeburúa, E., & Subijana, I. J. (2008). Guía de buena práctica psicológica en el tratamiento judicial de los niños abusados sexualmente [Guide to good psychological practice in the judicial treatment of sexually abused children]. *International Journal of Clinical and Health Psychology,* 8(3), 733–749.

Egan, V., Hughes, N., & Palmer, E. J. (2015). Moral disengagement, the dark triad, and unethical consumer attitudes. *Personality and Individual Differences*, 76, 123–128. doi.org/10.1016/j.paid.2014.11.054.

Elshout, M., Nelissen, R., & Van Beest, I. (2016). Conceptualising humiliation. *Cognition & Emotion*, 31, 1–14. doi.org/10.1080/02699931.2016.1249462.

Emery, R. E., Otto, R. K., & O'Donohue, W. T. (2005). A critical assessment of child custody evaluations: Limited science and a flawed system. *Psychological Science in the Public Interest*, 6(1), 1–29. doi.org/10.1111/j.1529-1006.2005.00020.x.

Erard, R. E. (2016). Maybe the sky isn't falling after all: Comment on Kleinman and Kaplan (2016). *Journal of Child Custody*, 13(1), 88–96. doi.org/10.1080/1537941 8.2016.1130597.

Erzi, S. (2020). Dark triad and schadenfreude: Mediating role of moral disengagement and relational aggression. *Personality and Individual Differences*, 157. doi. org/10.1016/j.paid.2020.109827.

Escudero. A., González, D., Méndez, R., Naredo, C., Pleguezuelos, E., Vaccaro, S., & Pérez, A. M. (2010). *Informe del grupo de trabajo de investigación sobre el llamado síndrome de alienación parental* [Report of the working group research called parental alienation syndrome]. Ministerio de Sanidad, Política Social e Igualdad del Reino de España.

Espejo-Siles, R., Zych, I., Farrington, D. P., & Llorent, V. J. (2020). Moral disengagement, victimization, empathy, social and emotional competencies as predictors of violence in children and adolescents. *Children and Youth Services Review*, 118, 105337, doi.org/10.1016/j.childyouth.2020.105337.

Eveland, W. P., & McLeod, D. M. (1999). The effect of social desirability on perceived media impact: Implications for third-person perceptions. *International Journal of Public Opinion Research*, 11(4), 315–333. doi.org/10.1093/ijpor/11.4.315.

Exline, J. J., Baumeister, R. F., Bushman, B. J., Campbell, W. K., & Finkel, E. J. (2004). Too proud to let go: Narcissistic entitlement as a barrier to forgiveness. *Journal of Personality and Social Psychology*, 87(6), 894–912. doi. org/10.1037/0022-3514.87.6.894.

Eysenck, H. J. (1952). The effects of psychotherapy: An evaluation. *Journal of Consulting Psychology*, 16(5), 319–324.

Farrell, P. (2001). Special education in last twenty years: have things really got better? *British Journal of Special Education*, 28(1), 3–9

Fenigstein, A. (2015). Milgram's shock experiments and the Nazi perpetrators: A contrarian perspective on the role of obedience pressures during the Holocaust. *Theory & Psychology*, 25(5), 581–598. doi.org/10.1177/0959354315601904.

Fermann, I., & Habigzang, L. F. (2016). Caracterização descritiva de processos judiciais referenciados com alienação parental em uma cidade na região sul do Brasil [Descriptive characterization of judicial processes referenced with parental alienation in a city in south region of Brazil]. *Ciencias Psicológicas*, 10(2), 165–176.

Fernández-Dols, J. M. (1993). Norma perversa: Hipótesis teóricas [Perverse norm: Theoretical hypotheses]. *Psicothema*, 5, 91–101.

Ferreiro, X. (2005). La víctima en el proceso penal [The victim in the penal process]. *La Ley*.

Fincham, F. D., Beach, S. R. H., Harold, G., & Osborne L. N. (1997). Marital satisfaction and depression: Different causal relationships for men and women? *Psychological Science*, 8(5), 351–356.

Finkelhor, D. (1988). The trauma of child sexual abuse: Two models. In G. E. Wyatt & G. J. Powell (Eds.), *Lasting effects of the child sexual abuse*. Sage.

Finkelhor, D. (1997). The victimization of children and youth: Developmental victimology. In R. C. Davis, A. J. Lurigio, & W. G. Skogan (Eds.), *Victims of crime*. Sage.

Fiske, A. P., & Rai, T. S. (2014). *Virtuous violence: Hurting and killing to create, sustain, end, and honor social relationships*. Amazon. doi.org/10.1017/CBO9781316104668.

Furman, W., & Buhrmester, D. (1992). Age and sex-differences in perceptions of networks of personal relationships. *Child Development*, 63(1), 103–115. doi.org/10.1111/j.1467-8624.1992.tb03599.x.

Galtung, J. (1990). Cultural violence. *Journal of Peace Research*, 27(3), 291–305.

Galtung, J., & Fischer, D. (2013). Positive and negative peace. In J. Galtung, *Springer Briefs on Pioneers in Science and Practice* (vol 5, pp. 173–178). Springer. https://doi.org/10.1007/978-3-642-32481-9_17-

Garcia, D., & Rosenberg, P. (2016). The dark cube: Dark and light character profiles. *PEERJ*, 4, e1675. doi.org/10.7717/peerj.1675.

Garcia, J. R. (2015). Using a critical race praxis to examine and resist the discursive practices that reproduce racism, misogyny, and homophobia. *Qualitative Inquiry*, 21(3), 315–323. doi.org/10.1177/1077800414557829.

García Díaz, V., Ana Fernández-Feito, A., Rodríguez-Díaz, F. J., López-González, M. J., Mosteiro-Díaz, M. P., & Lana-Pérez, A. (2013). Violencia de género en estudiantes de enfermería durante sus relaciones de noviazgo [Gender violence in nursing students during their dating relationships]. *Atención primaria*, 45(6), 290–296.

García-Pablos, A. (1988). *Manual de criminología. Introducción y teorías de la criminalidad* [Handbook of criminology. Introduction and theories of crime]. Espasa.

García-Piña, C. A., & Loredo-Abdalá, A. (2009). Guía para la atención del abuso sexual infantil. *Acta Pediátrica Mexicana*, 30(2), 94–103.

Gardner R. A. (1985). Recent trends in divorce and custody litigation. *Academy Forum*, 29, 3–7.

Gardner, R. A. (1991). Legal and psychotherapeutic approaches to the three types of Parental Alienation Syndrome families. When psychiatry and the law join forces. *Court Review*, 28(1), 14–21.

Gardner, R. A. (1992). *The Parental Alienation Syndrome: A guide for mental health professionals*. Creative Therapeutics.

Gardner, R. A. (1998). *The Parental Alienation Syndrome*. Cresskill, NJ: Creative Therapeutics.

Gardner, R. A. (1999). Family therapy of the moderate type of Parental Alienation Syndrome. *The American Journal of Family Therapy*, 27, 195–212.

Gardner, R. A. (2004). The relationship between the Parental Alienation Syndrome (PAS) and the False Memory Syndrome (FMS). *The American Journal of Family Therapy*, 32, 79–99.

Gardner, R. A., Sauber, R. S., & Lorandos, D. (Eds.). (2006). *The international handbook of Parental Alienation Syndrome: Conceptual, clinical and legal considerations*. Charles C Thomas Publisher.

Garry, M., Manning, C. G., Loftus, E. F., & Sherman, S. J. (1996). Imagination inflation: Imagining a childhood event inflates confidence that it occurred. *Psychonomic Bulletin & Review*, 3(2), 208–214. doi.org/10.3758/BF03212420.

Garver, N., & Friedenberg, E. Z. (1968). What violence is. *The Nation*, 209, 817–822.

Garzón-Azañón, M. A., & Barahona-Esteban, M. N. (2018). Diferencias personales en el perdón en universitarios españoles en función del sexo [Personal differences in forgiveness in Spanish university students based on sex]. *Cauriensia*, 13, 175–192. doi.org/0.17398/2340-4256.13.175.

Geng, Y. G., Chang, G. S., Li, L., Zhang, R. X., Sun, Q. B., & Huang, J. Y. (2016). Machiavellianism in Chinese adolescents: Links to internalizing and externalizing problems. *Personality and Individual Differences*, 89, 19–23. dx.doi.org/10.1016/j.paid.2015.09.037.

Gergen, K. (1992). Social psychology and the phoenix of unreality. In S. Koch & D. Leary, *A century of psychology as a science* (pp. 528–557). American Psychological Association.

Gilbert, S. (1981). Another look at the Milgram obedience studies: The role of the gradated series of shocks. *Personality and Social Psychology Bulletin*, 7(4), 690–695.

Glaser, B. A., Horne, A. M., & Myers, L. L. (1995). A cross-validation of the Parent Perception Inventory. *Child & Family Behavior Therapy*, 17(1), 21–34. doi.org/10.1300/J019v17n01_02.

Glick, P., & Fiske, S. T. (1996). The ambivalent sexism theory. Differentiating hostile and benevolent sexism. *Journal of Personality and Social Psychology*, 70, 491–512.

Gomez, J., Ortega, R., Clemente, M., & Casas, J. A. (2021). Intimate partner aggression committed by prison inmates with psychopathic profile. *International Journal of Environmental Research and Public Health*, 18, 5141. doi.org/10.3390/ijerph18105141.

Gomide, P., Cunha, I., Camargo, E. B., & Fernandes, M. G. (2016). Analysis of the psychometric properties of a Parental Alienation Scale. *Paidéia* (Ribeirão Preto), 26(65), 291–298. doi.org/10.1590/1982-43272665201602.

Goodwin, G. P., & Darley, J. M. (2008). The psychology of meta-ethics: Exploring objectivism. *Cognition*, 106, 1339–1366. doi.org/10.1016/j.cognition.2007.06.007.

Gottlieb, L. (2012). *The Parental Alienation Syndrome: A family therapy and collaborative systems approach to amelioration*. Charles C. Thomas.

Gray, H., & Wegner, D. (2007). Dimensions of mind perception. *Science*, 315, 619. doi.org/10.1126/science.1134475.

Green, B. L. (1994). Psychosocial research in traumatic stress: An update. *Journal of Traumatic Stress*, 7(3), 341–362.

Grosjean P. (2014). Conflict and social and political preferences: Evidence from World War II and civil conflict in 35 European countries. *Comp. Econ. Stud.*, 56 (3), 424–451.

Gunnthorsdottir, A., McCabe, K., & Smith, V. (2002). Using the Machiavellianism instrument to predict trustworthiness in a bargaining game. *Journal of Economic Psychology*, 23(1), 49–66. doi.org/10.1016/S0167-4870(01)00067-8.

Guterman, S. (1970). *The Machiavellians*. University of Nebraska Press.

Gutiérrez de Piñeres-Botero, C., Coronel, E., & Andrés-Pérez, C. (2009). Revisión teórica del concepto de victimización secundaria [Theoretical review of the concept of secondary victimization]. *Liberabit*, 15(1), 49–58.

Halmos, M. B., Parrott, D. J., Henrich, C. C., & Eckhardt, C. I. (2018). The structure of aggression in conflict-prone couples: Validation of a measure of the Forms and Functions of Intimate Partner Aggression (FFIPA). *Psychological Assessment*, 32(5), 461–472. doi.org/10.1037/pas0000806.

Halty, L., & Prieto, M. (2011). Psicopatía subclínica y la triada oscura de la personalidad [Subclinical psychopathy and the dark triad of personality]. Editorial Académica Española.

Hartman, C. R., & Burgess, A. W. (1989). Sexual abuse of children: Causes and consequences. In D. Cicchetti & V. Carlson (Eds.), *Child maltreatment: Theory and research on the cause and consequences of child abuse and neglect*. Cambridge University Press.

Hartman, C. R., & Burgess, A. W. (1993). Information processing of trauma. *Child Abuse & Neglect*, 17(1), 47–58. doi.org/10.1016/0145-2134(93)90007-R.

Hayes, B. E., & Kopp, P. M. (2020). Gender differences in the effect of past year victimization on self-reported physical and mental health: Findings from the 2010 National Intimate Partner and Sexual Violence Survey. *American Journal of Criminal Justice*, 45(2), 293–312. doi.org/10.1007/s12103-019-09510-7.

Hazzard, A., & Christensen, A. (1983). Children's perceptions of parental behaviors. *Journal of Abnormal and Child Psychology*, 11 (1), 49–59.

Hazzard, A., Kleemeier, C. P., Pohl, J., & Webb, C. (1988). *Child sexual abuse prevention: Teacher training workshop curriculum*. Atlanta: Emory University School of Medicine.

Hedges, R., Drysdale, K., Drysdale, K., & Levick, W. R. (2015). The Children's Memory Questionnaire-Revised. *Applied Neuropsychology-Child*, 4(4), 285–296. doi.org/10.1080/21622965.2014.925806.

Hernández, J., & Miranda, M. (2005). ¿Deben declarar los menores victimizados en el acto del juicio oral? [Should victimized minors testify in the oral proceedings?] *Revista La Ley*, 6335, 1–5.

Hernandez-Guzman, L., Gonzalez-Montesinos, M., Bermudez-Ornelas, G., Freyre, M. A., & Alcazar-Olan, R. (2013). Parental Practices Scale for Children. *Revista Colombiana de Psicología*, 22 (1), 151–161.

Hine, B., Noku, L., Bates, E. A., & Jayes, K. (2020). But, who is the victim here? Exploring judgments toward hypothetical bidirectional domestic violence scenarios. *Journal of Interpersonal Violence*, UNSP 0886260520917508. doi.org/10.1177/0886260520917508.

Isoke, Z. (2014). Can't I be seen? Can't I be heard? Black women queering politics in Newark. *Gender, Place and Culture*, 21(3), 353–369. doi.org/10.1080/09663 69X.2013.781015.

Jackson, J. C., Choi, V. K., & Gelfand, M. J. (2019). Revenge: A multilevel review and synthesis. *Annual Review of Psychology*, 70, 319. doi.org/10.1146/annurev-psych-010418-103305.

Jane, E. A. (2015). Flaming? What flaming? The pitfalls and potentials of researching online hostility. *Ethics and Information Technology*, 17(1), 65–87. doi.org/10.1007/s10676-015-9362-0.

Jarnecke, A. M., Ridings, L. E., Teves, J. B., Petty, K., Bhatia, V., & Libet, J. (2020). The path to couples therapy: A descriptive analysis on a veteran sample. *Couple and Family Psychology: Research and Practice*, 9(2), 73–89. doi.org/10.1037/cfp0000135.

Jia, T. L., Ing, H. K., & Lee, M.Ch. Ch. (2016). A review of personality factors on relationship infidelity. *Jurnal Psikologi Malaysia*, 30(1), 126–141. https://doi.org/10.1016/j.paid.2009.11.003.

Johnson, M. K., & Raye, C. (1981). Reality monitoring. *Psychological Review*, 88, 67–85.

Johnson, M. P. (2006). Conflict and control—Gender symmetry and asymmetry in domestic violence. *Violence against Women*, 12(11), 1003–1018. doi.org/10.1177/1077801206293328.

Johnson, M. P., & Ferraro, K. J. (2000). Research on domestic violence in the 1990s: Making distinctions. *Journal of Marriage and Family*, 62(4), 948–963. doi.org/10.1111/j.1741-3737.2000.00948.x.

Johnson, S. J., & Moore, T. M. (2020). The role of impulsivity and stress mind-set in understanding the mindfulness-intimate partner aggression relationship. *Journal of Interpersonal Violence*. doi.org/10.1177/0886260520917506.

Jonason, P. K., & Davis, M. D. (2018). A gender role view of the dark triad traits. *Personality and Individual Differences*, 125, 102–105. dx.doi.org/10.1016/j.paid.2018.01.004.

Jonason, P. K., Li, N. P., & Buss, D. M. (2010). The costs and benefits of the dark triad: Implications for mate poaching and mate retention tactics. *Personality and Individual Differences*, 48(4), 373–378. doi.org/10.1016/j.paid.2009.11.003.

Jonason, P. K., Li, N. P., Webster, G. D., & Schmitt, D. P. (2009). The dark triad: Facilitating a short-term mating strategy in men. *European Journal of Personality*, 23(1), 5–18. doi.org/10.1002/per.698.

Jonason, P. K., Luevano, V. X., & Adams, H. M. (2012). How the dark triad traits predict relationship choices. *Personality and Individual Differences*, 53(3), 180–184. doi.org/10.1016/j.paid.2012.03.007.

Jonason, P. K., Oshio, A., Shimotsukasa, T., Mieda, T., Csatho, A., & Sitnikova, M. (2018). Seeing the world in black or white: The dark triad traits and dichotomous thinking. *Personality and Individual Differences*, 120, 102–106. dx.doi.org/10.1016/j.paid.2017.08.030.

Jonason, P. K., Valentine, K. A., Li, N. P., & Harbeson, C. L. (2011). Mate-selection and the dark triad: Facilitating a short-term mating strategy and creating a volatile environment. *Personality and Individual Differences*, 51(6), 759–763. doi.org/10.1016/j.paid.2011.06.025.

Jones, D. N., & Paulhus, D. L. (2014). Introducing the short dark triad (SD3): A brief measure of dark personality traits. *Assessment*, 21(1), 28–41. doi.org/10.1177/1073191113514105.

Jones, D. N., & Weiser, D. A. (2014). Differential infidelity patterns among the dark triad. *Personality and Individual Differences*, 57, 20–24. doi.org/10.1016/j.paid.2013.09.007.

Kaminer, D., Stein, D., Mbanga, I., & Zungu, N. (2000). Forgiveness: Toward an integration of theoretical models. *Psychiatry*, 63, 344–357. doi.org/10.1080/0033 2747.2000.11024928.

Kaplan, S. (2011). *The Routledge Spanish bilingual dictionary of psychology and psychiatry*. Taylor & Francis.

Kashy, D. A., & DePaulo, B. M. (1996). Who lies? *Journal of Personality and Social Psychology*, 70(5), 1037–1051. doi.org/10.1037/0022-3514.70.5.1037.

Kaufman, M., & Kimmel, M. (2011). *The guy's guide to feminism*. Seal Press.

Kiire, S. (2017). Psychopathy rather than Machiavellianism or narcissism facilitates intimate partner violence via fast life strategy. *Personality and Individual Differences*, 104, 401–406. doi.org/10.1016/j.paid.2016.08.043.

Kiire, S. (2019). A "fast" life history strategy affects intimate partner violence through the dark triad and mate retention behavior. *Personality and Individual Differences*, 140, 46–51. doi.org/10.1016/j.paid.2018.07.016.

Kim, I. H. (2015). Legal and institutional measures to reform participatory trials for sex crime cases. *Asian Women*, 31(2), 53–84.

Kleinman, T., & Kaplan, P. (2016). Relaxation of rules for science detrimental to children. *Journal of Child Custody*, 13(1), 72–87.

Kobak, R. (2009). Defining and measuring of sttachment bonds: Comment on Kurdek (2009). *Journal of Family Psychology*, 23(4), 447–449. doi.org/10.1037/a0015213.

Kobau, R., Seligman, M. E., Peterson, C., Diener, E., Zack, M. M., Chapman D., & Thompson, W. (2011). Mental health promotion in public health: Perspectives and strategies from positive psychology. *American Journal of Public Health*, 101 (8), e1–9. doi.org/10.2105/AJPH.2010.300083.

Koladich, S., & Atkinson, B. (2016). The dark triad and relationship preferences: A replication and extension. *Personality and Individual Differences*, 94, 253–255. doi.org/10.1016/j.paid.2016.01.023.

Kopsaj, V. (2016). Blood feud and its impact on the Albanian criminality. *Mediterranean Journal of Social Sciences*, 7(3), 88–95.

Kreuter, E. A. (2006). *Victim vulnerability: An existential-humanistic interpretation of a single case study*. Nova Science.

Kubany, E. S., & Haynes, S. N. (2001). Traumatic Life Events Questionnaire. Manual. Second draft. Western Psychological Services.

Kuijpers, K. F. (2020). Partner disagreement on the occurrence of intimate partner violence among a national sample of heterosexual young-adult couples. *Violence against Women*, 26(8), 889–909. doi.org/10.1177/1077801219850343.

Kurdek, L. A. (1998). Relationships outcomes and their predictors: Longitudinal evidences from heterosexual married, gay cohabiting, and lesbian cohabiting couples. *Journal of Marriage and the Family*, 60, 553–568.

Kurdek, L. A. (1999). More differences about gender differences in marriage: A reply to Beach, Davey, and Fincham (1999). *Journal of Family Psychology*, 13(4), 669–674. doi.org/10.1037/0893-3200.13.4.669.

Kurdek, L. A., & Berg, B. (1987). Children's beliefs about parental divorce scale: Psychometric characteristics and concurrent validity. *Journal of Consulting and Clinical Psychology*, 55, 712–718. doi.org/10.1037/0022-006X.55.5.712.

Lameiras, M. (Ed.). (2002). *Abusos sexuales en la infancia. Abordaje psicológico y jurídico* [Sexual abuse in childhood. Psychological and legal approach]. Biblioteca Nueva.

Landrove, G. (1998). *La moderna victimología* [The modern victimology]. Tirant lo Blanch.

Lang, A., & Birkas, B. (2015). Machiavellianism and parental attachment in adolescence: Effect of the relationship with same-sex parents. *Sage Open*, 5(1). dx.doi.org/10.1177/2158244015571639.

Latham, G. (2006). *Work motivation: History, theory, research, and practice.* Sage.

Laxminarayan, M. (2012). Procedural justice and psychological rffects of criminal proceedings: The moderating effect of offense type. *Social Justice Research*, 25(4), 390–405. doi.org/10.1007/s11211-012-0167-6.

Lerner, J. S., & Tiedens, L. Z. (2006). Portrait of the angry decision maker: How appraisal tendencies shape anger's influence on cognition. *Journal of Behavioral Decision Making*, 19(2), 115–137. doi.org/10.1002/bdm.515.

Lewis, Y. (2003). The self as a moral concept. *British Journal of Social Psychology*, 42(2), 225–237. doi.org/10.1348/014466603322127229.

Leymann, H. (1990). Mobbing and psychological terror at workplaces. *Violence and Victims*, 5, 119–126.

Leymann, H. (1996). The content and development of mobbing at work. *European Journal of Work and Organizational Psychology*, 5(2), 165–184.

Limbaugh, R. (1993). *See, I told you so.* New York: Atria.

Loftus, E., Miller, D., & Burns, H. (1978). Semantic integration of verbal information into a visual memory. *Journal of Experimental Psychology: Human Learning and Memory*, 4, 19–31. doi.org/10.1037//0278-7393.4.1.19.

London, K., Bruck, M., Ceci, S., & Shuman, D. (2005). Disclosure of child sexual abuse. What does the research tell us about the ways that children tell? *Psychology, Public Policy, and Law*, 11, 194–226.

Lonsway, K. A. & Fitzgerald, L. F. (1995). Attitudinal antecedents of rape myth acceptance: A theoretical and empirical reexamination. *Journal of Personality and Social Psychology*, 68(4), 704–711. doi.org/10.1037/0022-3514.68.4.704.

López, F. (1993). La intervención educativa y terapéutica en los casos de abusos sexuales de menores [Educational and therapeutic intervention in cases of sexual abuse of minors]. In J. F. Navarro & F. J. Bustamante (Eds.), *Ensayos y conferencias sobre prevención e intervención en salud mental* [Essays and lectures on prevention and intervention in mental health]. Junta de Castilla y León.

López, F., Hernández, A., & Carpintero, E. (1995): Los abusos sexuales de menores: Concepto, prevalencia y efectos [Sexual abuse of minors: Concept, prevalence and effects]. *Infancia y Aprendizaje*, 71, 77–98.

Lorandos, D., Bernet, W., & Sauber, S. R. (2013). *Parental alienation: The handbook for mental health and legal professionals.* Charles C. Thomas.

Malesza, M., & Ostaszewski, P. (2016). The utility of the dark triad model in the prediction of the self-reported and behavioral risk-taking behaviors among adolescents. *Personality and Individual Differences*, 90, 7–11. doi.org/10.1016/j.paid.2015.10.026.

Manzanero, A. (2001). Procedimientos de evaluación de la credibilidad de las declaraciones de menores víctimas de agresiones sexuales [Procedures for evaluating the credibility of the declarations of minor victims of sexual assaults]. *Psicopatología Clínica. Legal y Forense*, 1(2), 51–71.

Manzanero, A. L., & Diges, M. (1993). Evaluación subjetiva de la exactitud de las declaraciones de los testigos: La credibilidad [Subjective assessment of the accuracy of witness statements: Credibility]. *Anuario de Psicología Jurídica*, 3, 7–27.

Mappes, D., Robb, G., & Engels, D. (1985). Conflicts between ethics and law in counseling and psychotherapy. *Journal of Counseling & Development*, 64(4), 246–252.

Marshall, L. L. (1999). Effects of men's subtle and overt psychological abuse on low-income women. *Violence and Victims*, 14, 69–88. dx.doi.org/10.1097/OLQ.0000000000000302.

Martín, J. L., & De Paúl, J. (2004). Trastorno por estrés postraumático en víctimas de situaciones traumáticas [Post-traumatic stress disorder in victims of traumatic situations]. *Psicothema*, 16(1), 45–49.

Martín-Corral, S. (2002). El consentimiento informado y el dictamen pericial psicológico [Informed consent and psychological expert opinion]. In J. Urra (Ed.), *Tratado de psicología forense* [Forensic psychology treatise] (pp. 837–844). Siglo XXI.

Martínez-Calcerrada, L. (1970). Independencia del poder judicial [Independence of the judiciary]. *Revista de Derecho Judicial*, 7, 1647–1652

Masip, J., & Garrido, E. (2001). La evaluación psicológica de la credibilidad del testimonio [The psychological evaluation of the credibility of the testimony]. In F. Jiménez (Ed.), *Evaluación psicológica forense. Fuentes de información, abusos sexuales, testimonio, peligrosidad y reincidencia* [Forensic psychological evaluation. Sources of information, sexual abuse, testimony, dangerousness and recidivism] (pp. 141–204). Amarú.

Masip, J., & Garrido, E. (2007). *La evaluación del abuso sexual infantil. Análisis de la validez de las declaraciones del niño* [The evaluation of child sexual abuse. Analysis of the validity of the child's statements]. Eduforma.

Maslach, C. (1976). Burned-out. *Human Behavior*, 5, 16–22.

Maslach, C., & Jackson, S. (1986). *Maslach Burnout Inventory manual.* Consulting Psychologist Press, Inc.

Mastroianni, G. R. (2015). Obedience in perspective: Psychology and the Holocaust. *Theory & Psychology*, 25(5), 657–669. doi.org/10.1177/0959354315608963.

Mavin, S., Grandy, G., & Williams, J. (2014). Experiences of women elite leaders doing gender: intra-gender micro-violence between women. *British Journal of Management*, 25(3), 439–455. doi.org/10.1111/1467-8551.12057.

Mazza, M., Marano, G., Lai, C., Janiri, L., & Sani, G. (2020). Danger in danger: Interpersonal violence during COVID-19 quarantine. *Psychiatry Research*, 289. doi.org/10.1016/j.psychres.2020.113046.

McConnell, T. (2014). Moral dilemmas. In E. N. Zalta (Ed.), The Stanford encyclopedia of philosophy. plato.stanford.edu/entries/moral-dilemmas/ (accessed on January 30, 2021).

McCormack, M. (2011). Hierarchy without hegemony: Locating boys in an inclusive school setting. *Sociological Perspectives*, 54(1), 83–101. doi.org/0.1525/sop.2011.54.1.83.

McCullough, M., Kurzban, R., & Tabak, B. (2012). Cognitive systems for revenge and forgiveness. *The Behavioral and Brain Sciences*, 36, 1–15. dx.doi.org/10.1017/S0140525X11002160.

McGue, M., Elkins, I., Walden, B., & Iacono, W. G. (2005). Perceptions of the parent-adolescent relationship: A longitudinal investigation. *Developmental Psychology*, 41(6), 971–984. doi.org/10.1037/0012-1649.41.6.974.

McLeer, S. V., Deblinger, E., Henry, D., & Orvaschel, H. (1992). Sexually abused children at high risk for post-traumatic stress disorder. *Journal of the American Academy of Child and Adolescent Psychiatry*, 31(5), 875–879.

Međedović, J., & Petrović, B. (2015). The dark tetrad. *Journal of Individual Differences*, 36, 228–236. dx.doi.org/10.1027/1614-0001/a000179.

Meere, M., & Egan, V. (2017). Everyday sadism, the dark triad, personality, and disgust sensitivity. *Personality and Individual Differences*, 112(1), 157–161. doi.org/10.1016/j.paid.2017.02.056.

Melo, O., & Mota, C. P. (2014). Conflitos interparentais e o desenvolvimento de psicopatologia em adolescentes e jovens adultos [Interparental conflicts and the development of psychopathology in adolescents and young adults]. *Paidéia*, 24(59), 283–293. doi.org/10.1590/1982-43272459201402.

Milgram, S. (1963). Behavioral study of obedience. *Journal of Abnormal and Social Psychology*, 67(3), 371–378.

Milgram, S. (1965a). Liberating effects of group pressure. *Journal of Personality and Social Psychology*, 1, 127–134.

Milgram, S. (1965b). Some conditions of obedience and disobedience to authority. *Human Relations*, 18, 57–75.

Milgram, S. (1974). *Obedience to authority: An experimental view*. Harper & Row.

Milner, J. S. (1993). Social information processing and physical child abuse. *Clinical Psychology Review*, 13, 275–294.

Miner-Rubino, K., & Cortina, L. M. (2004). Working in a context of hostility toward women: Implications for employees' well-being. *Journal of Occupational Health Psychology*, 9(2), 107–122. doi.org/10.1037/1076-8998.9.2.107.

Miner-Rubino, K., & Cortina, L. M. (2007). Beyond targets: Consequences of vicarious exposure to misogyny at work. *Journal of Applied Psychology*, 92(5), 1254–1269. doi.org/10.1037/0021-9010.92.5.1254.

Moll, A. (1931). *Perversions of the sex instinct: A study of sexual inversion based on clinical data and official documents*. Julian Press.

Montero, I., & León, O. G. (2007). Guía para nombrar los estudios de investigación en psicología [Guide to naming research studies in psychology]. *International Journal of Clinical and Health Psychology*, 7, 847–862.

Moshagen, M., Hilbig, B. E., & Zettler, I. (2018). The dark core of personality. *Psychological Review*, 125(5), 656–688. doi.org/10.1037/rev0000111.

Mosteiro, M. P. & Lana, A. (2013). Violencia de género en estudiantes de enfermería durante sus relaciones de noviazgo [Gender violence in nursing students during their dating relationships]. *Atención Primaria*, 45(6), 290–296.

Mota, A., Matos, A. P., Pinheiro, M. R., Costa, J. J., & Oliveira, S. (2015). Familial relationships perceived by parents and adolescent depression: Psychosocial functioning moderating effect. In Z. Bekirogullari & M. Y. Minas, *European proceedings of social and behavioural sciences* (pp. 21–37), 6.

Moya, M. (1998). Social identities and interpersonal relationships. In S. Worchel, J. F. Morales, D. Páez, & J. C. Deschamps, *Social identity: International perspectives* (pp. 154–165). Sage.

Moya, M., Páez, D., Glick, P., Fernández, I., & Poeschi, G. (2002). Masculinidad-feminidad y factores culturales [Masculinity-femininity and cultural factors]. *Revista Electrónica de Motivación y Emoción* [Spanish Journal of Motivation and Emotion], 3, 127–142.

Murrie, D., Martindale, D. A., & Epstein, M. (2009). Unsupported assessment techniques in child sexual abuse evaluations. In K. Kuehnle & M. Connell (Eds.), *The evaluation of child sexual abuse allegations: A comprehensive guide to assessment and testimony* (pp. 397–420). John Wiley & Sons.

Nam, Y., & Maxwell, S. R. (2020). Assessing the effects of witnessed parental conflict and guilt on dating violence perpetration among South Korean college students. *Journal of Family Violence*, 36(3), 293–305. doi.org/10.1007/s10896-020-00155-3.

Nichols, A. M. (2014). Toward a child-centered approach to evaluating claims of alienation in high-conflict custody disputes. *Michigan Law Review*, 112(4), 663–688.

Nicholson, I. (2015). The normalization of torment: Producing and managing anguish in Milgram's "obedience" laboratory. *Theory & Psychology*, 25(5), 639–656. doi.org/10.1177/0959354315605393.

Norris, F. H. (1992). Epidemiology of trauma: Frequency and impact of different potentially traumatic events on different demographic groups. *Journal of Consulting and Clinical Psychology*, 60, 409–418.

Nowak, K., Olmez, O., & Song, S. Y. (2014). Partial geometric difference families. *Journal of Combinatorial Designs*, 24(3), 112–131. doi.org/10.1002/jcd.21416.

Nyika, N. (2014). Discourses of ethnicity in Zimbabwe: Deliberative democracy or online misogyny? *Language Matters*, 45(3), 342–359. doi.org/10.1080/10228195.2014.975832.

Oceja, V., & Fernández-Dols, J. M. (1992). El reconocimiento de la norma perversa y sus consecuencias en los juicios de las personas [The recognition of the perverse norm and its consequences in the trials of people]. *Revista de Psicología Social*, 7(2), 227–239.

O'Donohue, W., Benuto, L. T., & Bennett, N. (2016). Examining the validity of parental alienation syndrome. *Journal of Child Custody*, 13(2–3), 113–125. dx.doi.org/10.1080/15379418.2016.1217758.

Okeke, N., Rothman, E. F., Mumford, E. A. (2020). Neighborhood income inequality and adolescent relationship aggression: Results of a nationally representative, longitudinal study. *Journal of Interpersonal Violence*, UNSP 0886260520908024. doi.org/10.1177/0886260520908024.

Omar, A. (2006). *Victimization, justice individualism-colectivism victimization—* Justicia individual y colectiva. Xalapa.

O'Meara, A., Davies, J., & Hammond, S. (2011). The psychometric properties and utility of the Short Sadistic Impulse Scale (SSIS). *Psychological Assessment*, 23, 523–531. dx.doi.org/10.1037/a0022400.

Ost, F. (1993). Júpiter, Hércules, Hermes: Tres modelos de juez [Jupiter, Hercules, Hermes: Three models of judge]. *Doxa: Cuadernos de Filosofía del Derecho*, 14, 169–194. doi.org/10.14198/DOXA1993.14.10.

Oware, M. (2014). (Un)conscious (popular) underground: Restricted cultural production and underground rap music. *Poetics*, 42, 60–81. doi.org/10.1016/j.poetic.2013.12.001.

Paciello, M., Fida, R., Tramontano, C., Lupinetti, C., & Caprara, G. V. (2008). Stability and change of moral disengagement and its impact on aggression and violence in late adolescence. *Child Development*, 79(5), 1288–1309. doi.org/10.1111/j.1467-8624.2008.01189.x. PMID: 18826526.

Padilla-Racero, D. (2013). El síndrome de alienación parental no es un transtorno mental, problema relacional ni de conducta. Es una feroz resistencia a los avances en la igualdad entre hombres y mujeres [Parental Alienation Syndrome is not a mental disorder, behavioral or relational problem. It is a fierce resistance to advances in equality between men and women]. *Infancia, Juventud y Ley*, 4, 58–73.

Padilla-Racero, D. (2015). El papel de la memoria y los recuerdos en la credibilidad del testimonio de los menores en las denuncias de abuso sexual infantil [The role of memory and memories on the credibility of the testimony of minors in allegations of child sexual abuse]. *Diario la Ley*, XXXVI (8651), 1–7.

Padilla-Racero, D. (2016). Credibilidad de las denuncias de maltrato infantil y el falso Síndrome de Alienación Parental [Credibility of reports of child maltreatment and the false Parental Alienation Syndrome]. Derecho y Proceso Penal, 42, 379–395.

Padilla-Racero, D., & Clemente, M. (2018a). El Síndrome de Alienación Parental: Una herramienta acientífica que desprotege a los menores en el sistema de Justicia [The Parental Alienation Syndrome: An unscientific tool that protects minors in the justice system]. Tirant lo Blanch.

Padilla-Racero, D. & Clemente, M. (2018b). ¿Obedecer o no obedecer? Protección del menor versus obediencia judicial [Obey or not obey? Child protection versus judicial obedience]. *Revista Aranzadi de Derecho y Proceso Penal*, 49.

Palacio, M. (2001). *Contribuciones de la victimología al sistema penal* [Contributions of victimology to the penal system]. Jurídicas Gustavo Ibáñez C.

Palacios, J., Moreno, M. C., & Jiménez, J. (1995). El maltrato infantil: Concepto, tipos, etiología [Child abuse: Concept, types, etiology]. *Infancia y Aprendizaje*, 71, 7–21.

Pandey, J., & Rastogi, R. (1979). Machiavellianism and ingratiation. *The Journal of Social Psychology*, 108, 221–225. doi.org/10.1080/00224545.1979.9711635.

Parkin, R., & Stone, L. (2007). *Antropología del parentesco y de la familia* [Anthropology of kinship and family]. Editorial Universitaria Ramón Areces.

Pastor, G. (1982). *Síndrome frío de personalidad sagaz: Psicología social del maquiavelismo* [Cold shrewd personality syndrome: Social psychology of Machiavellianism]. Universidad Pontificia de Salamanca.

Patterson, D. (2011). The linkage between secondary victimization by law enforcement and rape case outcomes. *Journal of Interpersonal Violence*, 26(2), 328–347. doi.org/10.1177/0886260510362889.

Paulhus, D. L., & Jones, D. N. (2015). Measures of dark personalities. In G. J. Boyle, D. H. Saklofske, & G. Matthews (Eds.), *Measures of personality and social psychological constructs* (pp. 562–594). Elsevier Academic Press. doi.org/10.1016/B978-0-12-386915-9.00020-6.

Paulhus, D. L., & Williams, K. M. (2002). The dark triad of personality: Narcissism, Machiavellianism, and psychopathy. *Journal of Research in Personality*, 36(6), 556–563. doi.org/10.1016/S0092-6566(02)00505-6.

Pazos, M., Oliva, A., & Hernando, A. (2014). Violencia en relaciones de pareja de jóvenes y adolescentes [Violence in relationships of youth and adolescents]. *Revista Latinoamericana de Psicología*, 46(3), 148–159.

Pedzich, J. (2014). The high-conflict custody battle: Protect yourself & your kids from a toxic divorce, false accusations & parental alienation. *Library Journal*, 139(20), 117–117.

Pereda, N. (2009). Consecuencias psicológicas iniciales del abuso sexual infantil [Initial psychological consequences of child sexual abuse]. *Papeles del Psicólogo*, 30(2), 135–144.

Pereda, N., & Arch, M. (2009). Abuso sexual infantil y síndrome de alienación parental: Criterios diferenciales [Child sexual abuse and parental alienation syndrome: Differential criteria]. *Cuadernos de Medicina Forense*, 15(58), 279–287.

Pereda, N., & Arch, M. (2012). Exploración psicológica forense del abuso sexual en la infancia: Una revisión de procedimientos e instrumentos [Forensic psychological exploration of childhood sexual abuse: A review of procedures and instruments]. *Papeles del Psicólogo*, 33 (1), 36–47.

Pereda, N., & Forns, M. (2007). Prevalencia y características del abuso sexual infantil en estudiantes universitarios españoles [Prevalence and characteristics of child sexual abuse in Spanish university students]. *Child Abuse & Neglect*, 31, 417–426.

Pereira, A., & Van Prooijen, J. W. (2018). Why we sometimes punish the innocent: The role of group entitativity in collective punishment. *PLoS ONE*, 13(5), e0196852. doi.org/10.1371/journal.pone.0196852.

Perez, J. A., Páez, D., & Navarro, E. (2001). Conflicto de mentalidades; cultura del honor frente a la liberación de la mujer [Conflict of mentalities; culture of honor in front of the liberation of women]. *Revista electrónica de motivación y emoción*, 4(8–9) 1–23.

Philipp, R. M. R. (2013). *Investigaciones actuales de las mujeres y del género* [Current research on women and gender]. Universidad de Santiago de Compostela.

Phipps, A., & Young, I. (2015). Neoliberalisation and 'lad cultures' in higher education. *Sociology: The Journal of the British Sociological Association*, 49(2), 305–322. doi.org/10.1177/0038038514542120.

Pignotti, M. S. (2014). Parental alienation diagnosis. A modern and effective subtype of domestic violence, endemic in italian courts. *Italian Journal of Pediatrics*, 40(1), 419.

Pineda, D., Piqueras, J. A., Galán, M., & Martínez-Martínez, A. (2021). Everyday sadism: Psychometric properties of three Spanish versions for assessing the construct. *Current Psychology: A Journal for Diverse Perspectives on Diverse Psychological Issues*. doi.org/10.1007/s12144-021-01434-y.

Plouffe, R., Saklofske, D., & Smith, M. (2016). The assessment of sadistic personality: Preliminary psychometric evidence for a new measure. *Personality and Individual Differences*, 104. doi.org/10.1016/j.paid.2016.07.043.

Pope, K., & Bajt, T. (1988). When laws and values conflict: A dilemma for psychologists. *American Psychologist*, 43(10), 828–829.

Popper, K. R. (1959). *The logic of scientific discovery*. Basic Books.

Popper, K. R. (1962), *La lógica de la investigación científica* [The logic of scientific research]. Tecnos.

Posner, R. A. (2008). *El análisis económico del derecho (Politica y Derecho)* [The economic analysis of Law (Politics and Law)]. Fondo de Cultura Económica.

Powell, J., Cheng, V., & Egeland, B. (1995). Transmisión del maltrato de padres a hijos [Transmission of abuse from parents to children]. *Infancia y Aprendizaje*, 18 (3), 99–110.

Pozueco, J. M., Romero, S. L., & Casas, N. (2011). Psicopatía, violencia y criminalidad: Un análisis psicológico-forense, psiquiátrico-legal y criminológico (Parte II) [Psychopathy, violence and criminality: A psychological-forensic, psychiatric-legal and criminological analysis (Part II).]. *Cuadernos de Medicina Forense*, 17(4), 175–192. dx.doi.org/10.4321/S1135-76062011000400002.

Ramirez, M., Botella, J., & Carrobles, J. A. (1999). Creencias infantiles sobre la separación parental [Children's beliefs about parental divorce]. *Psicología Conductual*, 7(1), 49–73.

Randolph, M. K., & Gold, C. A. (1994). Child sexual abuse prevention—Evaluation of a teacher-training program. *School Psychology Review*, 23(3), 485–495.

Raskin, D. C., & Esplin, P. W. (1991a). Assessement of children's statements of sexual abuse. In J. Doris (Ed.), *The suggestibility of children's recollections. Implications for eyewitness testimony*. American Psychological Association.

Raskin, D. C., & Esplin, P. W. (1991b). Commentary: Response to Wells, Loftus, and McGough. In J. Doris, *The suggestibility of children's recollections: Implications for eyewitness testimony*. American Psychological Association.

Raskin, R. N. (1980). Narcissism and creativity: Are they related. *Psychological Reports*, 46, 55–60.

Raskin, R. N., & Hall, C. S. (1981) The Narcissistic Personality Inventory: Alternate form reliability and further evidence of construct validity. *Journal of Personality Assessment*, 45, 159–162.

Raskin, R. N., & Hall, C. S. (1979). A narcissistic personality inventory. *Psychological Reports*, 45(2), 590. doi.org/10.2466/pr0.1979.45.2.590.

Rauthmann, J. (2012). The dark triad and interpersonal perception: Similarities and differences in the social consequences of narcissism, machiavellianism, and psychopathy. *Social Psychological and Personality Science*. 3, 487–496. doi. org/10.1177/1948550611427608.

Raven, B. H. (1992). A power interaction model on interpersonal influence: French and Raven thirty years later. *Journal of Social Behavior and Personality*, 7(2), 217–244.

Reay, K. M. (2015). Family reflections: A promising therapeutic program designed to treat severely alienated children and their family system. *American Journal of Family Therapy*, 43(2), 197–207. dx.doi.org/10.1080/01926187.2015.1007769.

Recover, T. (2006). La prueba pericial practicada por psicólogos. Referentes deon-tológicos y regulación en la nueva Ley de Enjuiciamiento Civil [The expert test practiced by psychologists. Deontological references and regulation in the new Civil Procedure Law]. In J. C. Sierra, E. M. Jiménez, & G. Buela-Casal (Eds*.), Psicología forense: Manual de técnicas y aplicaciones* (pp. 116–128). Biblioteca Nueva.

Redondo, C., & Ortiz, M. R. (2005). El abuso sexual infantil [Child sexual abuse]. *Boletín de la Sociedad de Pediatría de Asturias, Cantabria, Castilla y León*, 45, 3–16.

Reilly, M. E., Lott, B., Caldwell, D., & De Luca, L. (1992). Tolerance for sexual harassment related to self-reported sexual victimization. *Gender & Society*, 6(1), 122–138. doi.org/10.1177/089124392006001008.

Robertson, S. (2003). "If I let a goal in, I'll get beat up": Contradictions in masculin-ity, sport and health. *Health Education Research*, 18(6), 706–716. doi.org/10.1093/her/cyf054.

Rochat, F., & Modigliani, A. (1997). Authority: Obedience, defiance, and identifica-tion in experimental and historical contexts. In M. Gold (Ed.), *A new outline of social psychology* (pp. 235–246). American Psychological Association.

Rodríguez-Castro, Y., Lameiras, M., Carrera, V., & Vallejo, P. (2012). Estereotipos de género y la imagen de la mujer en los mass media [Gender stereotypes and the image of women in the mass media]. In I. C. Iglesias-Canle & M. Lameiras (Coord), *Comunicación y justicia en violencia de género* [Communication and justice in gender violence]. Tirant lo Blanch.

Rodríguez-Castro, Y., Lameiras, M., Carrera, V., & Vallejo, P. (2013). Validación de la escala de homofobia moderna en una muestra de adolescentes [Validation of the scale of modern homophobia in a sample of adolescents]. *Anales de Psicología*, 29(2), 523–533.

Rodríguez-Villagra, O., Padilla-Mora, M., & Fornaguera-Trías, J. (2010). Validez y confiabilidad de tres escalas para evaluar conductas sociales en preescolares y escolares [Validity and reliability of three scales to evaluate social behaviors in preschoolers and school children]. *Anales de Psicología*, 26(1), 104–111.

Romeder, J. M., & McWhinnie, J. R. (1978). Le développement des annéspotentielles de vie perdues comme indicateur de mortalité prematurée [The development of potential years of life lost as an indicator of premature mortality]. *Revue d'Epidémiologie et de Santé Publique* [Epidemiology and Public Health], 26, 97–115.

Ross, K., & Blush, G. (1990). Sexual abuse discriminators on the divorced or divorcing family. *Issues in Child Abuse Accusations*, 2, 1–6.

Rothstein, B., & Teorell, J. (2008). What is quality of government? A theory of impartial government institutions. *Governance*, 21(2), 165–190. doi.org/10.1111/j.1468-0491.2008.00391.x.

Rozanski, C. (2013). El Síndrome de Alienación Parental (SAP) y otras formas de silenciar niños abusados [Parental Alienation Syndrome (SAP) and other forms of silencing exploited children]. *Infancia, Juventud y Ley*, 4, 74–80.

Rubio-Garay, F., Carrasco-Ortiz, M. A., & García-Rodríguez, B. (2019). Moral disengagement and violence in adolescent and young dating relationships: An exploratory study. *Revista Argentina de Clínica Psicológica*, 28(1), 22–31.

Russell, N. J. C., & Gregory, R. J. (2005). Making the undoable doable: Milgram, the Holocaust and modern government. *American Review of Public Administration*, 35, 327–349.

Russell, N. J. C., & Gregory, R. J. (2011). Spinning an organizational "web of obligation"? moral choice in stanley milgram's "obedience" experiments. *The American Review of Public Administration*, 41(5), 495–518.

Sakalaki, M., Richardson, C., & Thepaut, Y. (2007). Machiavellianism and economic opportunism. *Journal of Applied Social Psychology*, 37(6), 1181–1190. doi.org/10.1111/j.1559-1816.2007.00208.x.

Samper, P., Cortés, M. T., Mestre, V., Nácher, M. J., & Tur, A. M. (2006). Adaptación del "Child's Report of Parent Behavior Inventory" a población Española [Adaptation of the "Child's Report of Parent Behavior Inventory" to Spanish population]. *Psicothema*, 18(2), 263–271.

Sánchez, A., & Iglesias, A. (2008). Curriculum oculto en el aula; Estereotipos en acción. Educar en la ciudadanía [Hidden curriculum in the classroom; Action stereotypes. Educating for citizenship]. In R. Cobo (Coord), *Educar en la ciudadanía. Perspectivas feministas* [Educating citizens. Feminist perspectives] (123–149). Ediciones La Catarata.

Sau, V. (2002). *Diccionario ideológico feminista* (Vol. I) [Ideological feminist dictionary (Vol. I)]. Icaria

Saunders, D. G., & Oglesby, K. H. (2016). No way to turn: Traps encountered by many battered women with negative child custody experiences. *Journal of Child Custody*, 13(2–3), 154–177. doi.org/10.1080/15379418.2016.1213114.

Save the Children. (2012*). La justicia española frente al abuso sexual infantil en el entorno familiar: Un análisis de casos a la luz de los estándares internacionales de derechos humanos* [Spanish justice in the face of child sexual abuse in the family environment: An analysis of cases in light of international human rights standards]. Ministerio de Sanidad, Servicios Sociales e Igualdad del Reino de España.

Schacht, S. P. (1996). Misogyny on and off the "pitch"—The gendered world of male rugby players. *Gender & Society*, 10(5), 550–565. doi. org/10.1177/089124396010005004.

Schaefer, E. S. (1965a). A configurational analysis of children's reports of parent behavior. *Journal of Consulting Psychology*, 29 (6), 552–557. doi.org/10.1037/ h0022702.

Schaefer, E. S. (1965b). Children's reports of parental behavior: An inventory. *Child Development*, 36, 413–424.

Schludermanna, E., & Schludermanna, S. (1970). Replicability of factors in Children's Report of Parent Behavior (CRPBI). *The Journal of Psychology: Interdisciplinary and Applied*, 76(2), 239–249. doi.org/10.1080/00223980.1970.9916845.

Shaw, M. (2016). Commentary for "Examining the use of 'parental alienation síndrome.'" *Journal of Child Custody*, 13(2–3), 144–146. dx.doi.org/10.1080/15379 418.2016.1219244.

Shim, H., & Shin, E. (2016). Peer-group pressure as a moderator of the relationship between attitude toward cyberbullying and cyberbullying behaviors on mobile instant messengers. *Telematics and Informatics*, 33(1), 17–24.

Shoebridge, A. (2014). Social winners and losers: A case study of press construction. *Media International Australia*, 153, 21–30.

Sichko, S., Borelli, J. L., Rasmussen, H. F., & Smiley, P. A. (2016). Relational closeness moderates the association between maternal overcontrol and children's depressive symptoms. *Journal of Family Psychology*, 30(2), 266–275. doi. org/10.1037/fam0000155.

Sigusch, V. (2012). The Sexologist Albert Moll—between Sigmund Freud and Magnus Hirschfeld. *Medical History*, 56(2), 184–200. https://doi.org/10.1017/mdh .2011.32

Sijtsema, J. J., Garofalo, C., Jansen, K., & Klimstra, T. A. (2019). Disengaging from evil: Longitudinal associations between the dark triad, moral disengagement, and antisocial behavior in adolescence. *Journal of Abnormal Child Psychology*, 47(8), 1351–1365. doi.org/10.1007/s10802-019-00519-4.

Silbey, S. S. (2005). After legal consciousness. *Annual Review of Law and Social Science*, 1, 323–368. doi.org/10.1146/annurev.lawsocsci.1.041604.115938.

Silva, R. C., & Lemos, P. A. (2015). Misogyny in heart disease? *Catheterization and Cardiovascular Interventions*, 85(5), 898–898. doi.org/10.1002/ccd.25881.

Smith, B. V. (2012). Uncomfortable places, close spaces: Female correctional workers' sexual interactions with men and boys in custody. *UCLA Law Review*, 59(6), 1690–1745.

Smith, W. A., Allen, W. R., & Danley, L. L. (2007). "Assume the position . . . You fit the description": Psychosocial experiences and racial battle fatigue among African American male college students. *American Behavioral Scientist*, 51(4), 551–578. doi.org/10.1177/0002764207307742.

Smith, W. A., Yosso, T. J., & Solorzano, D. G. (2007). Racial primes and black misandry on historically white campuses: Toward critical race accountability in educational administration. *Educational Administration Quarterly*, 43(5), 559–585. doi.org/10.1177/0013161X07307793.

Sowan-Basheer, W. (2020). The effect of gender on negative emotional experiences accompanying Muslims' and Jews' use of verbal aggression in heterosexual intimate-partner relationships. *Journal of Aggression Maltreatment & Trauma*, 29(3), 332–347. doi.org/10.1080/10926771.2018.1546246.

Steller, M., & Köhnken, G. (1989). Criteria-based content analysis. In D. C. Raskin (Ed.), *Psychological methods in criminal investigation and evidence* (pp. 217–245). Springer-Verlag.

Stotzer, R. L. (2014). Law enforcement and criminal justice personnel interactions with transgender people in the United States: A literature review. *Aggression and Violent Behavior*, 19(3), 263–277. doi.org/10.1016/j.avb.2014.04.012.

Sukys, S., Lisinskiene, A., & Tilindiene, I. (2015). Adolescents' participation in sport activities and attachment to parents and peers. *Social Behavior and Personality*, 43(9), 1507–1518. doi.org/10.2224/sbp.2015.43.9.1507.

Summit, R. C. (1983). The child sexual abuse accommodation syndrome. *Child Abuse & Neglect*, 7, 177–93.

Tejedor, 2006. *El síndrome de alienación parental: Una forma de maltrato* [Parental alienation syndrome: A form of abuse]. EOS

Thau, S., Aquino, K., & Poortvliet, P. M. (2007). Self-defeating behaviors in organizations: The relationship between thwarted belonging and interpersonal work behaviors. *Journal of Applied Psychology*, 92(3), 840–847. doi.org/10.1037/0021-9010.92.3.840.

Theimann, M. (2016). School as a space of socialization and prevention. *European Journal of Criminology*, 13(1), 67–91.

Tortosa, F. (1998). Una historia de la psicología moderna [A history of modern psychology]. McGraw-Hill Interamericana de España.

Trampotova, O., & Lacinova, L. (2015). Children drawn into the interparental conflict: Critical review and comparison of contemporary conceptions. *Ceskoslovenska Psychologie*, 59(1), 57–70.

Tran, U. S., Bertl, B., Kossmeier, M., Pietschnig, J., Stieger, S., & Voracek, M. (2018). I'll teach you differences: Taxometric analysis of the dark triad, trait sadism, and the dark core of personality. *Personality and Individual Differences*, 126, 19–24. dx.doi.org/10.1016/j.paid.2018.01.015.

Tripp, T. M., & Bies, R. J. (2010). "Righteous" anger and revenge in the workplace: The fantasies, the feuds, the forgiveness. In M. Potegal, G. Stemmler, & C. Spielberger (Eds.), *International handbook of anger: Constituent and concomitant biological, psychological, and social processes* (pp. 413–431). Springer Science & Business Media. doi.org/10.1007/978-0-387-89676-2_24.

Tulving, E., & Thomson, D. M. (1973). Encoding specificity and retrieval processes in episodic memory. *Psychological Review*, 80(5), 352–373. doi.org/10.1037/h0020071.

Twenge, J., & Campbell, W. K. (2003). "Isn't it fun to get the respect that we're going to deserve?" Narcissism, social rejection, and aggression. *Personality & Social Psychology Bulletin*, 29, 261–72. doi.org/10.1177/0146167202239051.

UN. (1999). Guide for police maker. www.uncjin.org/Standards/policy.pdf

UN. (2007). *Commentary on The Bangalore Principles of Judicial Conduct.* United Nations Office on Drugs and Crime.

Vandenberg, D. (1996). Caring: "Feminine ethics or materialistic misandry?" A hermeneutical critique of Nel Noddings' phenomenology of the moral subject and education. *Journal of Philosophy of Education*, 30(2), 253–269. doi. org/10.1111/j.1467-9752.1996.tb00394.x.

Vardi, Y., & Weitz, E. (2004). Misbehavior in organizations: Theory, research, and management. Lawrence Erlbaum Associates Publishers.

Varni, J. W., Seid, M., & Rode, C. A. (1999). The PedsQL (TM): Measurement model for the pediatric quality of life inventory. *Medical Care*, 37(2), 126–139. doi. org/10.1097/00005650-199902000-00003.

Vázquez-Mezquita, B., & Calle, M. (1997): Secuelas postraumáticas en niños. Análisis prospectivo de una muestra de casos de abuso sexual denunciados [Post-traumatic sequelae in children. Prospective analysis of a sample of reported cases of sexual abuse]. *Revista de Psiquiatría Forense, Psicología Forense y Criminología*, 1, 14–29.

Verrocchio, M. C., Marchetti, D., & Fulcheri, M. (2015). Perceived parental functioning, self-esteem, and psychological distress in adults whose parents are separated/divorced. *Frontiers in Psychology*, 6, 1760. doi.org/10.3389/fpsyg.2015.01760.

Vilalta, R. J. (2011). Descripción del Síndrome de Alienación Parental en una muestra forense [Description of Parental Alienation Syndrome in a forensic sample]. *Psicothema*, 23(4), 636–641.

Vrij, A., Mann, S., Kristen, S., & Fisher, R. P. (2007). Cues to deception and ability to detect lies as a function of police interview styles. *Law and Human Behavior*, 31(5), 499–518. doi.org/10.1007/s10979-006-9066-4.

Walters, M. G., & Friedlander, S. (2016). When a child rejects a parent: Working with the intractable resist/refuse dynamic. *Family Court Review*, 54(3), 424–445. doi. org/10.1111/fcre.12238.

Warshak, R. A. (2015a). Poisoning parent-child relationships through the manipulation of names. *American Journal of Family Therapy*, 43(1), 4–15. dx.doi.org/0.10 80/01926187.2014.968066.

Warshak, R. A. (2015b). Ten Parental Alienation fallacies that compromise decisions in court and in therapy. *Professional Psychology: Research and Practice*, 46(4), 235–49. dx.doi.org/10.1037/pro0000031.

Weitzer, R., & Kubrin, C. E. (2009). Misogyny in rap music: A content analysis of prevalence and meanings. *Men and Masculinities*, 12(1), 3–29. doi. org/10.1177/1097184X08327696.

Wells, G. L., & Loftus, E. (1991). Commentary: Is this child fabricating? Reactions to a new assessment technique. In J. Doris (Ed.), *The suggestibility of children's recollections. Implications for eyewitness testimony*. American Psychological Association.

Wemmers, J. A. (2005). Victim policy transfer: Learning from each other. *European Journal on Criminal Policy and Research*, 11, 121–133. doi.org/10.1007/ s10610-005-3624-z.

Westermann, C., Kozak, A., Harling, M., & Nienhaus, A. (2014). Burnout intervention studies for inpatient elderly care nursing staff: Systematic literature review. *Int J Nurs Stud*. 51(1), 63–71.

Whitaker, D. J., Haileyesus, T., Swahn, M., & Saltzman, L. (2007). Differences in frequency of violence and reported injury between relationships with reciprocal and nonreciprocal intimate partner violence. *American Journal of Public Health*, 97(5), 941–947. doi.org/10.2105/AJPH.2005.079020.

Whiteman, S. D., Solmeyer, A. R., & McHale, S. M. (2015). Sibling relationships and adolescent adjustment: Longitudinal associations in two-parent African American families. *Journal of Youth and Adolescence*, 44(11), 2042–2053. doi.org/10.1007/s10964-015-0286-0.

WHO/OMS. (2015). Gender. www.who.int/topics/gender/es/.

Willis, J. W., Bund, M.A., & Friswell, J. H. (2005). *La Rochefoucauld. Reflections; or sentences and moral maxims*. Simpson Low, Son, and Marston.

Wilson, J. M., & Smirles, K. (2020). College students' perceptions of intimate partner violence: The effects of type of abuse and perpetrator gender. *Journal of Interpersonal Violence*, UNSP 0886260520908025. doi.org/10.1177/0886260520908025.

Wilson, N. J., Parmenter, T. R., Stancliffe, R. J., Shuttleworth, R. P., & Parker, D. (2010). A masculine perspective of gendered topics in the research literature on males and females with intellectual disability. *Journal of Intellectual & Developmental Disability*, 35(1), 1–8. doi.org/10.3109/13668250903496351.

Wolfe, D. A. (1987). *Child abuse: Implication for child development and psychopathology*. Sage.

Wolfe, D. A. (1991). *Preventing physical and emotional abuse of children*. Guilford Press.

Wolfe, D., Sas, L., Wekerle, C. (1994). Factors associated with the development of posttraumatic stress disorder among child victims of sexual abuse. *Child Abuse and Neglect*, 18, 37–50.

Wolfsberger, F. (2015). La tríada oscura de la personalidad. Narcisismo, psicopatía o maquiavelismo [The dark triad of personality. Narcissism, psychopathy, or Machiavellianism]. *Mente y Cerebro*, 75, 46–52.

Yoshimura, S. M., & Boon, S. D. (2014). Exploring revenge as a feature of family life. *Journal of Family Theory & Review*, 6(3), 222–240. doi.org/10.1111/jftr.12041.

Young, L., Scholz, J., & Saxe, R. (2011). Neural evidence for "intuitive prosecution": The use of mental state information for negative moral verdicts. *Social Neuroscience*, 6(3), 302–315. dx.doi.org/10.1080/17470919.2010.529712.

Zicavo-Martínez, N., Celis-Esparza, D., González-Espinoza, A., & Mercado-Aravena, M. (2016). Escala ZICAP para la evaluación de la alienación parental: Resultados preliminares [Preliminary psychometric properties of a scale to evaluate parental alienation (ZICAP-Scale)]. *Ciencias Psicológicas*, 10(2), 177–187.

Zimbardo, P. G. (2007). *The Lucifer effect: How good people turn evil*. Rider.

Index

About the Author

Miguel Clemente received his master's and PhD in social psychology from the Universidad Complutense de Madrid. He is currently a full professor at the Department of Psychology at Universidad de A Coruña, Spain, and a researcher in legal psychology and protection of children. Clemente has authored about 20 books, 200 articles in scientific journals, and over 70 book chapters.

www.ingramcontent.com/pod-product-compliance
Lightning Source LLC
Chambersburg PA
CBHW022311280326
41932CB00010B/1057